Praise for Gus Lee's earlier, *Courage: The Backbone of Leadership*

"Gus Lee, in this well-written and useful book, demystifies courage and reveals what it is made of: integrity, competence, and good judgment."

—Warren Bennis
Distinguished Professor of Business, University of Southern California, Founder, Modern Leadership Development

"When it comes to leadership, Gus Lee has walked the walk and talked the talk. Now, in his latest book, he offers all of us, who call ourselves leaders, a primer on how to gain and maintain in ourselves and our organizations that critical element that makes the difference: courage!"
—H. Norman Schwarzkopf
General, US Army (Ret.)

Praise for *The Courage Playbook: 5 Steps to Overcome Your Fears and Become Your Best self*

"Gus Lee, who is not only very smart but also has an abundance of common sense, has written a terrific book about a perennial problem facing all of us: developing the courage to conquer our fears."

—John J. Mearsheimer, R. Wendell Harrison
Distinguished Service Professor of Political Science, University of Chicago

"Gus's training changed my life. He uses courage to shape us 'weeble wobbles'—and to help us stand firm even after we wobble and get knocked down, time and time again. The tools and concepts provided in *The Courage Playbook* challenged my approach to leading and communicating, by not just understanding and assessing my own courage but also by identifying practical applications of courageous behaviors. As Gus writes, 'courage is more action than abstraction and is more behavioral than theoretical.' As a combat veteran, entrepreneur, and business executive, I didn't need to think more about courageous actions; I needed to act more courageously and more quickly. Through *The Courage Playbook*, Gus personally coached me, provided me tremendous insights on myself, and empowered and encouraged me with practical ways to live the first of human qualities."
—Chris Miller
SVP Flippen Group, West Point Class of 1998, Operation Iraqi Freedom

"Meeting Gus Lee changed my life; his book will change yours. *The Courage Playbook* is a 5-alarm wake-up call to self-awareness, recognizing we control how we show up for others each day. We choose cowardice or courage in all our interactions—just getting along, or really getting it right. Gus's Leaders of Character, LOC Biography Form 5 inventory was my jump-start in understanding the painful truth of my lack of 'real' courage. Yet, I was not left lost, without a way forward. Gus provides the roadmap and all the GPS tools necessary for navigating the difficult terrain in becoming one's best self—a true person of courage."
—Joe LeBoeuf, PhD
COL, US Army, Retired Former Academy Professor, USMA; Professor of the Practice Emeritus, Duke University

"*The Courage Playbook*'s practical tools are universal game-changers. From the time Gus Lee was my mentor at West Point he has helped me and others in evaluating and forming ethical solutions for those who desire to be the best they can be. The Third Step helped me stop reactions to fear that I'd retained in a career that demanded courageous leadership and physical bravery as an Air Cavalry combat leader in Vietnam. *The Courage Playbook*'s comprehensive tool sets have enhanced my life, especially in a profound respect for others, no matter race, religion or sexual preference. It's improved my relationships in my community, and I will continue to use it to constantly improve my character and quality of life."

—**William Malkemes**
COL, US Army (Ret.)

"*The Courage Playbook*'s focus on practice, not theory, was essential to my ability to transition from a performance-based junior executive to a growth-based chief executive. The concept of UPR is easy but doing it every day takes a lot of practice. I used the 10-week UPR Behavioral Practice continuously to value and develop every member of my organization. Every quarter I spent 10 weeks going down the checklist. Then I spent the last three weeks of the quarter personally praising every member for their contribution. That's how you build a high-performance company with little employee turnover."

—**Steve Wilson**
Founder and CEO of an INC 500 Company

"We took Gus's advice to heart as my team took action and developed leadership rules to live by and demonstrate courage to build trust. By remembering that courage is an expression of caring, we overcame the barriers to sharing feedback and hitting hard issues head-on. In the business world we face tough issues every day, and by remembering to approach interactions and address shortcomings from a position of caring, we learn to be courageous. *The Courage Playbook*'s tools provide the guide for putting high core values into action and cementing them into our behaviors at work and at home. I am constantly reminded of the lessons I learned from *Courage*, and when I know I am facing an untenable situation I prepare myself, dig deep, take a big gulp and leap across that river of fear. I am pleased to share that I have yet to drown but learned at times of my shortcomings and succeeded beyond my expectations with others."

—**Jena Holtberg-Benge**
General Manager, John Deere Reman

"*Yes Kids, Try This at Home*. Forty years working with community leaders taught me about courage. *The Courage Playbook* helped me bring that skill home to confront fear and change avoidant behavior. Using the skills-practice based approach, the skills themselves, and 'memory cards,' I replaced my contempt for incompetence with 'Unconditional Positive Respect' and resolved a long-running dispute with a global company in two days. Then, I answered the question: 'What does my husband most want me to change?'—so we stopped yelling at each other, and a frustrating home improvement project was finished in a night. The skill, courage, is easy to understand yet hard to do. With *The Courage Playbook* I am deploying it where it is most needed, at home."

—**Jolie Bain Pillsbury, PhD**
Author of *Results Based Facilitation* and *Theory of Aligned Contributions*

"*The Courage Playbook* is not for those who only want to talk about courage. If you want to do the hard work of developing courage from the inside out, there's no other tool like it. I frequently face situations that require courage. This book was a great encouragement to me to stay the course and not give into fear. *The Courage Playbook* will lead you step by step from fear to fearless."

—**Eric Bolger**
Vice President for Academic Affairs and Dean of the College,
College of the Ozarks

"As a career soldier, I was often amazed by senior officers who would risk injury or even death in service to our nation, while also demonstrating an aversion for doing anything that might risk their careers. In this context, Gus Lee appropriately cites Mark Twain's observation, 'It is curious that physical courage should be so common in the world, and moral courage so rare.' I recommend *The Courage Playbook* to everyone in or desiring to be in a leadership position. It teaches you the right thing to do and how to do it. It is invaluable in learning to lead the toughest of all followers: yourself."

—**Gilbert S. Harper**
Brigadier General, US Army (Ret.)

"Kudos to Gus Lee for his amazing *Playbook*. I found his remarkable Step One assessment tool helped me identify that childhood relationships with parents and siblings can distort adult relationships. Identifying this 'baggage,' I was able to more fully listen to others and use his Courageous Communication tools. This has helped me enormously in patient care and made my personal relationships more rewarding. The CourCom tools help me see how internalized fears and anger result in disrespecting others and so shatter the trust and cooperation we all need for successful and rewarding collaboration with others."

—**Mary M. Zhu, MD, PhD, MPH, MA**

"*The Courage Playbook* finds me in a place in life where continuation of old comfortable habits and behaviors is untenable and counterproductive both professionally and personally. Fear, avoidance, and laziness of thought and execution have been my life's Achilles' heel. *The Courage Playbook* shines a bright and painful light on the effects of these mental and behavioral choices, calling them out but at the same time offering carefully drawn self-directed offers for change with clear instruction on how to use them and move forward toward self-mastery. The work is often painful, but in the words of someone who knows there is some pain, the gain is significantly more. By its design, it requires one to go through the fire to separate from old painful mind habits and move toward more life-affirming and supportive choices. Of all the projects, classes, 12-step programs and therapy sessions, *The Courage Playbook* is the most complete and compressive framework moving me towards a better version of myself. With gratitude and deep respect, I give my thanks to Gus Lee for having provided me the tools and skills to move forward on my pathway to a healthier life."

—**Dr. Toussaint Streat**
Physician

"In *The Courage Playbook*, Gus Lee takes all the tools and behavior-based guides he patiently taught me and puts them into an easy-to-understand, follow-the-steps practice guide. These tools have helped me overcome my fear and avoidance of conflict and set me on the path to becoming a courageous leader. As a husband, father, friend, and entrepreneur, improving my courage and character first and then those of others has transformed and deepened all my relationships. I encourage you to start on this journey today toward a more meaningful life."

—**Chris Kay**
COO, Water Harvesting, Inc.

"There are many good fire departments across the country, albeit only a few really great ones. After 46 years in the fire service, I believe this may be from the fire service's focus on discipline and the traditional nature of the job. The truly great fire agencies are made up of firefighters and officers that embrace Gus Lee's concept of self-governance, which requires a personal commitment to transformational change. For these individuals, continual growth becomes a passion that they embrace to the core of their being, requiring physical, mental, and most importantly, moral courage. Lee, in *The Courage Playbook*, provides a path for those willing to change. Is it a quick and easy fix? No, it is exceptionally hard. But for those who desire to embrace the challenge of truly creating a better life for yourself and those around you, apply these ancient principles. Life will never be the same."

—**Ron Lindroth**
Fire Chief

"Gus's first *Courage* book placed me on a 'high core values improvement plan.' While Gus does not know my cowardly foibles from firsthand observation, his *Playbook* calls me out as if he had been watching at my most fear-controlled moments for the last decade. His new book inspires with real-life examples and self-assessments that gnaw to the root of my fear while providing the tools to build back courage. The CLEAR model particularly exposed my lingering bad habits and provided a map for improvement. Now back to work I go."

—Jack Colwell
Co-Director, Public Safety Practice, The Arbinger Institute

"Gus Lee's *Playbook* is about courage, character and leadership. It's a practical set of revealing assessments and carefully crafted techniques designed to improve anyone's ability to make tough choices to do the right thing—every time—regardless of personal risk. That starts with a disciplined approach requiring unconditional respect for one another and consistently listening with humility and empathy. The courage to do so builds character and enables leadership. Not for the faint of heart, but well worth the effort."

—COL (Ret.) Larry White
Infantry: Vietnam, 1971–72; Korea, 1982–83; West Berlin, 1983–86; Kabul, 2009–10

"A delightful guide full of important information for those of us who want to understand fear and recognise how it works in our lives and discover characters we can look up to, to position us for freedom. While answering the questions in *The Courage Playbook*'s Assessments, I recognized how fear worked in my life, how it impacted my behaviors, and with the tools provided in the book, they are giving me courage to change. With small progress each day, it will develop into a habit."

—Beata Negumbo
Programme Assistant, FAO Representation in Namibia

"Throughout my life and career, I could choose inaction by relying on the phrase, 'Discretion is the better part of valor.' In *The Courage Playbook*, Gus Lee's deep dig into courage, he delivers a gut punch; the words come from the lips of a cowardly braggart in Shakespeare's *Henry IV*. Lee observes that the discretion wording 'gives modern cowards an excuse to avoid conflict.' What a life lesson. This book is for those of us who desire to shun avoidance and change our mindset. Eminently readable and research-based, it is in a class all its own: literary nonfiction. It gives us practical tools for reversing our fearful mentality and for implementing the changes necessary to be courageous in both ordinary and extraordinary conflicts we all face. I wish I had read it sooner."

—Robin Shakely
former Assistant Chief Deputy District Attorney, 39-year career prosecutor, mother, wife, and reforming coward

"*The Courage Playbook* puts courage into action. As a law enforcement leader, my life and legacy were transformed after reading Gus's earlier *Courage* book. I am excited to see so many ideas about living courageously laid out in such a helpful way in this new book. It is what I desperately need to figure out how courage looks and works in my family and professional life. Courage helps me lead my family, and myself, in our darkest and most challenging days and has shaped me into a leader who first looks in the mirror, as I strive to lead and serve others in my organization and my life. Courage has become the virtue that I take with me into every interaction. I'm so thankful that Gus Lee has put such a practical guidebook together for living a courageous life. It has helped me make sense of so much that I learned through trial and experience. If you're picking up *The Courage Playbook*, your time and investment into the process of living out courage will be worth every sacrifice. Be willing to cross the River of Fear—the journey on the other side is a life that is not perfect—but well worth living."

—Roy Bethge
Chief of Police, Cherry Valley Police Department, Illinois

"Under pressure and unsure in tough situations, you can refer to *The Courage Playbook* to get your bearings, survive and succeed. Gus Lee's Five Steps have improved how I treat and educate others and beats the heck out of painful and grueling effort that ends in foreseeable failure. Gus effortlessly convinced me of two primal things, refined in this book: first, respect for everyone, all the time, is the key; second, you need courage to exercise that respect. *The Courage Playbook* is the civilian *Ranger Handbook* of doing the right thing. It will bring you home."

—**Dr. James P. Sullivan**
Sullivan Engineering; Professor, Purdue University, Army aviator

"Moments in life that call for moral courage are not rare; they pop up every single day of our lives with friends, family, coworkers, and strangers. Oftentimes we miss these moments as we justify our behavior with 'I'm too busy,' 'It's too hard,' and 'It won't change anything.' Gus Lee's *The Courage Playbook* cuts through our fears and offers us a practical set of tools to recognize these moments and courageously do the right thing with unwavering respect for others. This book will change how you see the world and transform your relationships for the better. I use *The Courage Playbook*'s quick references every day to help me become the man I want to be at work and at home."

—**Ben Bain**
national security professional

"Gus Lee knocks it out of the park and makes a difference with *The Courage Playbook*, which gives us tools to improve effectiveness in leading and in life. In Step Three, he strips bare common human inhibitors to leadership and gives us a practical way to defeat them. I witnessed Gus apply these principles, know that they came from the school of hard reality, and that they actually work. In my career and interface with Gus, I've used his applications to promote my ability and that of others to be self-examining leaders in a guided personal journey of reflection and improvement."

—**Tom Rozman**
Past Director, Collective Training Directorate, Deputy Chief of Staff for Training, US Army Training and Doctrine Command; past Director Central Region, Virginia Department of Labor and Industry

"Gus Lee has penned a road map for those of us striving to overcome our compulsive tendency to prefer faux self-preservation over courageous moral action. The 3 NOs helped me more clearly understand the compounding effects of my self-deception and better equipped me to take ownership for the quality of my relationships. I remain grateful for the ways in which the practical lessons that constitute *The Courage Playbook* continue to unfold in my personal and professional life."

—**Major Chip Huth**
30 years, Kansas City Missouri Police Department

"Informed, honed, intentional and deliberately acquired courage, which Gus Lee presents in *The Courage Playbook*, walked me through meaningful exercises that led to my making serious decisions and direction changes with clarity and precision. Gus describes how courage can be developed, sharpened, and used to raise decisions and people to greater heights and avoid reckless actions that in truth are not courage. He writes with clarity, wit, wisdom and research and lives the way he writes. Down to earth, boots-on-the-ground illustrations make concepts come alive and applicable. *The Courage Playbook* is readable, poignant, and practical."

—**Dick Stenbakken, EdD, MDiv, MEd, MA**
Chaplain (Colonel) US Army, Retired Director of Family Life Ministries

"The Assessment tools helped me get a bead on behaviors that were controlling me—I was trapped without joy. Step Two actions equipped me to stop my self-lying, sharp self-interest, blaming and anger, with huge benefits to my company. Steps Three and Four are saving my marriage and our daughter from constantly seeking approval of others. Thank you for the immediate action steps and the fundamental planning truths in Step Five. Sharing your work and experience with others is producing blessings."

—**Rock Adams**
President, Rock Hard, Inc.

"Several years ago, I was blessed with the opportunity to work with Gus Lee. *The Courage Playbook* and other Gus Lee books represent what is possible in our lives when we commit to practice, experience, learn, overcome, and share our big life lessons. Gus has faced substantial challenges, refused to quit or give in to an easier path and remained resolute to a higher calling and purpose. Gus is the real deal; he shows up every day as a respected moral and courageous teacher and leader. This book lays down a very effective road map that we can use to create a more positive and intentional way in our own lives and model to strangers and to those we love and care about. It equips us to face difficulties and opportunities, to make the conscious choice to not become bitter but better. Using Unconditional Positive Respect and seeking the Highest Moral Action, we steadily become more courageous in every part of our lives. This is Gus's gift to us. His life story, experience, and wisdom have greatly impacted my life. Implementing the insights and practices shared in *The Courage Playbook* will challenge and reward you with the ability to experience a more inspired life. Enjoy the journey!"

—**Rob Knauer**
Vistage Worldwide, Chicago Chair, leads high-performing CEO Peer Advisory Boards; CEO, Black Ocean Advisors, Inc.

"*The Courage Playbook* uniquely provides the structure to help those aspiring to become their best self. Gus created the tools for anyone to grow in self-awareness and understanding on a journey to become a better follower and leader with intent and practice. I found the book's assessments challenging and had to talk with family and others to ensure I was being honest with myself. *The Courage Playbook* is well worth revisiting with changing professional and personal challenges. It joins a short list of books that add value with each reread and periodic reevaluation and refocusing to update our best practices, which I now do as I systematically develop and coach leaders to be their best."

—**Scott Tessmer**
Retired Naval Officer

"I appreciate the introspective tools Gus uses in *The Courage Playbook*, especially the Three NOs. They are a living checklist for me to mentally review before tough conversations, when I've been blindsided, and when I automatically react out of fear. Remembering to show unconditional respect, to not let fear control me, and to remember that I can choose courageous actions to do the right thing are but samples of the essential tools Gus equips us with in his new book."

—**William A. Salmon**
Fire Captain (Ret.), Poudre Fire Authority

"During my 23 years as an NFL side judge, including three Super Bowls and more than a dozen playoff games, I encountered innumerable challenges. The NFL is a high-stakes enterprise where officials' mistakes garner considerable scrutiny and criticism. I wish that I had *The Courage Playbook* to guide me during my career. Gus Lee's principles and lessons would have given me even more confidence to act with courage, confidence, and clarity. In retirement, I am still a husband, father, and grandfather. I teach at the college level, volunteer with the police and serve on our city's parks, beaches and recreation commission. *The Courage Playbook* is my blueprint for doing what is right in every sphere, thus strengthening me to make a greater difference for my family and communities. What a gift!"

—**Dr. Laird Hayes**
NFL Side Judge, known for making the biggest call in Super Bowl history (SB XLVI)

THE
COURAGE
PLAYBOOK

GUS LEE

THE
COURAGE
PLAYBOOK

FIVE STEPS TO **OVERCOME YOUR FEARS**
AND BECOME YOUR BEST SELF

WILEY

Published by John Wiley & Sons, Inc., Hoboken, New Jersey.
Published simultaneously in Canada.

For general information on our other products and services or for technical support, please contact our Customer Care Department within the United States at (800) 762-2974, outside the United States at (317) 572-3993 or fax (317) 572-4002.

Wiley publishes in a variety of print and electronic formats and by print-on-demand. Some material included with standard print versions of this book may not be included in e-books or in print-on-demand. If this book refers to media such as a CD or DVD that is not included in the version you purchased, you may download this material at http://booksupport.wiley.com. For more information about Wiley products, visit www.wiley.com.

Library of Congress Cataloging-in-Publication Data:

Names: Lee, Gus, author.
Title: The courage playbook : five steps to overcome your fears and become your best self / Gus Lee.
Description: Hoboken, New Jersey : Wiley, [2022] | Includes index.
Identifiers: LCCN 2021058276 (print) | LCCN 2021058277 (ebook) | ISBN 9781119848905 (cloth) | ISBN 9781119848950 (adobe pdf) | ISBN 9781119848943 (epub)
Subjects: LCSH: Courage. | Fear. | Interpersonal communication.
Classification: LCC BF575.C8 L44 2022 (print) | LCC BF575.C8 (ebook) | DDC 179/.6—dc23/eng/20211210
LC record available at https://lccn.loc.gov/2021058276
LC ebook record available at https://lccn.loc.gov/2021058277

Cover Design and Image: Wiley

SKY10033159_022522

To our children, grandchildren, and next generations for their faith, love, and courageous service to others.

Contents

Foreword   *xv*

Acknowledgments   *xvii*

      Introduction   1

Part I   **The Courageous Self**   **13**

Chapter 1   Step One: Where Am I? I Assess Myself   15

Chapter 2   Step Two: Who Am I, Really? I Admit
                and Quit the 3 NOs   39

Chapter 3   Step Three: Getting It Right—The 3 GOs   73

Part II   **Courage with Others**   **121**

Chapter 4   Step Four: Playsets for Basic CourCom   123

Chapter 5   Step Five: Playsets for CourCom Conflicts   147

Part III   You Decide: Choosing Your Core   **189**

Chapter 6   Your Identity: Naming, Claiming, and Aiming   193

Chapter 7   The Individual Courage Advancement Plan: ICAP   197

Chapter 8   Crossing the River   209

Epilogue   217

Appendix: Cut-out Memory Cards   219

Notes   223

Glossary of Acronyms   245

About the Author   247

Index   249

Foreword

AFTER READING GUS Lee's *Honor and Duty*, I believed that its author would provide our students at the St. Mark's School of Texas with a sound example of fine writing. So we invited Gus to campus as a visiting scholar. During that visit, we concluded that Gus would provide us with more than lessons in how to think and write, but on how to become better people. Coincidentally, Gus and Diane were in the process of writing *Courage: The Backbone of Leadership*.

The rest became history. In subsequent years, Gus challenged us to think afresh and more clearly and intelligently about our core values. He has taught us to simplify our objectives by directing our attention to key fundamentals—courage, honesty, integrity—and residing there no matter what the difficulty or cost.

Clearly, we were fortunate to be introduced to Gus. The principles of *Courage* became deeply embedded in our Character and Leadership program, providing the basis on which we have taken our young men along the Path to Manhood in a thoughtful, ethical, and courageous manner. It was Gus who motivated us to formalize the program and who inspired us to reach further than we otherwise would have dreamed.

Gus advocated that we be ardently committed to our convictions about making our hopes a practical reality and encouraged us to make formal that which was being taken for granted. Without intentionality, he said, we would miss opportunities to take our students into the moral "weight room of life."

What Gus prompted us to achieve has been enduring and has made generations of our boys better men, leaders, and community members. So many conversations at the school include references to the words of Gus Lee. Innumerable interactions begin with Unconditional Positive Respect and doing the Highest Moral Action despite risk to self-interest. Our students and faculty have learned to disagree well by respecting others, listening first, articulating their discerned conclusions, and making tough decisions with strength and civility.

The Courage Playbook takes these concepts to new levels of self-awareness in clearly stated ways. What might have been simply noble and vital aspiration becomes tangible, measurable practice—character made real. One's courage is not questioned, but is only expanded to appear more consistently in everyday behavior through empirical suggestions and steps. This work is a superb guide to helping us become our best selves despite fear and stress. By following the recommendations included herein, one will become stronger and find ways to make one's organizations and teams more productive and effective, thriving in ways that might not otherwise have been imagined. In any era, and perhaps especially in today's climate of blaming, name-calling, and judging others, their actions, and beliefs categorically, *The Courage Playbook* provides us with a clear and decisive road map to follow. Through courage, Character first. Character last. Character always.

I am eager to learn how *The Courage Playbook* impacts my former school and all others. From this vantage point, I envision tomorrow's leaders will exhibit courage, be unafraid to take necessary and intelligent risks, and will hold close the greater good and the well-being of others as their personal desires. Forward we go with courage!

Arnie Holtberg, Eugene McDermott Headmaster, St. Mark's School of Texas (Retired); Principal, Hong Kong International School; and former NY Yankees minor league catcher

Acknowledgments

To DIANE, FOR her guidance in writing *The Playbook* and all of our books, and mostly for her love and for everything in everything.

To the many who rescued, encouraged, and trained me in courage. Special appreciation to those who make the world a better place by having dedicated their lives to the development of courage, character, and leaders of character, with my personal thanks to Coaches Antonio Gallo and Bonifacio Tizon; Toussaint Streat, MD; Terry Stein, MD; Professors Warren Bennis, Kwang-ching Liu, and James R. Edwards; CEOs Christopher A. Kay and Richard K. Eitel; Dr. Tim Keller, and to those who have done so at West Point and in the US Army: Dr. James "Sully" Sullivan; COL (Ret) Larry "Whitey" White; CSM (Ret) Theodore L. Dobol; CSM (Ret) George Kihara; GEN (Ret) H. Norman Schwarzkopf; GEN (Ret) Fred M. Franks, Jr.; COL (Ret) Douglas Boone; LTG Ronald P. Clark; and COL (Ret) Glenn A. Waters. My special thanks to national security professional Ben Bain for his wise inputs.

Many thanks to my clients and to Gary, Aiden, Bella, Alicia, Caleb, Anita, Sean, David, Josh, Gracie, Clifton, Alphonse, and Deke, who continue to instruct and inspire others.

Our gratitude and love, always, to Jane Dystel and Miriam Goderich of Dystel, Goderich & Bourret, Literary Agents, our dear friends who have made writing possible and enjoyable while keenly shepherding my career. Thanks to my sister, Amy Tan, who opened the door. Thanks to Zachary Schisgal, Dawn Kilgore, Donna J. Weinson, Manikandan Kuppan, and the art and marketing teams at Wiley for their professional support and teamwork in bringing *The Playbook* to life.

Introduction

"All we have to decide is what to do with the time that is given us."
—Gandalf, in J.R.R. Tolkien's The Fellowship of the Ring

IN THE YEARS since the publication of *Courage: The Backbone of Leadership*,[1] we as a country have seen our levels of conflict, fears, and anxieties soar like an Elon Musk rocket. The first casualties? Our already questionable abilities to respect all people and to actually listen to each other.

The Playbook challenges us to do the highest moral action in the routines of everyday life. It's not about the rarely needed physical bravery of running into burning buildings. It's really about authentically respecting others in the here and now to instill a strong and meaningful rhythm in our daily lives. When do we need courage? Every time we interact with someone or face any manner of decision. Where does this need arise? At home, in families, during commutes, at work, in relationships, in the gym, and out with friends—whenever moments quietly call upon our actual ability to be courageous. Often, we don't even notice or, fearing discomfort, we look the other way. Every day, we lose opportunities to become our best selves. Based on my own history of weakness, I know we can do better. I train people to overcome their fears. Long experience with diverse clients has taught me to focus on two principles:

1

First, as individuals and as a people, we need to use UPR, Unconditional
Positive Respect.

Second, UPR is achieved by practice. Practicing UPR takes courage.

What's courage? It's the deep, mystic chord with which we can
lead our lives and inspire others to become their best selves. It
seamlessly equips us to improve who we are. It optimizes how we use
the time given us. Courage fuels our brave adventuring into a life of
deeper meaning, of helping others, of serving a higher, unselfish cause
in a grand narrative, of becoming who we always wished to be. It is
doing that liberating right thing which at first seems undoable.

Courage counts because we often allow our anxieties, fears, and
doubts to play with us like a kitten with ball of yarn. We sweat out
energy worrying about the external and forget that we were internally
wired to practice courage so that we can lead and live with this great,
unflinching, untapped, life-uplifting source of strength. Courage, like
a world-class runner in the blocks, merely awaits our decision to run
the race of life with a stronger purpose.

Courage is many things. For starters, courage is more an action
than an abstraction, and is more behavioral than theoretical. Courage
is doing the highest and grandest right thing.

As a child, I had many disadvantages with the special decision-
making ability of a defective video game character. This led to a life of
fear and flight, of dwindling in the face of challenges. I let myself slide
into cowardice. But courage was chasing me. I knew it was there, just
beyond reach. I couldn't see it and I couldn't name it—but I could
sense it. Later, being coached by selfless men and women forced me to
accept that even I could become courageous.

"Life," wrote Anais Nin, "expands or shrinks in proportion to one's
courage."[2] Gaining courage stopped my shrinkage. It changed
everything, like *Peanuts*' Charlie Brown, the hapless cartoon character
never again losing the kite and now always getting to kick the football.

"The Y," said Coach Tony, "ain't a boxing factory. None o' you are
likely to go pro. The Y's here for you to get inner courage. Build your
character. Uh, 'specially *you*, kid."

Can anyone acquire courage? Certainly. But today, many can only
sense courage the way I did as a child. We know in a vague way that

courage is there. But we see it incompletely and understand it imperfectly, with an ancient fear that courage is full of promise but in reality is an unwinnable lottery ticket.

Critically, we forget that courage is a set of practiced behaviors, a way of life, and a fundamental form of human identity.

Courage recruited me, an All-American Chicken Little. I feared everything, ran from my own fears, and couldn't find "courage" in the dictionary. It methodically equipped me to obey my coaches, practice doing the right thing, train others to beat their fears, and to care for those whom I could reach. Courage gave me life. Because it can be acquired by anyone, never again would I find myself running on empty and fleeing discomfort on the fumes of my fears.

A result is *The Courage Playbook*, your personal invitation to flex your essential courage muscles before they atrophy from unthinking neglect. Here, intellect, emotions, actions, and inner spirit unite in a principled way so you can become who you were always supposed to be.

This differs from other books on leading your life and the like. It departs from the popular, mainstream leader and self-development efforts that rely on listening to speakers rather than actually acquiring practical on-the-ground skills and focusing on self-gain rather than on helping others. Per professor-psychologist-aviator-humorist-writer-and-boxer Dr. James P. Sullivan, we win greatness of ability by practicing the skills of courage instead of listening to people talk about them. Crucially, we gain courage for the common good.

The difference is captured in a simple axiom: We get courage by doing courage.

How do we do courage? By practicing its now-forgotten behaviors.

The Courage Playbook walks you through those actions in five basic Steps.

The ideas and exercises in *The Playbook* come from a revolutionary courage training program that has equipped individuals and organizations to overcome their fears so they can act with unfettered freedom, resolute confidence, and a sense of humor, all for the right reasons.

It's not how I used to do it. For decades, working for top global and national leader development institutions and business schools, we taught leadership knowledge as if it were an academic subject like

English or math. Thousands of smart, experienced, and educated participants took notes, enjoyed personality insights, simulation games, camaraderie, and meals and gave us 4.5 stars. They left emotionally refreshed. But their behaviors hadn't changed. Our binders sat brightly on the shelf, but the learning hadn't installed practical interpersonal abilities. They knew more than before, yet the fears they had on arrival were waiting for them when they returned. The glow lasted about a week. Yet they had not functionally improved as leaders or individuals. We'd taught *intellectual theory*; we hadn't trained in *actual courage and skills*.

The participants' organizations continued to practice denial and blame, avoid glaring problems, tolerate toxic managers and be stymied by poor performance, disrespect, turnover, dishonesty, and divided cultures. They drove for profits instead of quality; picked on others for not improving while refusing to change themselves; didn't want to hear the truth; chose short-term results over sustainability and became bad companies—sadly, the very issues that had brought them to us for training. In business and in personal lives, they knew more about why they struggled, but didn't know how to implement courageous actions for authentic improvement, to become who they were supposed to be. Courage had been left out of the training schedule. It's as if they had attended a running clinic without stepping outside the classroom; they hadn't learned and then conscientiously practiced the fundamental plays, leaving them to hesitate once the starter gun sounded.

In the language of the earlier book on courage, they had read about crossing the River of Fear—the barrier between us and our best selves—but they hadn't practiced doing it and hence didn't know how to pull it off.

I realized that leadership shouldn't be only for those with rank, and courage can't be only for those who can afford an executive coach. The very definition of courage requires that it be available to everyone and that it not be for you alone; when you gain it by practice, you'll then generously share it.

Courage is essential in leadership—it's impossible to lead and inspire others to be their best selves while being anxious about approval, constantly fearing failure, or avoiding difficulties. But courage is rarely presented as central to human effort and is almost never the subject of actual, practical behavioral training. Research into our national efforts to develop positive work, family, and community cultures through leadership training has confirmed what I'd observed and learned through decades of experience.

Acutely lacking leaders, the United States spends $170 billion every year ($520 per capita) to develop them—without producing effective leaders.[3] We've tried agility, change theory, conceptualization, do what you feel, emotional intelligence, execution, fishbones, going to Gemba, pursuing Kaizen, chasing habits, laws, Lean Six Sigma, rules, break the rules, forget the rules, no rules, perseverance, positivity, quality programs, Root Cause Analysis, scrums, speed, sprints, strengths, transparency, trust, and vision.

The results? Per John Kotter of Harvard, we suffer a 400 percent deficit in leaders at every level.[4] Dr. Paul Brand, an international medical missionary, noted that Americans, who live with greater physical comforts than most in the world, are unequipped to cope with simple discomfort and are especially vulnerable to sharp disappointments.[5]

Brimming with good ideas, we have found ourselves back where we began.

We are missing something, and it's big.

What happened? I'll tell you what happened: we lost our courage, and watching endless PowerPoint presentations and taking personality assessments and doing simulations have sadly failed to bring it back. With brains, universities, and a big economy, we sit on the fence of positive action, suffer great falls, and can't put Humpy Dumpty together again.

We've created and then fallen face-first into a yawning Courage Gap.

But when I was engaged in one-on-one executive and private coaching, I did things differently. By guiding clients to courageously stop basic and common negative habits, practice key courageous behaviors, and to be actually accountable, the coaching became personal, relational, and impactful. They became dramatically stronger as listeners, communicators, teambuilders, and effective solvers of tough, recurring problems at work. But beyond that, more importantly, they were able to repeat the same behaviors in their private lives, the place that counts the most. By changing themselves, they inspired change in others. We laughed, not at preplanned jokes to warm up participants, but from experiencing the spontaneous and deeper mirth from the lost art of courageously realizing our foibles. And they then practiced the behaviors of courage, which locked key skills into mind-muscle-heart memory, and shared their courage with others. The results were often life-changing.

I found myself looking more carefully at the goals of leader development and at how to create a training model for real results.

Pitching thought-based education from a platform or stage, I'd let the university habit of only gathering knowledge to override the practice of courage to equip us to rightly live and lead so we could then actually apply cognitive data.

The first courage book was written for that simpler time and I used boxing examples to illustrate an approach for facing fear. But to train people to actually *overcome* fear, I had to rely on deeper matters of moral instruction, core identity, family repair, relationship reconciliation, marriage, and parenting.

Half of us are football fans, so half of us aren't,[6] but the sport is instructive regardless of what we like. So I studied the training methods of a once-obscure college football coach named Bill Walsh. Walsh then took over the worst franchise in sports history—the San Francisco 49ers—and transformed the organization, improved the game, and saw his teams win five Super Bowls. It's helpful to know the answer to: How'd he do it?

First, to form a selfless and unified team structure, he picked morally courageous players instead of egotistical superstars. His prime example was Jack "Hacksaw" Reynolds, a tough, old, slow, over-the-hill linebacker. Jack was the "most telling personnel move I ever made," said Walsh. "He set an example for everybody. . . that single addition was the key to our success."[7]

Many heard the word—a failing organization was saved by hiring a humble, nondescript, overlooked leader of character—and preferred to focus on the players that Reynolds led to greatness.

Walsh also picked Joe Montana ("too skinny") and Steve Young ("too reckless") because he needed smart and studious (vs. big, huge-armed) quarterbacks who knew his playbook to fluently call, "Green RT Slot Z Opp Fake 98 Toss Z and watch that safety,"[8] and had the mental calmness to make off-schedule plays. Second, and most importantly, Walsh coached his players to acquire mastery by *practice*,

practice, practice. His coaches identified the skills required for each position. They memorized and practiced hundreds of plays from a huge playbook. Offensive linemen had to personally master 38 specific skills in realistic drills that required more brains than mass. Bobb McKittrick, the bald, well-read, world-traveling offensive line coach, turned Walsh's high-character, undersized, low-draft picks into 19 Pro Bowl selections.[9]

"That's the essence," said Walsh, "repetition developing skills and then under pressure, being able to perform."[10]

The Playbook does the same, without the bruising or the need for ice baths and physical therapy. And without the weight of Walsh's *Oxford English Dictionary*–sized game manual.

How many plays do most of us know, and how many of us get coached in courage?

Only a precious few. Thus, *The Playbook.*

Courage is not a life panacea but it comes awfully close. In the steps of this playbook, you'll see courage acted out by parents and teens, managers, firefighters, nurses, doctors, teachers, C-levels, and the jobless. People of every background who saw themselves as good but never brave, and then found their courage because they practiced it. They became effective leaders as courage countered individual fears, natural disrespect, bias and discrimination.

Aristotle was the great thinker who invented useful things like empirical research, character training, and the happiness formula. Despite being the scorned alien, he persisted in earnestly training Athenians because they needed his wisdom. He remains fresh for reminding us that courage is the single virtue that helps us navigate hard times of fear and stress in order to achieve our best personhood.

Aristotle also saw that sadness, difficulty, and struggle—the hard signs of our times—can help us break unhealthy habits, inspire us to gain what we're missing and to prep moral meals from disregarded ingredients. Professor Brené Brown found strength in our vulnerabilities. Researcher Dr. Angela Duckworth discovered that low points can lead to high ones.

The data tells us that we can leverage sadness and dismay to defuse old habits of fear, find our forgotten courage, reframe poorly defined mindsets, and even overwrite sad pasts.

Courage, unlike avoidance, is a positive, heroic verb. Unlike utopia, it's not a fictional notion. Like sports, it becomes real with practice. Courage is the unique virtue that gives us deep values like self-control, integrity, respect, generosity, love, justice, trust, and an authentic caring for others—the sweet higher order goods that represent our deepest, heartfelt desires.

J.M. Barrie, polymath educator and creator of *Peter Pan*, recognized courage as a life goal. He bluntly warned college graduates: *"If courage goes, then all goes."*[11]

We no longer speak or act courageously at work, in our families, or in the public square. We privately say totally wrong things to ourselves that deepen our fears and separate us from our courage. We seek comfort by hopefully reciting that we're special while not remembering that courage calls us to see what is unique in others.

Despite a deep inner need, courage has few followers, fewer advocates, and no network. It lacks a central, unified curriculum and has no cultural platform and few champions. It faces powerful and corrupt foes in business, government, and society. Once the path of the good life and the renewable fuel for human thriving, courage is now a boutique answer to an arcane trivia question and a distant theory. It seems to be a pleasant thought without boots on the ground.

We think we're okay without it. We think practicing it is unnecessary.

This is a huge mistake.

It's unwise to unfriend courage, gaslight ourselves with barrages of bad news, and nurture our fears as if they were household pets. It's wrong to ignore the practice of courage to be captives of our anxieties.

Global poverty experts Brian Corbett and Steve Fikkert find there is little courage left in the world.[12] Courage has been asked to leave our cultural stage. But all has not yet gone. It remains the approved solution to undo our impulsive reliance on negativity, criticism, bias, and self-harm. Long before handheld screens and the discovery of the coffee bean, we were prewired to be courageous and thereby free of self-perpetuating fears.

But how do we go from a *capacity* for courage to becoming courageous?

We practice its behaviors.

Those who practice sing better than those who do not. If you exercise, you tend to be more fit and will feel and function better than when you only sit. When we practice honoring all persons we chip away at the monoliths of self-centeredness and racism.

"String Bean," said Coach Bonifacio, his nickname for my less than impressive physique. Coach B was a *wing chun gong-fu si fu*, a martial arts master on a work visa from Manila.

"You think courage out of reach. You think you can't punch your way out of a wet paper bag. But courage made just for you, the weak of heart."

Practicing courage with others makes us courageous leaders for others.

Singing well, boxing, acting rightly, reconciling conflicts, solving moral problems, and leading courageously when stressed are not inborn gifts or accidents of nature. They directly result from behavioral practice. Thus, the need for a courage playbook.

Living in our shape-shifting, conflicted culture, we forget that we own a very real personal capacity for courage.

Courage is race and gender neutral, honors all faiths, and favors no party. It requires neither unique powers nor specific intelligence, unusual gifts, or a generation with a special name.

"*Cowardice,*" said Dr. Martin Luther King Jr., "*seeks to suppress fear and is mastered by it. Courage faces fear and thereby masters it.*"[13]

How can you be like Dr. King? You *practice the behaviors of courage*, which you will soon own. *The Playbook* trains you to face fear and master it, to ascend the five practical and logical steps to courage.

Gangly and socially awkward, Sir Edmund Hillary was the first to reach the peak of Mount Everest. Suddenly a world sensation, he was asked about reaching that deadly summit.

"It is not the mountain we conquer," he said, "but ourselves." Conquering our fears is Tolkien's and Lucas's classic moral struggle. Can Frodo find the courage to give up the ring? Will Aragorn overcome the terrors of his painful past? Can Solo defeat his smugness, Leia her sarcasm, and C3PO his nervous frights? The great saga turns on the single, eternal issue of our heroic identity: *Can Luke master his anger? Can you?*

Our battle isn't against Sauron, Vader, or a virus. It's against fear and our worst reactions in an epic, personal struggle against our own weaknesses.

After 10 years of tutelage by my YMCA coaches, I lucked into West Point despite scoliosis, flat feet, and visual and pulmonary disqualifiers. In the Infantry and in Asia, with people of all colors, I worked to improve my Courage Quotient,[14] learn new tongues, and lead others while my knees knocked together. Many colleagues had also been poor, unfed, and unwanted by their families of origin. But we practiced and overcame our worst poverty—the lack of courage—to selflessly work toward what we can call the *heroic moral ideal.*[15] We were able to experience a new freedom by serving something greater than ourselves without hungering for personal honors or recognition. Those days of trust, camaraderie, and low pay remain the happiest among my many jobs.

In the earlier book, I described the importance of behaviors of courage. I got feedback asking for a practical step-by-step playbook to make acting courageously and defeating our fears as spontaneous as smiling at a beautiful sunset.

The Courage Playbook is that solution. It trains you in the key behaviors that we individually and collectively need most. Emerson might say that it gives you a plan, a goal, and a dominating thought process to possess the courage to do the right thing. The *Playbook* lets you move from the unseen to the seen, from the passive to the active, from the ordinary to the courageous. It is a precise distillate of our best understanding of behavioral courage, integrity, character, and courageous, effective leadership. It has three parts.

Part I is about you—the equipping of *The Courageous Self.* Here you'll friend courage and paint a personal courage-colored portrait. You'll stop your worst fearful reactions to create space for the behaviors of courage.

Part II is about relationships—*Courage with Others.* There you will deploy[16] basic courage plays and behaviors while interacting with others in communication, teamwork, leadership, management, and personal relationships. You'll learn the central, radiating power of courageously respecting all persons to consistently do the Highest Moral Action.

Finally, in Part III, *Choosing Your Core*, you'll select your personal identity—your operating principles—draft your Individual Courage Advancement Plan for continued assessment and forward navigation, and then Cross the River of Fear.

You need an Executive Courage Coach to guide you through each step, to equip you to own the courage to live intentionally, robustly, and even happily. For the short span of this shared journey, I would like to be that coach.

I equip people to face fear and to find, build, forge, and share their courage in a process older than *Exodus*, *The Iliad*, and *The Analects*. The best of Greek and Eastern wisdom literature was created during plagues, crises of fear, ethnic wars, and conflict.

Take this opportunity to play in a different realm in which no one is denied the right to personal courage. With it, you will enter a deeper country of brave lions and fearless leaders in which you can take extraordinary and unprecedented actions. Those actions—our key verbs—equip you to become who you were always supposed to be.

Acquiring courage is one of the greatest human adventures.

The risks lie not on the journey, but in avoiding it. For who among us has already conquered fear, mastered courage, perfected one's true core identity, and achieved a complete firmness of character? Who doesn't want better plays on the great and exciting field of life?

Will you join me on this courageous journey?

PART

I

The Courageous Self

"What lies behind us and what lies before us are tiny matters compared to what lies within us."

—*Ralph Waldo Emerson*

"My heartache," said Dr. Gary Persons, "is Dr. Aiden Bellevue.[1] He's brilliant and wins Blue Ribbons for loving himself. When he's not ticking people off, he's threatening them. He's Teflon-coated against HR counseling, discipline, and pay cuts. The more I try to correct Aiden, the harder he fights me. I love his brain but hate his character and he's hurting a mission-essential project. If I keep him, I fear key folks will quit. If I fire him, he'll tie us up in litigation and probably wreck the project. So, what's your wise counsel?"

Our responses to discomfort and tough questions say much about where we are and how well we cope with challenges in a highly competitive world.

Dr. Persons is a tall and trim science leader who looks like an ambassador to a very important place. Impeccable apparel suggested attention to detail. A sharp, unblinking gaze said he didn't suffer fools and didn't want to hear about an easy, shiny-object, quick-fix idea. He'd heard those before from consultants whom he concluded had mostly tried to make him feel better without helping find the fix.

What is wise counsel? Upon what do you usually base your decisions?

We often rely on feelings to make decisions. Feelings are emotional states that can overcome rational thinking and do great damage. Luckily, conscience and experience can mitigate impulses and prevent us from giving in to blame and anger.

Dr. Gary Persons owned a 200-pound brain, command of the Scientific Method, and success in career advancement but was stymied by Dr. Bellevue. Gary had tried many clever, quick, expedient, short-term options which had only made matters worse.

I asked, "Where do Dr. Bellevue and your heartache begin?"

He hesitated. "I was going to blame Aiden, but truly, my heartaches are mine. Ergo, it's very possible that it begins with me."

I was impressed with Dr. Persons' speed in moving from blaming others to courageously looking at his opportunities to improve as a colleague, a leader, and as an individual.

1

Step One: Where Am I? I Assess Myself

"If you do not change direction, you may end up where you are heading."
—*Lao Tzu*

THE FIRST STEP in the Scientific Method is to objectively observe phenomena. To advance our courage, we must first calmly assess ourselves.

I said, "Gary, as we discussed earlier, we begin the journey to courage with the Biography Form to figure out our starting point. It gives us insights about how we can better handle ourselves and relate to and even lead others. Those insights might link your personal life history with your Aiden Bellevue heartache."

Gary completed a biography form and we now jump in so you can do the same.

The LOC Biography Form 5

An Army buddy was a brave and brilliant wounded combat veteran with a PhD. Conditioned to face discomfort and tough it out, he ignored persistent chest pains. Candid as a professional, he wasn't honest with his VA physician or his friends, so he'd survived the terrible and constant dangers of deadly close-quarters combat only to let heart disease kill him as he was peacefully gardening.

Looking at ourselves often involves discomfort, and we feel like using denial to get a momentary illusion that we can avoid unpleasant feelings. Denial is the opposite of courage.

Thus, I want you to be brutally honest in filling out the Bio. Doing the Bio is a once-in-a-lifetime opportunity to get candid and highly useful information on where you are, what you value, and how you treat yourself and others.

The Bio uncovers key data. We then leverage your honesty about your past and present to build your courageous abilities for the future.

After each question you'll see a general courage-based comment in italics.

Do your best to not read the comment until after you've thoughtfully answered the question.

Ready to be totally and courageously honest with yourself? Take a deep, diaphragmatic breath, slowly exhale completely, begin, and enjoy!

> *"Courage doesn't happen when you have all the answers. It happens when you are willing to face the questions that you have been avoiding your whole life."*
> —Shannon L. Alder, author[1]

LOC Biography Form 5©

This form asks 53 personal insight questions. It has 3 sections:
Personal Information | Reflections | Courage
It will take about an hour. This is like driving; do not do this if you are tired.

If uncertain about an answer, pick what people who know you would probably choose.

Section I: Personal Information (13 Questions)

1. Words that describe the quality of the relationships with your parents & siblings
   a. As an adolescent

   ┌───┐
   │   │
   │   │
   │   │
   │   │
   └───┘

   Your answer above is a reminder of the power of our pasts. Many find that patterns of relationships in adolescence have an impact on how we now relate to people in general.
   b. Today

   ┌───┐
   │   │
   │   │
   │   │
   └───┘

   Improving difficult family relationships shows you can do the same with other people. If stress persists in these situations, you'll find that The Playbook will offer possible solutions.

2. What were the *actual* living conditions of your home life from earliest memory to age 18? Read across each row in Figure 1.1 and check the one that is closest to your experience.

   Per Professor J. Garbarino, early childhood trauma returns to haunt us. Do your answers tell you something? Do they form a pattern? What does the pattern tell you? Items C, D, E, G, I, and K can play significant roles on your path to courage. You might want to pay particular attention to these items if you answered them in the Y and Z columns. I had many Z responses and dedicated time to go through therapists until I found an effective, change-based one.

	COLUMN X	COLUMN Y	COLUMN Z
A	☐ Economically stable	☐ Economically inconsistent	☐ Economically unstable
B	☐ Emotionally nourishing	☐ Emotionally inconsistent	☐ Emotionally unsafe/ traumatic
C	☐ Unconditional affection	☐ Some affection	☐ Little affection
D	☐ Very high ethical principles	☐ Some ethical principles	☐ Whatever works
E	☐ Consistent fairness	☐ Some fairness	☐ Little fairness
F	☐ High responsibility	☐ Some responsibility	☐ Little responsibility
G	☐ No depression	☐ Some depression	☐ Depression was common
H	☐ Trained to do the right thing	☐ Some training to act rightly	☐ Little training to act rightly
I	☐ Adults did the right thing	☐ Adults struggled to act rightly	☐ Adults seldom did the right thing
J	☐ Healthy arguing	☐ Unhealthy arguing	☐ Violent arguing
K	☐ Physically, emotionally safe	☐ Physically, emotionally uneven	☐ Physically, emotionally unsafe
L	☐ Regular meals with family	☐ Irregular meals	☐ I was on my own

Figure 1.1 Home Life Living Conditions

3. Many of us struggled in adolescence and junior high. Which of
your teenage personality traits were the most difficult?

*Many find that what was a challenge for us as teens can reappear
in adulthood. True for you?*

4. Read across the rows in Figure 1.2 and circle the one that **most
closely describes** you right now.

FEATURE 1		or	FEATURE 2	
Stressed	Often worried, anxious	or	**Untroubled**	Unworried, keeps calm
Pressured	Often harried, hurried, rushed	or	**Planful**	Unhurried, finishes early
Impatient	Irritable, frustrated, crabby	or	**Patient**	Understanding, forbearing
Self-serving	Ambitious, power-seeking	or	**Selfless**	Focuses on others' needs
Inner-focused	It's my needs, feelings, issues	or	**Other-focused**	Helps others improve
Abrupt	Often inattentive, thoughtless	or	**Respectful**	Attentive, caring
Agitating	Complains, carps, negative	or	**Peacemaking**	Calms others

Figure 1.2   Emotional Assessment

FEATURE 1		or	FEATURE 2	
Passive	Avoids controversies, hassles	or	Assertive	Communicates clearly
Worried	Feels weight of fallen world	or	Confident	Self-assured, positive
Perfectionist	Judgmental, not good enough	or	Understanding	Perceptive, helpful, patient
Tired	Often exhausted, worn out	or	Rested	Refreshed, renewed
Avoids conflict	Usually looks or turns away	or	Faces conflict	Addresses respectfully
Tough	Often inflexible, even mean	or	Compassionate	Humane, warm, caring
Preferential	Focuses on elites, favorites	or	Respects all	No cliques, no favoritism
Independent	Wants to work solo	or	Teaming	Cooperates, helpful
Prideful	Cocky, self-centered, arrogant	or	Modest	Unpretentious, unassuming
Disengaged	Can be aloof, isolated	or	Engaged	Relational, personable
Discouraged	Often down, pessimistic	or	Encourages	Supportive, strengthens
Angry	Quick-tempered, volatile	or	Peaceful	Harmonious, tranquil
Discontented	Restlessly malcontent	or	Contented	Satisfied, at equanimity

Figure 1.2　(continued)

Yes, you guessed it: you were asked to denote some negative and less flattering behaviors. The Courage Playbook *believes that while assets are important, the first step of a journey begins best on the first rung of the ladder so we can see our starting point.*

In questions 5–13: *Disagree* or *Agree* using the following Likert scale.

Note: The "cowardly number," 3, is *not* an option.

<u>1</u>	<u>2</u>	*	<u>4</u>	<u>5</u>
strongly disagree	disagree	—	agree	strongly agree

5. _____ I worry less about life in general than I did two years ago.

6. _____ I sleep more deeply than I did two years ago.

7. _____ I more quickly forgive those who disrespect or hurt me than I did two years ago.

8. _____ I am more physically fit than I was two years ago.

9. _____ I am more content emotionally than I was two years ago.

10. _____ I listen more closely to my spouse/significant other than I did two years ago.

11. _____ I have greater self-governance than I did two years ago in dealing with others.

12. _____ I have greater self-governance in eating than I did two years ago (i.e. junk food).

13. _____ I have greater self-governance than two years ago related to alcohol, drugs, addictions, and screen time.[2]

Per Mayo Clinic, if you routinely sit, you should get up and move every 30 minutes to forestall heart disease, obesity, and cardiovascular disease.[3]

The Bio reminded Gary that his father had punished him for getting less than perfect grades, for enjoying sports and expressing an opinion. His father wouldn't listen, frequently criticized his wife and kids, enjoyed hurting Gary and his brothers with sarcasm and disrespect, and refused to improve. Gary has taken on some of his father's worst reactive behaviors regarding people and stress and has become fatalistic about people's ability to change. As frustrations with Dr. Bellevue escalated, his positive coping skills and general health have declined.

Section II: Reflections (12 Questions)

14. How might your family background be affecting how you see your life and how you treat others today?

15. My 3 Best Personal Behaviors:

   o _____

   o _____

   o _____

16. My 3 Worst Personal Behaviors:

   o _____

   o _____

   o _____

We improve by using our strengths (such as intelligence, diligence, and creativity) to turn around our weaknesses (such as excuses, avoidance, and blame). As an assistant dean, I counseled inner-city Educational Opportunity Program (EOP) university students. Johnny was a billiards expert who struggled with books. I suggested that studying was like his 8-ball strategy (assessment, selection, key balls, position, angles, and obstacles). He began applying the diligence he had in one space to practicing it in an area of weakness. Johnny was in the leading edge of first EOP college graduates and became a CPA. Can you pair a best behavior of yours with a worst one to turn it around?

17. To improve as a person, what 3 behaviors would you change?

    o _____

    o _____

    o _____

    Your answers here are key.

18. In Figure 1.3, check **The One—only one**—that best states your core primary identity in life right now.

		Select only one that best describes you right now
☐	A	It's most important that I financially support myself/my family.
☐	B	My feelings inform me of what's right and how to navigate life.
☐	C	My intellect, reasoning, knowledge, and logic direct my life.
☐	D	A successful and rewarding career is #1 for me right now.
☐	E	More than anything, I am results-oriented in how I live.
☐	F	More than anything, I am my belief system about the world.
☐	G	My creative, artistic, aesthetic, and innovative abilities are truly at my central core.
☐	H	I am a family person; my family is number one.
☐	I	More than anything, I am a relational being; my relationships are at my central core.
☐	J	I am focused on being a good person who does not do wrong things.
☐	K	My physical health, fitness, and conditioning are the basis for being able to do all else.
☐	L	Other:

Figure 1.3   Core Primary Identity

We usually want to check more than one box. Here we discern our current, primary core identity. (Are you fundamentally your job, relationships, or values?) Research says that courageously doing the right thing positively influences everything from A to L.

19. Reflecting on your life, what essential thing have you yet to accomplish?

```
┌──────────────────────────────────────────────────┐
│                                                    │
│                                                    │
│                                                    │
│                                                    │
└──────────────────────────────────────────────────┘
```

20. What might your answer to #19 reveal about who you are?

```
┌──────────────────────────────────────────────────┐
│                                                    │
│                                                    │
│                                                    │
└──────────────────────────────────────────────────┘
```

What we focus on is important.

21. What 3 behaviors would your spouse/significant other want you to change the most?

    o _____

    o _____

    o _____

The answers to this question can have a profound impact on you, your courage, and your life.

22. What factors have kept you from making those changes?

    o _____

    o _____

    o _____

23. When you look with brutal honesty at yourself, which behavior or habit do you dislike the most?

You showed good courage by answering this!

24. What do you say to yourself to not change?

Your brain runs on what you tell it.

25. What is your deepest, darkest fear?

Your brain can malfunction based on what you tell it to fear.

These reflections are like a Character Mirror that provides a rare look into the inner self. *Character* comes from the Greek word *charassein*, to engrave or impress deeply. Character includes our inborn disposition, developed temperament, mentality, mindset, worldview, imprinting of childhood reactions, psychology, fears, present constitution, and way of being—the sum of who we are. More importantly, character is a measure of the actual quality of the self— how we measure up to an ideal standard when tested by difficulty.

If you glanced at someone, it would be hard to see the inner person. But if a person ignored a bully beating a child, or respectfully intervened, either behavior would reveal much about their courage and character.

Section III: Courage (28 Questions)

In questions 26–53: *Disagree* or *Agree* using the following Likert scale. Note: the "cowardly number," 3, is *not* an option.

<u>1</u>	<u>2</u>	*	<u>4</u>	<u>5</u>
strongly disagree	disagree	—	agree	strongly agree

26. _____ I'm not fully attentive when others speak.

27. _____ I find it hard to respect people who disagree with me.

28. _____ It's very difficult for me to accept negative feedback from others.

29. _____ I tend to deny my own faults.

30. _____ I tend to worry about work and health without having a plan to change.

31. _____ I mostly avoid conflict.

32. _____ Under stress, I'll make excuses or rationalize what I'm doing.

33. _____ When things go wrong, I tend to automatically think others are responsible.

34. _____ I find it easier to shift responsibility than to look hard at myself.

35. _____ I can easily become defensive by blaming others.

36. _____ I'm quickly impatient with or easily frustrated by people.

37. _____ I hate it when people get angry at me, but I express anger at others.

38. _____ I don't always listen very carefully to my spouse/S.O./ family members.

39. _____ I don't always respect all people—especially when arguing with someone I dislike.

40. _____ I normally don't respectfully challenge biased or bigoted comments or behaviors.

41. _____ I am not unselfish or self-centered.

42. _____ I don't consistently improve how I treat others.

43. _____ I don't always govern my emotions when highly stressed or anxious.

44. _____ I don't always learn from my mistakes and I find myself repeating them.

45. _____ I don't see and then improve my deepest faults in every situation.

46. _____ I really don't treat all people as being at least as important as I think I am.

47. _____ I don't always use reason, wiser people, and conscience to see the highest right.

48. _____ I don't consistently value doing the right thing over getting results.

49. _____ I seldom coach others to do the right thing.

50. _____ Seeing a wrong, I don't consistently discern the right action and then do it.

51. _____ When I see someone act wrongly, I almost never ask that person about it.

52. _____ I tend to try "quick fixes" instead of focusing on a problem's moral root cause.

53. _____ I seldom attempt the Highest Right solution because of feared pushback.

These aren't easy but they're important. We'll spend time on them in Steps Three and Four.

Thank you very much for your candor.

Personal inventories can cause discomfort; completing Form 5 is an act of courage.

Take a well-deserved break!

"The Bio surprised me," said Gary. "And the last questions, 25 to 53, were tough. I always thought of myself as being calm under pressure. But in Questions 16 and 21, about worst and most disliked behaviors, I realized that I'm quick to judge and I'm impatient. I react badly to negative situations. I eviscerate others with a hard look or sarcastic word. Worst, I let my direct reports bully their people. I'm excited about what we're going to do with this."

"Good, Gary. Those things stood out to me, too. We'll definitely use them. And Aiden?"

"Aiden," he said, "underperforms. But when I'm about to fire him, I get a twinge of conscience. Like I'm doing something wrong, or I'm being controlled by my emotional reactions. I think about the impact on his family if I fire him. What's the right thing? I can see that I started my decision-making cycle out of fear. I think more about fixing things in the moment instead of figuring out the right thing to do. And I don't have a rational way to discuss things with him in a competent way."

"Good points," I said. "Research shows we should heed those signals from our conscience,[4] our instinctive moral sense of right and wrong. And to not confuse them with our instinctive signals of fear. The truth is that we simply can't reason effectively when we're fearful. We all face tough situations and need a way to reconcile our feelings with doing the right thing. Luckily, we have a tool."

Completing the Bio has probably raised your awareness of how you relate to your world. It was designed to help you see where you are now as you begin to overcome your fears and become your best self. This is where I start with large groups or individuals.

Another tool I use in courage coaching and teaching that helps us assess where we are is the Tier 4 GPS Tool.

The Tier 4 GPS Tool

"Endless confusion about actions and results can be avoided by simply asking if each choice is correct in the moral frame."

—Robert Galbreath[5]

We saw in the Introduction that we need courage to live without constant anxiety and worry. We also need courage to truly love, to be deeply loved, to actually know others, and to be authentically known. We need courage to know the right thing and to then do it. We need courage to first lead ourselves, and then lead others.

The process of knowing the right from the wrong should be simple, but we clutter up a straightforward sequence with old fears, new stresses, and anxious habits. Finding a tool to help us came about in a surprisingly easy way. My wife, Diane, and I were in remote western Kenya, visiting our daughter and her husband. Each was the CEO of a nonprofit that together brought clean water wells and women's health care to over a million people in eleven African nations. We were in the small village of Lwala, playing Hearts. It's a game that begins by ridding yourself of bad cards and I was able to quickly recognize them. I wondered if we could just as easily and systematically discard poor choices in life—the ones driven by fear, stress, and self-destructive habits—to leave us better options? The thought became the Tier 4 GPS tool.

Tier 4 quickly helps us to eliminate our worst alternatives, leaving us with the wiser ones. Figure 1.4 reflects this.

Gary Persons and another client, Bella Cruz, would find this helpful. Bella is the director of a health care system's addiction treatment services. She's smart, capable, and hardworking, which won her early promotions. She's young, short, speaks English as a second language, and can be quiet with superiors, all of which have invited disrespect. Gary Persons is stuck with Aiden Bellevue and Bella Cruz is pinned between hard times and a mean boss.

"We hurt before the COVID-19 hit us," said Bella. "Staff and budget have been slashed and OD deaths and patient numbers exceed our ability to cope. Now I've been told to cut more staff and to increase service delivery. My staff is tired and angry and pushing back. My boss, he is not a nice man, he said I can be replaced. I don't complain, but Gustavo, I'm a single mom."

TIER 4 KEY INFO	TIER 1	TIER 2	TIER 3	TIER 4
My Fears	Losing power	Losing control	Losing	Not doing the right thing
Core	It's all about me or you will suffer	I get my way or else	I live on stress to get results	Help others to be their best selves
People are	Things to abuse	Things to control	Good for making deals	To be given Unconditional Positive Respect (UPR)
Behaviors	Cruelty, abuse, harassment, criminal acts	Disrespects, bullies, acts selfishly, intimidates	Nice to some, depends on mood	UPR
Method	Fear, abuse, harm	Fear, threats, pain	Use, do deals	Courageously inspire and lead
The Self	◄────── SELF- INTERESTED ──────►			OTHER- INTERESTED

Figure 1.4   Tier 4 GPS Tool Overview

How would you advise Bella Cruz? Fear impairs good decision making. Tier 4 can help us identify and then discard fear's worst impulses.

Bella asked me, "But, Gustavo, isn't fear a great motivator?"

"Yes, it is. But it's not a good one."

Author Daniel Pink found that the stick of fear, even with the promise of the carrot, kills intrinsic motivation and spurs negative behaviors, cheating, and unethical practices.[6] Wharton Professor Andrew Carton finds that fear momentarily motivates, and leads to destructive paralysis, deep demoralization, personal health problems and then, as we'll see, invites ultimate failure.[7]

Yet fear has an important use. Gavin de Becker points out that fear warns us of dire physical threats. But without training, our simple fears can turn us into victims by making us panic and freeze.[8] Humans who did not behaviorally train themselves to face fear became predator food. *The Playbook* isn't a physical survival guide against criminals, mountain lions, or grizzlies; it's a practice handbook for becoming our courageous selves in a modern jungle of our anxieties.

Here's an example. Let's say that your work team is asked to give inputs on the selection of a critical vendor. Your team leader might respond in one of the following ways depending on the Tier in which they operate.

- **Tier 1:** I always need more power and will die before I share it. People? They're just things to exploit, threaten, and harm. I'll go into rages and fire people who try to lead.
- **Tier 2:** I always have to control others and will seldom share my power. People are things; I use them to get what I want. I give in to anger, belittle, criticize, dispirit, depend on hand puppets, and demote those who try to be leaders.
- **Tier 3:** I try to know my stuff and survive by going with the majority and the flow. I do deals and favors to get results and look the other way when I see or hear Tier 1 and 2 actions.
- **Tier 4:** I always try to do the right thing and am miserable when I don't. I help others and don't complain when I'm disrespected. I promote warm, universal respect, forgiveness, and teamwork.

Author Robert Gilbreath wrote that we can be free of endless confusion by simply asking which of our choices is right in "the moral frame." As "moral" can be a hotly loaded term, let's do a quick time-out and take a cool look at its definition: *Moral* means to be "concerned with principles of right and wrong and the goodness or badness of human character; holding or manifesting high principles for proper conduct; sanctioned by or operating on one's conscience or ethical judgment."[9] That's not too painful. The definition pulls us from our passions and biases toward weighing our actions with a cool and clinical look at doing the right thing.

This has a particular focus on how we relate to humans. In this consideration, as we'll later see, there is nearly universal agreement.

If the number "one" customarily represents something at its best, why, in Tier 4 GPS Tool, does Tier 1 describe us at our worst? It's because courage is a progressive competence. We're working on Step One to reach Step Five. In discerning the best actions, we begin at Tier 1's malignant selfishness to progress through better options to reach the heroic moral ideal of Tier 4.

I said that we can start using the Tier 4 Tool by asking: *What are my fears in this situation?*

Gary fears that Aiden will sink a key project. Deep down, he fears he'll be seen as ineffective, which could harm his career. Bella's afraid of failing her patients, her staff, and her boss, and of losing her job. Deep down, she fears her children will go hungry.

What do you fear?

Our answers give us our first look at what we call the River of Fear. More on that later.

We then ask ourselves four questions—one in each Tier.

Tier 1: Malignant drive for power. *What's the very worst reactive thing I could do?* Attila the Hun might say: *Destroy every human being in my path.* The tyrannical individual does the worst things imaginable to exert power over others and get their way. It's fear controlling our lowest, most inferior, self-serving, narcissistic hungers. Scarlett O'Hara, a slave-owner with a Civil War–ruined plantation in *Gone with The Wind*, fiercely vows with a clenched fist, "I'm going to live through this, and when it's all over, I'll never be hungry again—no, nor any of my folks! If I have to lie, steal, cheat, or kill!" This is the Tier 1 manifesto and we see this in violent parents and criminals and cheating executives.

In Tier 1, people say, "I'll crush anyone to get my way," to include lawbreaking, sexual crimes and harassment, racism, extortion, discrimination, bribery, threats, fraud, theft, abuse, domestic violence, and murder. They then deny responsibility and take vengeance against those who don't cave in to their will. Tier 1 people reward a few blindly obedient people of similarly deficient character with money and position. When they punish, they are often brutal.

Tier 1 social groups operate on fear and power. Spouses have little independence and children are commonly disrespected, tyrannically controlled, and abusively neglected.

Tier 2: Compelling self-interest. *What's the worst thing I can do without breaking a law?* The hated, toxic, controlling manager threatens a rival; coerces employees using unwarranted criticism and bullies, intimidates, deceives, manipulates, steals credit, and micromanages for control, status, money, and personal gain. This person does everything short of criminal activity to get their way.

In Tier 2, people say, "I'll do whatever it takes and I'll do what I want when I feel like it," from being biased, breaching ethics, lying, backstabbing, and disrespecting to faking data and inflating stats. Tier 2 is Tier 1 with lip gloss or a bow tie. In Tier 2, people deny responsibility, blame others, and justify their ditching of ethical and organizational standards by saying, "Everyone else does it." Many Tier 2 people, often using rationalizations and justifications, believe that these are right choices.

Tier 2 family groups are often overly controlled. Spouses can become unduly compliant. Children can be forgotten or driven to overachieve to satisfy parental expectations. Appearing to be normal, happy, and content is more important than the inner reality of their lives.

Tier 3: Benign self-interest: success via results. *What do I have to do to not fail?* This person tries to survive in a harshly competitive world. Tier 3 people struggle for results and success. They try to please those in power, are often yes-people, quickly take credit, make no waves, avoid controversies and conflicts, look away when others are being harmed, curry approval and seek comfort, and are perpetually worried and stressed. A minority of them work hard; most just try to get by. Individuals in Tier 3 see themselves as "good people" who won't do wrong. But neither will they stand for principles, choosing to be "nice" in moral situations instead of courageously and respectfully doing the right thing, face-to-face.

In Tier 3, bending to their fears, people say, "What can you do? It'll never change." "Don't fight City Hall." "He doesn't want to hear that." "People don't change." "Really, it's none of my business." "Let them take care of it." "He was asking for it, anyway." "Thankfully, I don't have to take responsibility." "It's not the right time to bring it up." "We're not covering things up—we're protecting the integrity of our [family or organization]." "I'm not being dishonest—I'm just discreet." "I'm not a coward; I'm just conflict avoidant."

In families, children are usually not taught skills to discern the highest right action. Nor are they routinely guided to unconditionally respect all persons. Worse, they routinely overhear harsh and vicious language—not from screens—but from parents who angrily criticize people who hold different opinions. This can cultivate in children a persona of extreme intolerance. Further, they're seldom trained in practical behavioral problem solving or taught how to cope and persevere in the face of disappointment.

Most of us have pitched our tents in the center of Tier 3 country, which is compelling proof of our Age of Fear.

Tier 4: The heroic moral ideal. *After consciously eliminating the lower-tier options, what's the absolute best, ideal thing that I can do?* In Tier 4, one courageously discerns that action, boldly does it despite risks to self-interest, generously trains others to do the same, and does the Five Steps to Courage to improve in everything one does.

In Tier 4, people say to others, "I admire you the most for doing the right thing." "How are you doing with that? Can I help you?" "I'm not understanding this decision. Could you tell us more?" "You may be right, but I need to understand your reasoning before I support it." "Thank you for seeing me in private. I was disappointed by what you said to Biff in our meeting." "You're blaming her but it was my fault."

Tier 4's right action can at times include not taking immediate action because we need more time to discern, to gather more critical information, or because the greater good requires withdrawal. When I was in law enforcement, a man had witnessed a criminal gang member, who lived in his neighborhood, murder a rival. The witness received a message that his family would be killed if he merely went to court. Unable to provide round-the-clock protection for him and his family, I chose not to subpoena him. That decision still bothers me, but I discerned that it wouldn't have been the highest right action to compel him to risk the lives of his family.

"What percentage of people," asked Bella Cruz, "live in Tier 4?"

"Sadly, not many," I said. "Some in the leader development guild believe it's less than 5 percent. We've lost the language and the skills of doing the right thing. It's a terrible loss."

"I agree," said Gary. "I've gotten decades of training and I still struggle to solve basic relationship challenges. But which Tier produces the best results?"

I showed them the table in Figure 1.5:

"Fifteen-hundred percent greater profits?" asked Gary. "Where did you get that?"

TIER 4 KEY INFO	TIER 1	TIER 2	TIER 3	TIER 4
FORTUNE 500 $ RESULTS	High rate of failure	High rate of failure	Achieves 30% of expectations	**Out-earns the general market by 1500%**

Figure 1.5 Tier 4 Earning & Results Power

"It's from Stanford Business School's longitudinal research. They identified the Fortune 500s that made the greatest profits over a hundred-year period—and how they managed to do it. They were shocked to learn that the few firms that consistently did the right thing far out-earned the entire results-oriented, profit-seeking US business system. It shows that when we focus on the bottom line, we tend not to get what we want. The best way to make money is to care about your people and your customers' welfare, and that takes care of the bottom line. It means that the actual bottom line is doing the right thing. The financial outcome is only a by-product."

"I have such a hard time believing," said Bella Cruz, "that Tier 1 and 2 people fail. They always seem to get ahead."

"Many do at first," I said. "But can anyone truly trust or really follow people who are malicious, cruel, and mistreat others? People in Tiers 1 and 2 get hate instead of love; good people leave them; and gutsy people confront them and even sue and prosecute them. Thieves cheat and steal, but they have to live in the shadows, unable to trust anyone. A few keep what they steal, but constantly waiting for a detective to ring the bell is a bad life. Their own people are likely to give them a harsh ending. In business, studies tell us that most results-only and unethical firms fail."

Bella slowly nodded her head. "But they sure hurt a lot of people before that happens."

"And they'll continue as long as people don't practice their courage."

I then asked Gary and Bella to each fill in a blank Tier 4 table (Figures 1.6 and 1.7).

TIER 4 KEY INFO	TIER 1 WORST I COULD DO	TIER 2 ALMOST WORST	TIER 3 SHORT-TERM RESULTS	TIER 4 THE BEST POSSIBLE
GARY PERSONS	Fire Aiden & ruin him personally	Fire him & ruin his career	Pressure and threaten Aiden to improve	?

Figure 1.6   Gary's Tier 4 Table

TIER 4 KEY INFO	TIER 1 WORST I COULD DO	TIER 2 ALMOST WORST	TIER 3 SHORT-TERM RESULTS	TIER 4 THE BEST POSSIBLE
BELLA CRUZ	Don't lay off staff & don't tell the boss	Lay off people & try to get boss fired	Worry, bad-mouth the boss & hope for the best	?

Figure 1.7   Bella's Tier 4 Table

Reader, in which Tier are you, right now? Check your space.

	TIER 1	TIER 2	TIER 3	TIER 4
MY IDEAL CORE				
ME, RIGHT NOW				

Figure 1.8   My Tier 4 Table

Gary and Bella said they felt the strong tug of Tier 1 or 2 options. Seeing them laid out in front of them helped them decide to not go that way. They said that they hoped they wouldn't do Tier 3. Neither was ready to guess at a Tier 4 action.

"That's okay," I said. "First, the tool shows us how fear affects our decisions. Second, it invites us to practice not impulsively giving in to fear and anxiety in decision making. In Step Three, we'll see what Tier 4 options look like and begin practicing them."

Before we finish Step One with the Mindfulness Pivot, let's stretch and breathe. Try to breathe slowly and deeply. Fill the diaphragm and let your belly push outwards. James Nestor found that inhaling through the nose and exhaling through the mouth is best for normal breathing.[10] We'll see that breathing in this methodical way also reduces tension and uncertainty. (I've just paused writing to breathe and stretch.)

When Gary cajoled, punished, and played Tiers 1–3's reactive game of carrot-and-stick, he became mired in a protracted war of wills with Dr. Bellevue. Gary saw he couldn't control Aiden's behaviors.

But he could first improve himself.

Gary had experienced the Tier 4 Mindfulness Pivot. It's the radical shift from spending your precious energy on anger and fear to instead calmly correcting the self.

Psychologist Dr. Seth Gillihan finds that our fears inflate discomfort into existential threats.[11] As Gary feared Aiden, Bella Cruz had given her energy to counting the reasons for failure and her terrible personal risks. Each had developed the habit of being anxious about having anxiety and fearing the fact that they had fears; they'd doubled their suffering to create a constant, negative, and troubled mindset. Bella's Mindfulness Pivot happened when she saw the reality that she and her department were doing well, that she could survive a disrespectful boss, and that she had endured far worse. She realized that anxiety and worry weren't helping her or her children, and that she could stop giving in to her unrealistic fears.

That pivot becomes real when we consciously and systematically recognize and then stop negative reactions to pressures and stress. That is our next step.

2

Step Two: Who Am I, Really? I Admit and Quit the 3 NOs

"Courage is the first of human qualities for it is the only quality that guarantees the others."

—*Aristotle*

THINKING I WAS courageous, I feared conflict. Judging others, I couldn't handle criticism. I denied my weaknesses, made excuses, was quick to resent, to blame, to project my anger onto others, and to then justify things I said or did while knowing they were wrong. I struggled to govern food intake, alcohol, love, and even success. I lacked integrity in how I treated others. Ethical at work, I was comfort-seeking in private. The tight grip of self-absorption meant I couldn't hold on to a compelling and noble purpose. Amid all this, there was the irresistible sense that something was chasing me. But studying the frozen mountains of Manchuria, walking in the heat of the Maasai Mara and in the hostile country of my demons, I discovered there was no place on earth where I could either hide from courage or not need it.

In *The Lord of the Rings*, loyal Samwise Gamgee, committed to helping Frodo reach the Dark Tower and Mount Doom, finds himself exhausted and finally defeated.

But even as hope died in Sam, or seemed to die, it was turned to a new strength. Sam's plain hobbit-face grew stern. . . as the will hardened in him, and he felt through all his limbs a thrill, as if he was turning into some creature of stone and steel that neither despair nor weariness nor endless barren miles could subdue. . . he studied the next move.[1]

How did Sam, a small, humble, unheroic Hobbit, find such firmness? He knew courage is not the reckless aggression of evil Corsairs or the brassy boldness of greedy humans; courage is the physical practice of the resolve to help others in the face of fear and adversity. Sam had unexpectedly exercised, developed, and honed the behaviors of courage during his risky, half-year, thousand-mile trek from the soft comforts of the Shire. Practice had produced in him a deep internal purpose and a new, nonnegotiable identity in courage.

Self-concern felt good until I resented the personal troubles it caused; shame burned the back of my neck until I regretted hurting others with my selfishness. It took a newfound strength to condemn my cowardice and accept the reality of courage. Courage helped me rethink my purpose in life and reorganize how I treated others. It was deeper than self-help; doing the right thing meant quitting my favorite destructive habits that had come to define who I was so I could be a better model for others. I hadn't found courage by street tussles, boxing, soldiering, jumping from airplanes, or physically taking down bad guys. Courage, via principled mentors and a barking conscience, had chased me until I stopped running from what I was internally supposed to be.[2]

Courage also pursues you, not to make you admirable, popular, or rich but to equip you to encourage and help others, to bear selfless hopes in an unfair world, to fulfill deeper meaning, and to lead a life of moral purpose. Sam knew that courage—not brains, money, or fame—determines the quality of our lives. Given my past, I'm unworthy to represent courage, but fate and others trained me to advocate it, to tell you from brutal experience that if you wish to be a truly honest person who enjoys the happiness of high integrity and inspirational character, and, as a consequence, can serve as a truly effective leader, you must first find your courage.

> *"Hold yourself responsible to a higher standard. . . . Never excuse yourself."*
> —Henry Ward Beecher, Abolitionist leader

We can choose to be better. But sans courage it was tedious to hold myself to a higher standard. I hoped fears would leave, like acne, and courage would magically appear, like front teeth. But conscience whispered that I'd lost my way from who I was supposed to be. I was an aimless Nowhere Man, seeing only what I wanted to see.[3]

To improve my inner identity, I could do three things:

- **Admit** my NO behaviors and be brutally honest about who I really was.
- **Quit** bad habits to then meet a higher standard with the help of Battle Buddies.
- **Repair** my relationships by choosing right responses to stress and fear.

You're lucky because you are now at these key pivot points. Let's review.

In Step One, you took a deep look at your past history, you examined yourself in the Character Mirror and recorded key behavioral findings.

Now, in Step Two, you'll gain authority over commonly destructive fears to help you redefine who you really are. How? You're about to blow away your negative behaviors of disrespect, anger, and hideouts.

The 3 NOs Overview

We begin with a story about firefighters in the Mountain States region of the West. The scene you're about to enter isn't much different when trainees are ER docs, IT managers, nonprofit execs, nursing leaders, hurricane-chasing NOAA aviators, school principals, battle-toughened paratroopers, or thick-skinned CEOs. The technical trade language changes, but our human issues and reactionary NOs have remained unchanged since we lived in trees.

Let's join a top fire department on a bright sunny day filled with birdsong. The task? Equip them to stop harmful behaviors so they can practice courage as a verb.

I said to them, "Question 18 in the Bio asked you to select the best description of your current primary life motivation. It's asking, '*Who are you really?*' Not how you pose, but your true, inner identity. As firefighters, you've practiced and ingrained the *external*, physical bravery of lifesaving skills, even though you don't have to use them every day.

"Firefighters top the survey lists of admired people. But who are you really? Do you honestly see yourself? Do you truly cope with relationship stress? How do you treat others? Do you make wise decisions? Face conflict? Actually improve things or just go along? We need *internal courage* to get ourselves and our actions right, not just when you respond to an alarm, but a hundred times a day, every year, forever.

"Yet we don't practice these actions. So we don't ingrain them. They remain foreign to our lives and our work. Results? We royally screw up with each other and with leading and teaming, again and again, usually in exactly the same way. Look at your answers to Bio question #15 that you did in Step One."

You, the reader, are now a courage trainee. You identified your 3 worst personal behaviors in Bio question #16. Compare your answers to the most common responses from highly diverse courage trainees in other vocations and national cultures.

Anger	Anxious	Avoids people
Avoids conflict	Excuses	Power seeking
Blames	Fails to lead	Lousy self-control
Denies	Fears	Self-centered
Disrespects	Inattentiveness	Stressed

"What drives these reactions?"

Silence.

Then, "Fear," said one. "Fear," said others. "Anxiety." Most nodded: *Fear.*

"Yes! Fear is our human knockout punch. We're anxious and passive when we should act, and silent when we should speak. We don't face it; we turn away from it. We complain about intolerance, slurs, bullying, and cliques but do nothing to stop them in our own hearts. You're at a scene. A peer's messing up. Should've talked to him weeks ago, years ago, but you didn't and you lie and tell yourself, 'It's not the right time.' At the station, you're gassed, bloody, and grimy and need a hot shower to recoup, rinse out bad images, and clean gear. You'll tell him later. But you know later never happens. It's easier to say bad things behind his back than speak to him like a partner.

"Later, you tell a battalion chief there's a safety issue but he's busy. *Tell him and get the bad look?* You fear disapproval so you repeat The Big Lie, a thing you'd never say to a friend: *'You can't handle disapproval.'* But you listen to it and clam up. Sacrificing your good heart to your anxieties, you don't tell yourself the truth: that courage was built into you at birth and you are to use it for the good. Instead, you gossip and tolerate bullies and bias, junior high cliques and anger. Things that make you selfish and conniving and poison the air you breathe.

"Listen: you are not your skills, your bench presses, your buddies, time off, video games, or your things.

"Who are you? Courage has an impact on everything you do and don't do and who we actually are. We know it's true: your identity is your courage, or your lack of it."

The room was still. I recited their worst behaviors.

"That's why we adventure into the deeper country of courage. We're going to stop our worst personal and leader habits to do the hardest right and not the easier wrong.[4] Questions?"

"What if," said Evie, a captain, "we won't quit our bad, evil ways?" All laughed.

"Evie, here's a Jake Blues answer." I rolled a clip from *The Blues Brothers*. John Belushi plays Jake, a self-destructive ex-con who wears sunglasses to bed and steals your grandmother's hubcaps. He ditched his fiancée (Carrie Fisher) at the altar. She's caught him in a sewer to end his disreputable life. Jake clasps hands and pleads. "*. . . I ran out of gas! . . . I had a flat tire! Didn't have enough money for cab fare! My tux didn't come back from the cleaners! An old friend came in from out of town! Someone stole my car! There was an earthquake! A terrible flood!*

LOCUSTS! IT WASN'T MY FAULT, I SWEAR!"[5] We all laughed. The lights came on.

"If we don't quit our evil ways, we become Jake. You all practice coping with tough physical tests. But you keep your bad personal habits, hoping no one sees who you really are.

"Time-out. When did you last actually *practice* principled conduct under pressure? Practice not being selfish? Fixing your screwed-up relationships? Telling the truth to authority? Respecting those you dislike? Stopping blame and gossip? Defeating the fears you take home after shift? Challenging bigoted language? Forgiving people because deep down, you know it's right? Practice improving your marriage, parenting, screen habits, snacking, and sex life? Anyone here been part of character-based behavioral training?"

No hands.

"We talk about character but don't train in it. Mark Twain saw it's easier to be physically brave than morally courageous.[6] Observers see that we Americans are among the least capable of coping with discomfort and true adversity.[7] It would be easier if adversity were the problem.

"But it's not adversity in our stressful moral environment. Baby boomers didn't like distant parents so we began a culture of feelings. *Forget principles; just do what you feel like doing.* Well, we can feel fear. But courage, our human superpower, isn't an emotion; it's a set of practiced abilities. We feel fear down to our toes but we never *feel* courageous. We can't wait to feel courageous so we can act courageously. Courage is a decision.

"Because we can't feel it, courage seems unreal and out of reach, while anxiety sets up housekeeping in our chests and we're constantly jacked up on adrenaline.

"Integrity is doing the right thing inside yourself. Courage is doing the right thing in the world while we're awash in the jumping Neanderthal-like hormones of anxiety.

"Today, we struggle with anxiety without courage. We focus on the threats of external crises but ignore our internal need to be strong. To relieve anxiety, we deny, avoid, make excuses, blame others, and get angry. Letting our fickle fearful reactions control how we live is not fun. Worse, it's not smart.

"So we practice principled behaviors to *act like the courageous person you were always supposed to be.* With courage, each of us meets that higher standard of how we treat others."

Heads nodded. Arms uncrossed. People leaned forward. Some squirmed.

"Being lousy at facing discomfort, we inflict junk responses on each other, especially those closest to us. That junk quietly accumulates into a life of cowardice without love.

"Good news: we can boil down our bad habits to three human reactions to fear. Stop them and anxieties will evacuate your chest and firehouse. Ready for it?" I showed them the following table (Figure 2.1).

"Welcome to the 3 NOs. I'll say this gently. . .The 3 NOs are our stinking, thoughtless, lying, self-deceiving, and cowardly reactions to fear. They're disgraceful untruths that deceive you by saying it's okay to dump your courage and chicken out and then get angry.

"You do a NO, and you broadcast that you can't cope with discomfort. As Jack Nicholson famously accused in a fanciful movie, 'YOU CAN'T HANDLE THE TRUTH!'"[8]

REACTIONS	BEHAVIORS
DISRESPECTS OTHERS	Is inattentive, ignores, shuns, scorns, dishonors, shows bias, sexually harasses
GIVES IN TO ANGER	Yells, intimidates, curses, threatens, coerces, attacks, hits objects, abuses, harms others
HIDEOUTS: Avoids Conflict, Denial, Excuses, Blames	Denies the truth, "I have no problems, only you do." Avoids conflicts by looking the other way, fleeing, failing to help others. Makes excuses by rationalizing, covering up, and arguing. Blames others by gossiping, backstabbing, making accusations, or lying.

Figure 2.1   The 3 NOs Examples—Our Deceitful, Fearful, Cowardly Reactions to Fear

The first and second NOs are our more active and in-your-face. It's self-evident that they cause negative consequences. The third NO, Hideouts, initially appears to be more passive and benign. But as we'll see, these destructive outcomes can be as grave as the first two.

"Courage is the first of human virtues because it alone guarantees our other strengths and the qualities we truthfully love the most deeply. Disrespect is the worst of our weaknesses because it protects our worst selves and the traits we most dislike.

"But let's look at all 3 NOs as we begin to uncover our own reactions to stress and fear."

They wrote down the NOs.

"The first NO is DISRESPECTS OTHERS. Disrespect breaks our organizations. It directly fuels racism. Racists of all colors are cowards who disrespect people who are different; sexual harassers are cowards who dishonor others; elitists are cowards who look down on those who appear less gifted; criminals are cowards who disrespect everyone. I survived cancer to tell you that *disrespect is the moral cancer that would make cowards of us all*. Disrespect is like felony arson. Disrespect is the fire starter that burns down work, families, society, and life itself.

"The second, GIVES IN TO ANGER, destroys who I am and kills what I love.

"When I use the third one, the HIDEOUTS, I deny truth and pretend to be faultless. I avoid conflicts and become Chicken Little. I make excuses and turn into a sad Jake Blues; I ditch my duties and blame others.

"You know the NOs—they're the negative emotional reactions we all hate in others—and, if we're honest, in ourselves. We counter the NOs by stopping them—"

"HOLD ON!" roared Fitz Smith, a hulking battalion chief.[9] "Listen, we deal with life and death. A guy has a case of the slows, I'll yell at that SOB to get his ass in gear!"

Another firefighter said, "I get tired and I can get testy, but I'm not a racist and I DON'T harass." Others agreed.

"That's our challenge," I said. "We don't see ourselves as offenders in the extreme forms of the NOs. But most of us do some of the NOs under pressure. Let's take a break."

I met Fitz outside. "Thanks for your comment. Can I ask a question? If I outranked you, got in your face for being slow and yelled at you to move your butt, how'd you react?"

Fitz's jaw jutted. "I'd want to knock you out. But I wouldn't."

"Whew, good thing. Would you actually speed up?"

"You outrank me, right? Yeah, I'd do it, but I'd do it half-assed and half-stepping."

"What sticks to you better: actually improving, or getting ticked at me?"

"Being ticked." Aspens shimmered silver in a gentle wind. "Anger beats everything."

We regathered ourselves. The Stretch Master, a rotating volunteer from the audience, led us in stretches. We all felt better, and I thanked her.

By the way, we should stretch every 30 minutes.[10] Humans once walked seven miles a day.[11] Sitting for long periods increases risk of death by 200 percent.

"Tell me if I'm wrong: you are paid to NOT do the 3 NOs. You're paid to stretch yourselves to get more courage. Give in to a NO, what happens to you? A boomerang smacks you in the chops and fouls up performance and endangers lives. Author Tim Keller: 'It is no wonder that the angry get anger, haters are hated and cowards get abandoned.'"[12]

"Look at the verbs (Figure 2.2): *resent, dislike, fear, distrust* and *hate!* The NOs make you into what you detest. When we use NOs, we're like self-serving politicians—but perhaps I repeat myself.

"Every time you use a NO, you're lying to yourself and you're lying to others. Then you kill trust and your ability to lead. And, after all that cost to yourself, the NOs don't work. They end up making us look dumb when we were already looking bad.

"What I want you to do now is rank the NOs. Your top NO is the one you use first and most often. The third is the one you use last. Circle your top one. Here are mine (Figure 2.3)."

Reader, rank your 3 NOs in Figure 2.4. Circle your #1 NO.

	REACTIONS	SO OTHERS. . .	. . .AND	TRUST?
1	DISRESPECTS OTHERS	Resent you	Disrespect you	Distrust you
2	GIVES IN TO ANGER	Hate you	Hatefully retaliate	Distrust you
3	HIDEOUTS: Avoids Conflict, Denies, Excuses, Blames	Accept bullying and bias, resent you, fear you, dislike you	Are frustrated by your inaction, avoid you, conspire against you	Distrust you

Figure 2.2   The 3 NOs Boomerang Effect: Killing Trust

		RANK # 1-3
1	Disrespects others	2
2	Gives in to anger	3
(3)	Hideouts: avoids conflicts, denies truths, makes excuses, blames others	1

Figure 2.3   Gus's Deceitful, Fearful, Cowardly Reactions to Fear

		RANK # 1-3
1	Disrespects others	
2	Gives in to anger	
3	Hideouts: avoids conflicts, denies reality, makes excuses, blames others	

Figure 2.4   My Reactions to Fear

Record it here.

My #1 NO is:

   1. _____

I stood straighter. "I'm going to read out the 3 NOs. When I name your top NO, please stand if you can." They looked around. Doubts spread like an airborne virus.

Faces said, is this guy serious? I'd done the 3 NOs for 50 professions and industries from Antarctica scientists to Young Presidents and I have Courage Coached C-levels, business owners, couples, executives, engineers, physicians, prisoners, managers, teens, and warriors.

In each group, after an initial hesitation, everyone stood to admit their NOs.

Well, almost everyone.

I was about to train the top executive suite and 300 leaders of a global organization. I got a tap on my shoulder from a very senior person.

"Don't," he hissed, "do that exercise where we have to admit our fears."

I switched off my mic. I said that the NOs were fundamental to the training.

The MC said, "Please join me in welcoming Gus Lee. . ." Applause.

"I don't care!" he growled. "Don't do it!" The stage prompter motioned, Now!

Calmly and warmly, I quietly said, "Please let your leaders model courage. Thank you, sir." I shook his hand. I walked on stage; in the distance, I saw the executive leave, taking his top folks with him. Only one senior leader, a woman, remained.

Accepting discomfort as a normal condition of life is a puny admission price to being human. Avoiding adversity erases our toughness, lowers empathy for those who hurt, and ravages care and cooperation. Over decades of doing The 3 NOs Exercise, only these few managers ditched those they were paid to lead, denying the daily discomforts that we all face. They missed bonding in moral camaraderie and sharing a freeing laughter.

All their people stayed and courageously improved themselves. They stood to stop fearful emotional reactions not by command, but by an enlightened individual decision. As a recovering coward, I know those who crept away regretted chickening out from a chance to improve themselves. I later asked the woman why she stayed.

"They walked out for the reason we asked you to train us—to become courageous. It's weird. It's so strange. I think my colleagues worry about the discomfort of facing our weaknesses more than they fear total failure. We're engineers who lack complete logic."

On our journey toward courage, it's crucial to admit our current ways of being. Doing so precedes strategies for quitting ineffective and destructive behaviors so that we can later repair our character and our relationships.

The First NO: Disrespects Others

"Preservation of one's own culture does not require disrespect for other cultures."

—César Chávez[13]

Back to our firefighters. "Let's start with Number One, DISRESPECT. Here's an inventory. We all disrespect some people. Ego and biases, unchecked, become intolerance. Intolerance, unchecked, becomes racism and bigotry.

"Please check the boxes that apply to you."

Reader, please do the same. We'll revisit them in Step Three.

The First NO Inventory: Disrespects Others

Check all that apply to you.

☐ I'm not fully attentive when others speak.

☐ While arguing, I seldom say, "I see. Can you tell me more about that?"

☐ Some types of people can be obstacles and problems for me.

☐ Not everyone has earned my respect.

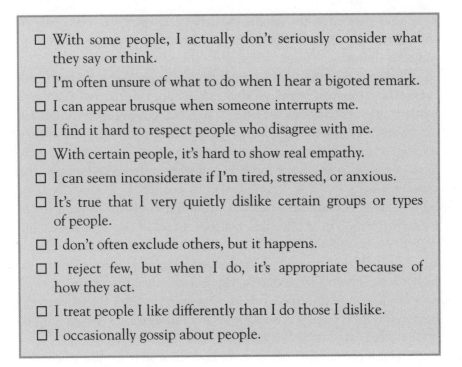

- [ ] With some people, I actually don't seriously consider what they say or think.
- [ ] I'm often unsure of what to do when I hear a bigoted remark.
- [ ] I can appear brusque when someone interrupts me.
- [ ] I find it hard to respect people who disagree with me.
- [ ] With certain people, it's hard to show real empathy.
- [ ] I can seem inconsiderate if I'm tired, stressed, or anxious.
- [ ] It's true that I very quietly dislike certain groups or types of people.
- [ ] I don't often exclude others, but it happens.
- [ ] I reject few, but when I do, it's appropriate because of how they act.
- [ ] I treat people I like differently than I do those I dislike.
- [ ] I occasionally gossip about people.

"When I disrespect others, even casually, I'm saying that I'm so much better than you and everyone else. We all look at people who differ from us and feel that primitive tug to disrespect the unfamiliar. But if we don't bear down to reverse this ancient impulse, we slide into intolerance, bias, discrimination, racism, and sexual harassment. Disrespect is our spiritual cancer. But we have a universal antidote, the cure of courage. It doesn't come free of charge; you get it by changing yourself. And that starts right now. Ready?

"If *disrespects others* is your number-one NO, please stand if you can or otherwise indicate that you own this behavior."

Breathlessly, they looked around. One stood. In a tension-breaking stadium wave, a fourth of them rose to their feet to admit what we all do—we disrespect others.

Reader: if this is your top NO, and you can do so, even if you're alone, please stand or otherwise indicate that you own this.

Some firefighters nodded in rare moral candor. "It was stupid," said one, "to say I wasn't doing these things when I was doing them in public."

Some glanced at the people they'd disrespected for years, only to find those people looking back at them. Boomerang. I let the moment simmer.

Flitting eye contact led to small nods. People that couldn't stand each other were now standing in a curious unison. Years of the bitter burdens of scornful disrespect and toxic group gossip began to lighten.

"Okay!" bellowed one. "Yeah!" said others with high fives as they inhaled a new freedom from the radioactive poison of trying to deny how they actually treat people. Laughter rippled through the training room.

"We live," I said, "on a planet with billions—who also want to get their own way. The predictable collision of all of our egos makes life messy. We're self-absorbed. That makes us mean. We worry about being embarrassed or rejected. We hunger for approval. We're resentful. Defensive. Touchy. We innately discriminate against certain types of people. Bingo, we disrespect others. Disrespect is fear's cheap, smooth, best-selling street drug. It hooks you in a microsecond, sets you up to do the other NOs, and kills who you want to be.

"Even if it's not your top one, we have to stop it. Unless you're the world's undiscovered perfect human, please stand if you can." Everyone stood.

Readers, please own this NO. Even if you already stood for this NO, to groove in the fact that this tells other people who we really are, please stand or acknowledge it again.

"Now, if you agree to truly admit this negative reaction and to tell the person closest to you in your personal life that you've admitted it, please shake hands with others standing who are also making the same agreements." The room became warmer with handshakes, laughter, hugs, and animated dialogue.

"You've personally admitted this reaction to fear. If you're ready to stop this response, you're going to need someone to hold you accountable. Let's call this person a 'Battle Buddy.'

"A Battle Buddy is someone who works closely with you and sees you in action. Most importantly, it's the kind of reliable person who'll give you a 'Buddy Check' when you take an off-ramp. Note the word, 'reliable.' So it can't be the kind of individual who says, 'Hey, I like you just the way you are. I really like your faults because they make me feel better about me.'

"There are two types of Battle Buddies:

- Work Battle Buddy: works near you and will respectfully tell you the truth
- Life Battle Buddies: in your personal life and will respectfully tell you the truth
  (Do not choose your "regular" friends who are accustomed to overlook or worse, trigger and even aggravate your faults, and invite you to participate in theirs.)

"As we go through the NOs, think about who this person should be. We'll pick our Work Battle Buddies at the end of this Step and your Life Battle Buddies later."

Physically brave people who enter burning buildings while others flee had pledged to stop a harmful personal and corporate habit. They'd stuck their boots into the shallow end of what we'll learn is the River of Fear, an exercise in which we intentionally venture into a deeper country of brave lions and courageous leaders.

The Fire Chief stood; they hushed up. "You," he said to his people, "are openly pledging to not give in to your anxiety by disrespecting others. Each handshake is your word. We know that we can do this if we have a partner by our side who won't BS us." Many nodded.

"Thank you, Chief," I said. "Having and being a Battle Buddy means giving Buddy Checks when we slip up. They let you keep your word today to be your best self tomorrow. We think we're lucky if we skate and no one sees our weaknesses. But it's not true: we're incredibly lucky when a buddy sees us mess up and respects us enough to want us to be better than we are.

"We all want to change but don't know how; now you do. We commit to change but we slip up; now you have the beginning of accountability so you can keep your word and stay on course.

"Disrespect is our most infectious NO. It permeates all we do and who we are. We're now ready to look at the Second NO."

The Second NO: Gives in to Anger

"Anger is the bitter wind which blows out the lamp of the mind."
—Robert Green Ingersoll, author and Civil War veteran

"DISRESPECT, the First NO, is the cancer that starts our decline in courage and character. ANGER, our Second NO, is The Killer. It's our ancient, fear-driven emotion that spurs abuse, cruelty, and violence. It's the First NO, disrespect, gone totally bad."

Diane and I were happily shopping for our wedding rings in San Francisco's glitzy Union Square. When a driver blew the traffic light, I pulled Diane back before he killed her. Fear, in a nanosecond, had triggered my primordial lizard response, shut down higher-order thinking, adrenalized my fight instinct, and my dumb limbic brain (also known as the hindbrain) commanded: *Give in to your anger, Gus. Destroy this threat to your beloved.* My chemistry overrode being an Army officer in uniform and an attorney, obligated to obey two higher professional standards of conduct—and I'd been a boxer, trained for 13 years to never punch out a civilian. But I gave in to anger and charged the driver who, also reacting chemically, left his car, making it easy for me to destroy him.

Diane thought I was a mild-mannered Army lawyer who jumped out of airplanes, as if it were like skydiving. (US Army paratroopers jump from a fast military cargo jet at an elevation of 1,000 feet with 50–160 pounds of gear strapped on their back and waist. The object is to execute a specific, well-practiced Parachute Landing Fall to limit exposure in the air and land fast with as much gear as humanly possible, so they can survive in enemy territory without any outside help. Traveling at 16-plus MPH, landing on one's feet will break back, hips, and legs and can be fatal. Military chutes don't maneuver and it's impossible to land without scrapes, bruises, and contusions and injuries are routine. In contrast, a sport parachutist or skydiver drops from a slow propeller-driven airplane with a fully maneuverable sports canopy to enjoy soaring. After running out of thermals, the sport parachutist simply flares the canopy, reducing the descent velocity to zero miles per hour and lands as if one were stepping from a sidewalk to the street. The object is to have a fun, recreational experience.) Her limbic brain commanded: *Protect your family.*

"NO!" she cried repeatedly, grabbing me and tugging with all her strength. Through a hormonal fog, I heard her and my own screaming conscience. The driver was elderly, in bad shape, and as able to defend himself as Barney Fife in a body cast. He, swept up by fear and anger, was as self-destructive as me. He lived to see another day and I would need therapy and physical self-governance practice to stop giving in to anger.

Emma Pattee wrote, "Anxiety is the most common mental illness in America. . . . Modern-day humans are basically a bunch of freaked-out Neanderthals in fight-or-flight mode, 24/7."[14]

"Without physical training to overcome fear," I said, "we slip into our worst selves. Despite knowing how self-destructive it is, I can be tempted to give in to my anger. Anger gives me a momentary illusion of power so I can display my intolerance for others and my inability to govern myself. Anger erases my reason and invalidates my expensive education. When angry, I act like a bigot. Anger, the poison I swallow to get even with someone, kills my courage, destroys relationships, compromises my health, invites heart attacks, and reduces longevity.[15] I can then spread fear and anxiety, like twin viruses, by incidental human contact.

"Everyone here," I said, "feels anger. Check the following boxes to see if giving in to anger is showing up in your life."

Reader, please check your behaviors in the following inventory. We'll revisit them in Step Three.

The Second NO Inventory: Gives in to Anger

Check those that apply to you.

- ☐ I'm quickly impatient with or easily frustrated by people.
- ☐ I hate it when people get angry at me, but I get angry at others.
- ☐ I can lash out if stressed by other people's continued failures or rudeness.

(continued)

(*continued*)

☐ Certain situations can make me become moody and withdrawn.

☐ I sometimes raise my voice if I'm angry.

☐ I'm probably edgier around people who are different from me.

☐ I can sometimes be quickly argumentative.

☐ I can occasionally verbally dress down certain people.

☐ Some people might occasionally see me acting like a bully.

☐ Like most, I can occasionally drink too much.

☐ I can struggle to be myself if I'm under extreme pressure.

☐ On rare occasions I hit objects such as desks or walls.

☐ Very, very seldom am I physically violent with some people (adults, children).

☐ I have had periods of depression after becoming deeply angry.

☐ I have had issues with controlling my temper.

☐ When others anger me, I can use profanity.

"If gives in to anger is your top NO, please stand if you can."

Fitz, the big battalion chief, suddenly leaped on top of his table.

I'd never seen anyone do this. A stunned silence, then loud applause, whoops, cheering, stomping boots, and laughter chased denial and fear from the room and birds from the trees. It was a huge wow in their community history. Fitz's quick and ferocious temper was the giant elephant in the room, in their lives, and in the department's damaged reputation. His anger scared people by day and tailed them home at night, spawning bad dreams to impair much-needed sleep.

Many others stood for this NO. But would they actually stop their anger? Would Fitz?

"You're standing," I said, "as the one person in the world with the moral authority and agency to stop your negative, angry reactions. Only you can control Almighty You.

"Lectures and magical thinking won't do it. Practiced courage gives you the strength to stop it. Before today, you stood out because you lacked the self-control you need to lead yourself and others. You're courageously standing to take command of yourself, to model what everyone needs. Medal of Honor recipient Colonel Jack Jacobs asks us, if not now, when?[16] If not you, then who? If not here, where? Will there ever be a better opportunity?

"Hey, guys," growled a battalion chief, "we're clicking it in. Anger's our big problem. I think we'd rather suck toxic fumes than do this kind of training, but this one helps."

"We now stop our anger," I said. "Do you commit to not give in to it, and to tell your significant other that you've publicly pledged to control your anger?" They shook hands, the room was abuzz as the angriest people in the group committed to stopping a bad behavior.

"Say a Battle Buddy sees me lose it. She says to me one-to-one, 'Gus, what happened? How can you fix it, right now?' If she can't pull me aside, she just quietly says, 'Buddy Check.'

"So I get it that I went off course. Instead of growling at her, I thank her."

During the break, I asked Fitz, "What made you jump on the table?"

"I saw they're really afraid of me. That hurt. But we operate in life-and-death situations. I have to crawl their butts. Anger gets their attention. Now, that kind of anger is okay, right?"

"Fitz, I know squat about fires. Can't blow out a match. But research reveals that fear can make your people jump, but it's a terrible motivator.[17] You have to keep upping the ante until, what? You execute them? Are you still making the same corrections with the same guys?"

He sighed. "Crap. Damn idiots! Shouldn't call them that. Man, they always tick me off. I'm probably getting crabbier. Yeah. It's true, it's always the same stuff."

"I know what you mean. Anger drowns our blood in hot fear hormones, and we get high on anger and get hooked on it. I once loved my anger more than the people I was supposed to lead. Anger is addicting. The angrier we get, the more anger we need the next time.[18] We blow our tops, proving we cope by going nuts and screaming."[19]

He thought about that. I knew Fitz admired Soldiers. I told him a story.

Colonel Robert L. Howard, US Army Special Forces officer and combat veteran, was known for doing the hardest right thing when most will not. A tough Soldier's Soldier, he never yelled in anger or swore. "I ask Soldiers to risk their lives. I don't disrespect them with profanity or loss of self-control."

Col. Howard received the Medal of Honor, the Distinguished Service Cross, the Silver Star, four Bronze Stars for Valor, and eight Purple Hearts—he was the only individual recommended three times for the Medal of Honor. Soldiers knew Bob didn't cuss to show he was "tough." Verbal self-discipline was a part of the practiced ability to govern (more than control) his emotions. He respected the enemy. He never expressed anger to his wife or children. Giving first aid to the enemy and carrying them from the battlefield to aid stations inspired his Soldiers to control themselves under fire, to help others in the face of fear, and to be their best selves even when wounded, anxious, and angry. They demonstrated moral courage and bravery in every situation.

"Fitz, can I ask you and one of your captains to help me with a role play?"

We reconvened.

I'm seated in front of the class on a work bench in an unfastened incident firefighter PPE jacket with luminous stripes, studying my phone. Fitz walks in. He does a violent double take.

"WHAT THE HELL ARE YOU DOING!" he roars. I jump up as all in the room flinch.

Captain Evelyn appears at Fitz's side to give a quick confidential Buddy Check, whispering loudly for the sake of the class. "Chief, Buddy Check: your anger."

Fitz grimly nods, takes a deep breath. "Thanks, Evelyn." He coughs. "Gus, sorry I raised my voice. I promised I wouldn't do that. Can I get a do-over?"

"You bet." Fitz leaves, I study my phone, he returns and says, "Hey, what's up?"

"Oh, hi, Boss." I stand. "Caught me goofing off. I'll clean up and get to work."

Fitz takes a breath and softly says, "How can I help you to not repeat this?"

Jaws drop across the training room.

"Did he control his anger?" Loud applause, whistles, boot stomps, gut-deep cheers. Instead of giving them heart attacks, Fitz was lifting their downtrodden spirits.

I thanked the demonstrators and said, "What's next?"

"Lunch!" said Michael Brian, wildfire expert, the fastest at carrying another firefighter in full kit, and owner of two master's degrees. Such is the quality of his cooking that every firehouse begs him to join their truck companies. "In honor," said Michael, "of Courage Training, enjoy German Beef Rouladen, a robust corn chowder, and classic Irish soda bread." He got three cheers, and we stood and stretched for a gourmet meal.

After lunch, they trained in the Third NO.

Reader, I'll now take you through our last—but not to be ignored—NO.

The Third NO: Hideouts (Avoids Conflict, Denial, Excuses, and Blame)

"All of us make mistakes. The key is to acknowledge them, learn and move on."
"The real sin is ignoring mistakes, or worse, seeking to hide them."
—Robert Zoellick, Deputy Secretary of State[20]

At the dawn of our Age of Fear, being a coward was so painful that, sneaky as mice, we dropped troublesome words like "cowardice" into the wastebasket of uncomfortable terms. We replaced cowardice, which made us feel bad, with a mash-up of two words that made us feel better. Now, if asked whether or not I'm a coward, I can say, without having to surrender a molecule of my fears, "Oh, no, I'm not a coward, I'm just conflict avoidant."

Research reveals that 95 percent of us avoid conflict because we find it uncomfortable.[21] Our HIDEOUTS are in large part ways to avoid conflict. Let's look at these reactions to discomfort and fear as we dig in to our last NO.

Avoids Conflict

"Pain in this life is not avoidable, but the pain we create avoiding pain is avoidable."

—R.D. Laing, Scottish psychiatrist[22]

Years ago, board members falsely accused our government liaison, a man of color, of interfering with their ability to communicate with a key client. He was innocent of the charge. Morally, I needed to come to his defense; politically I needed board votes to fund new initiatives. Cowardly, I said nothing. In this lamentable moment, I forgot that I'd been trained to do the right thing despite risk to self-interest. The attack on my colleague led to a catastrophic political cascade in which the corporation lost much of its justification for existence. Later, in shame, I apologized to him. I grimace today when I remember chickening out. Avoiding conflict provides a moment of fictional relief followed by an avalanche of moral regret and recrimination.[23]

For our AVOIDS CONFLICT discussion, let's look at a Seattle high-tech firm. Hard rain drummed on tall windows. Cal Kennedy, SpeedSprint's test director, was writing an email to the boss of Software Design, Lauren Gold. "Lauren, you set pitiful standards for yourself and fail to meet them. You're a despicable kiss-ass who rushes to production to plague us with defective product." Cal sighed, paused on the send button and quickly deleted the message, as was his habit.

In nearby Bellevue, Lauren Gold told COO Alicia Guerrero, on Zoom, "I send Cal Kennedy primo products and he wigs out on it. He's costing us clients and our time to market! Fire him!"[24]

Alicia told me, "Cal and Lauren and their divisions have hated each other for a decade. I've tried HR mediation, outside alternative dispute resolution consultants, high-rent retreats, and more time off. It's all *bupkis* and costing us millions in margin,[25] and they'll still be at it tooth and nail when I die of a heart attack. Probably, next week. They just fired my predecessor for not solving this terrible Hatfield-McCoy feud."

"What if," I asked, "you tried to reconcile their relationship?"

A soft laugh. "I don't think I have a software program for that."

"Do you think there's a chance that while you're focused on fixing the conflict, you've personally stayed out of it?"

"That's pretty harsh, Gus," she said. "But you're probably right."

I asked her to look at how she avoids conflict.

Reader, there's a 95 percent chance you avoid conflict, too. Please check your behaviors in the following inventory. We'll revisit them in Step Three.

The Third NO Inventory: Hideouts (Avoids Conflict)

Check those that apply to you.

☐ I mostly avoid conflict.

☐ I often avoid uncomfortable situations.

☐ I can avoid speaking up so I don't look foolish, wrong, incompetent, or stupid.

☐ I've often been grateful that dealing with bias and discrimination isn't my job.

☐ I tend to avoid difficult people and difficult conversations.

☐ If I tried to solve a conflict, I could fail and worsen the situation.

☐ I'll remain silent to avoid hurting someone's feelings.

☐ I sometimes change the subject if it's making me uncomfortable.

☐ I sometimes change what I'm thinking about because it's also uncomfortable.

☐ Discretion is the better part of valor.

Alicia checked five items. "But isn't the last one true: 'Discretion is the better part of valor?'"

I had to chuckle. "That's Falstaff's line in Shakespeare's play, *Henry IV*. Falstaff is a braggart and narcissist who plays dead during a battle and then pompously announces, 'The better part of valor is discretion.'[26] Shakespeare reveals Falstaff to be the coward of cowards, a counterfeit knight and a notorious liar, and has given modern cowards an excuse to avoid conflict.

"So, how have these behaviors helped you?"

"You're pretty funny. Not in any way that I can see."

"Agreed. What can you do with them that doesn't mean avoiding conflict?"

She reflected. "Tell them I'll evaluate the quality of their teamwork with each other."

"Good courage! It's always the best. If we're going to work together, I'd like to invite you to stop avoiding conflict and not do the Inventory behaviors you checked, from now on. Can do?"

"Ever again?" she asked. "That's a tough ask."

"You'll need Battle Buddies to help you build new habits. I'll explain the 3 NOs Process so you can do that."

Many people have taken classes in conflict resolution, managing conflict, tough conversations, and effective communication and in exceptionally valuable quality management processes. But none of these will be helpful if you don't have the courage to practice using the tools, first in training and then in actual conflicts and frustrating circumstances. If you're afraid of falling off the bike or losing a race, you'll never master riding or running. If you avoid the discomfort of a conflict, even when you know that it's wrong to do so, then all the conflict courses in the world will not help, and fear triumphs again over our good intentions. Truthfully, what's wrong with a little discomfort?

Denies the Truth

"How often it is that the angry man rages in denial of what his inner self is telling him."

—Frank Herbert[27]

Research finds that we're programmed to think we're right at all costs. We also strenuously deny all evidence to the contrary. This is a bad habit and it's now no surprise to us that "Unlearning and relearning [this] requires courage over comfort."[28]

Without courage, we disrespect others. Using DENIES TRUTH— about ourselves and the real world—infects your mindset and your actions.

In 1985, Roger Boisjoly (Boh-zhe-lay), a bullet-headed senior aerodynamicist who worked on NASA's Space Shuttle project, sent a memo. It said that a long history of engine O-ring failures and launching Space Shuttles in temperatures below 50°F will cause catastrophic O-ring failure, loss of life, and total Shuttle destruction.

In January 1986, it was near zero at the Kennedy Space Center as icicles formed on the booster rockets. Boisjoly, Allan McDonald (director of the Shuttle's boosters project), and others sent messages to delay launching *Challenger* to avoid total failure and loss of life.

NASA officials said they wanted to launch, but McDonald refused to sign the launch approval order. His superiors ignored the engineering No-Go. On January 28, 1986, the shuttle launched; frozen O-rings failed; and *Challenger* burned up after launch, killing all seven astronauts.[29]

Allan McDonald was in the audience during Commission hearings into the disaster. He heard false testimony—misleading words for a deceitful cover-up.

McDonald, being human, no doubt felt the temptation to deny reality. But he faced his fears and stated that he hadn't approved the launch.

"Who said that?" asked a commission member.

McDonald testified that NASA had denied the risk data and ordered the launch.[30] Boisjoly and McDonald were then demoted, shunned by colleagues and even by neighbors. McDonald had no regrets and both he and Boisjoly are now revered for their courage to do the right thing.[31] Boisjoly received the Prize for Scientific Engineering and Responsibility, became a top forensic scientist, and gave lectures on engineering ethics at over 300 colleges and civic groups.[32] Allan McDonald became an enduring and beloved symbol of the noble professional.

NASA's excuse for launching? *It wanted to.* Its executives used denial of the truth to do what they wished.

Stress and anxiety give birth to the use of denial to overcome education. Johns Hopkins found that our hospitals annually kill more than 250,000 patients by accident, replacing cancer as the third leading cause of death.[33] In a Midwest health care system, an audit found that a surgeon was routinely violating the hospital's patient safety standards, causing unintended deaths. The privileges committee reconfirmed his status. As a consultant, I was asked to encourage the committee to reconsider. I asked the committee for their reasoning.

"He's not our worst," said one. "Margin's too thin," said another, "to lose a top earner."

"He's in a bad divorce with child custody issues." "He has Type 2 Diabetes." "He takes Medicaid patients." "He's good in the community." "He has powerful friends." "Give him a break."

"Would you," I asked, "let him operate on your spouse or child?"

The committee revoted to retain the surgeon's privileges[34] and asked that I be investigated for an anti-physician bias. I later trained the committee to not do those behaviors.

Reader, please check your denial behaviors in the following inventory.

The Second NO Inventory: Hideouts (Denial)

Check all those that apply to you.

☐ I tend to deny my own faults.

☐ I'm not a liar, but I soften the truth if it hurts others.

☐ I don't spend a lot of time thinking about my weaknesses.

☐ I think my strengths far outweigh my weaknesses.

☐ I often deny the hard truths about those close to me.

☐ My faults seldom really hurt other people and if so, they usually get over it.

☐ I don't ask for candid, routine feedback on how I actually treat others.

☐ It's very difficult for me to accept negative feedback from others.

☐ I don't have a problem with diet, exercise, sleep, or addictive behaviors.

☐ I don't think I have a real problem dealing with bias or bullies.

I like denial. It deludes me into thinking that using it will get me off the hook. I can pretend to myself that I get a pass on my responsibilities. I ignore truths about me. Denial lets me rewrite narratives with cute ideas that make me feel better for a few seconds. I turn a blind eye to problems, so their root cause remains unfixed and problems don't get solved—they get worse. In denial, I lie and then deny that I lied and deflect feedback to the contrary. Of course, I'm nuts to think that any of this works. But fear bypasses our reason.

Making Excuses

> *"He that is good for making excuses is seldom good for anything else."*
> —Benjamin Franklin[35]

Our fourth NO is Jake Blues's disastrous choice of MAKING EXCUSES. Here, I disrespect everyone's intelligence while polluting my integrity. We all tell little white lies—really, how bad can that be? So I delude myself by thinking that the use of humiliating excuses is a good thing. Making Excuses is a puny effort to cover up truth and skip out on responsibility. Sadly, using feeble rationalizations, which we hope will help us feel better, only worsens the original sin. Okay, I goofed; but if I try to skate with an excuse, I'm now a cowardly liar who's also stupid. Just like the other hideout NOs, excuses lure us by masquerading as an easy way out, when in reality they're self-destructive and dishonest traps. It's an ineffective falsehood in a failed attempt to get your way.

What follows is a story from a Midwest fire department; firefighters constantly face fear and have much to teach us. In this instance, they suffered a flashover—a fast fire in a closed space with synthetic fuel (furniture, drapes) in which hot, unvented gases simultaneously ignite the fuel into a violent production of flame and smoke.[36]

Three young firefighters are putting water on a fast-moving structure fire in an old multistory apartment building. Their captain focuses on the troubled occupants. He misses the heavy, dark smoke, poor venting, fast-circling flames in low ceilings that need "fogging" to avoid a flashover. Suddenly, an 1,100°F burst of gases and flame engulfs the three men.

It's a very complicated situation when firefighters are injured. It's worse when excuses are being made to minimize the consequences and to blur the causes of the harm. Fortunately, they survived their burns.

The three firefighters were on extended medical leave and there was concern about their probable depression, and some worried about suicide attempts. I learned that none of their superiors were in contact with them. It was the elephant in the room.

When I pulled their superiors aside, they said, "We've got it covered." "We have excellent services available when one of us gets hurt." "They're tough and resilient." "We've already studied the incident." "I think the people at the scene have learned their lesson."

I didn't hear (1) an actual action plan that addressed the mental, emotional, and physical health of the injured men; (2) an After-Action Review of what went right, what went wrong, and what needed to be corrected to avoid another flashover; or (3) a training plan for the superiors at the incident. What I heard was a lot of excuses.

It's therefore important for us to read this section on making excuses and to reflect on the excuses inventory. Check the items that apply to you in the following inventory. It's for individual self-reflection and to build courage.

The Third NO Inventory: Hideouts (Excuses)

Check those that apply to you.

☐ I've made excuses to avoid blame or discomfort.

☐ I've justified to others my weak actions and poor decisions.

☐ Under stress, I'll make excuses or rationalize what I'm doing.

☐ I can disrespect others and explain it away by saying I'm tired, stressed, or hungry.

☐ I've said, "That's just who I am."

☐ It's often hard for me to admit mistakes or to own an error.

☐ I've made excuses when I actually knew I was wrong.

☐ I've made excuses for procrastinating or avoiding unwanted tasks.

☐ I can say, "I'm busy" or "Something came up," when neither may be true.

☐ I can say words to the effect of, "Look, I had a bad life" or "Give me a break."

Making excuses is a graphic reminder that each of the 3 NOs is a form of lying.

It's also a reminder that the power of our anxieties allows us to make excuses so routinely that it can become as natural as breathing and as irresistible as an unconscious habit.

Blames

"If at first you don't succeed, blame your parents."

—Marcelene Cox, author[37]

The term *blame* can mean fixing accountability for errors. But unlike acknowledgment or assignment, in Courage Training *blame* reflects disrespect, accusation, censure, rebuke, emotional attacks, and the absence of calm objectivity.

We focus on BLAME as my cowardly response to anxiety in which, in an effort to relieve my discomfort and protect my feelings, I accuse someone of doing or causing my mistake. Using this particularly gross form of disrespect diminishes my courage and lowers my character. It weakens my ability to model for others and to act as a courageous leader.

A familiar saying goes, "To err is human. To blame it on someone else shows management potential." In an East Coast school district, burdened by budget cuts, retirements of senior faculty, and conflicts over content, political struggles, and shifting priorities, disrespect hit everyone like an all-day-long plane crash. Parents and teachers blamed each other, principals blamed the school board, the school board went after the district, the district blamed the city, the union blamed others, and the media found itself in a target-rich environment.

With the wishful thinking that a short talk could solve 40 years of deeply embedded habits of fear, disrespect, and blame, I spoke to a gathering of high school principals about the practice of courage. Many liked the idea, but payback was in the air.

"It's hard to know," I replied, "what to do when what you've tried hasn't worked and has even made things worse. Let's do this: in your small groups, take 10 minutes to list the benefits and the costs of blaming others." I wrote their answers on a flipchart. There were no benefits. They could see the conclusion: blaming made things worse.

I was then asked, "But what's the alternative? Just sit and take getting blamed ourselves? That's not fair. Courage should mean we can defend ourselves and point out their faults."

"Let's take a time-out," I said. "Could you list the techniques you've used to improve dialogue with parents, the district, and union stewards?" On a flipchart, they wrote:

Active listening	Mediation
Emotional intelligence	Alternate dispute resolution
Candid conversation	Using "yes and"
Finding "yes"	

"Good interventions," I said. "Why haven't they worked?"

They admitted that they had "used the tools"—while blaming the other parties.

"Please check the ones that apply to you from this inventory."

Reader, please do the same in the following inventory.

The Third NO Inventory: Hideouts: (Blames)

Check those that apply to you.

☐ I've blamed others to avoid responsibility.

☐ I've blamed people I dislike when it wasn't truly their fault.

☐ Under stress, I'll point the finger at others who aren't present to defend themselves.

☐ I can blame others and explain it away by saying that I thought I was right at the time.

☐ I've said, "You made me blame you."

☐ It's often hard for me to admit mistakes.

☐ I've blamed a set of circumstances knowing that it wasn't completely true.

☐ I've blamed the institution for things that were actually my responsibility.

☐ I've blamed people for hurting me just to get even.

☐ I've pointed fingers to cover up my own errors.

They checked most of the descriptors. "Now, imagine using the positive techniques above, again. But this time, don't use blame."

"Ah," said Principal Anita Benoit (a pseudonym), "here's his courage message."

The new answers: no blame, no defensiveness, take responsibility.

Anita, broad-shouldered and straight-backed, said, "We started on the wrong foot with parents and the district. We tell kids to take responsibility and not blame, and here, we take first place in pointing fingers. Now what should we do in our remaining time?"

"Dr. Benoit, thank you. I think if you stop blaming—a nasty, unflattering reaction to fear—and instead use courageous behaviors to build steady, sustaining relationships with the other stakeholders, you'll also stop worsening a tough situation. That will create space for repairs. Before practicing some essential courageous behaviors, what if you pledged to each other to stop blaming?"

"That simple?" asked Anita.

"What do we have to lose?" I asked. "If this flops, you can blame me."

Finally, some laughter.

"Bring it on!" said Dr. Benoit.

They did the 3 NOs Process.

Reader, it's now your turn to use the process to stop blaming others.

Admit, Quit, and Repair

We've now completed our journey of considering the 3 NOs.

An important way to exercise your authority over the NOs is to assess beforehand the circumstances that trigger your use of them.

What situations trigger those reactions in you?

```
┌─────────────────────────────────────────────────────────────────┐
│                                                                   │
│                                                                   │
│                                                                   │
│                                                                   │
│                                                                   │
└─────────────────────────────────────────────────────────────────┘
```

ADMITTING to the NOs in our own chest automatically begins to detoxify us.

QUITTING means we're going to stop all 3 NOs.

Please stand if possible and do the 3 NOs process to agree to quit. Handshakes (virtual handshakes work). Our internal desire to stop a bad habit becomes more authentic when we deliberately connect that wish with another person.

As of this writing, Fitz has not completely stopped his anger but with Battle Buddy feedback, he visibly exercises more self-governance than before. Allan McDonald's lessons about not making excuses are still being taught in engineering classes and at NASA. The no-excuses training for the health care system's Privileges Committee has created stronger safety standards for physicians in one hospital but has not been adopted by the profession. Dr. Anita Benoit has continued to lead and to encourage others to process conflicts without blaming.

You, the courage trainee, have new insights into the real you. You have charted a path ahead away from cowardice by admitting and then committing to quit your NOs.

The next step is big and necessary, for no one comes to courage alone and no one comes to courage without the impulse to quit and go home.

It's now time to commit and choose your Work Battle Buddy—the reliably forthright coworker—who will help you stop your NOs. Select a person who has the guts to tell you the unvarnished truth when you go sideways on your journey to become your best self. Again, don't pick someone who likes your faults and may even secretly celebrate your weaknesses.

My Work Battle Buddy:

```



```

You have completed the ADMIT and QUIT in your journey to gain your courage. What remains is the process of REPAIR.

Here you replace your former responses with life-giving, life-sustaining actions that define your best self. You begin this when you tell your spouse, significant other, or the person closest to you, that you've committed to stop using the 3 NOs—and that you have a Work Battle Buddy to help you with accountability.

You then complete repair by also telling the people who have most often received your NO behaviors that you are committed to stopping.

Well done! You've completed Step Two. As you move up the ladder to Step Three, you'll gain new actions that will complete your repairs by replacing past habits.

So, take a deep diaphragmatic nasal breath and slowly exhale through the mouth. Stretch and stand, do planks and push-ups, if you can.

I've used this Step of *The Courage Playbook* to give you an overview of the 3 NOs. In the next three Steps, remember to honestly look at how you treat others, especially if (like me) in times of stress, you're prone to disrespecting people, denying the truth about yourself, avoiding conflict, making excuses, blaming others, or giving in to anger.

I'll apologize now for the discomfort you may have been experiencing. I congratulate you for finishing two Steps. What follows is the vital and very rare opportunity to actually improve both for your sake and for the sake of others.

Next, in Step Three, you'll learn and practice the behaviors of courage, and prepare to draft your Individual Courage Action Plan (ICAP). It all adds up to a life changer.

Please keep your eye on the goal: becoming your best and most courageous self to live above the common level of life. Stephen Covey advises us to be proactive and begin with the end in mind.[38]

Now, let's go get some courage.

3

Step Three: Getting It Right—The 3 GOs

"Courage is rightly esteemed the first of human qualities because it is the quality which guarantees all others."

—*Winston Churchill*[1]

IN THE BEST and worst of times we need to deeply understand the answer to the question: *What is courage?* Courage is singular but multidimensional. It is essential in life and vocation. It is unifying and is composed of many parts.

Courage is important because it gives us a heroic narrative in the unique pathway of our life. It leads to a courageously stable and coherent identity that overcomes our fears and equips us to be our true best self.

In practice, courage is a verb. As an ability, it is indifferent to background and status and is available to all. In reality, courage is a set of observable actions and becomes our key human competence when we practice its behaviors. Courage is moral prowess; it does the highest right thing. We need courage to be free of the dictatorship of our fears and to live freely and confidently without incessant anxiety. Courage equips us to do our best without the prohibitive costs of self-centeredness.

Most vitally, courage develops in us a strong, admirable, noble, and even heroic character. Courage is constructed and character is sustained by how we treat principles, humans, society, and existence and how we deal with the challenges of a world that blooms with innumerable tests.

Courage is grand but is expressed in humility. It is not an end in itself; we practice and build courage not to boast or become superior to others. We do so to better govern ourselves and to benefit others with optimum excellence.[2] Courage is the empowering aptitude, the hardworking mechanism, and the practiced means by which we become our best selves.

In ethics, courage is a virtue. A virtue is an apex of moral excellence. But courage isn't only a virtue; Aristotle learned it was the first virtue, *arête*, an ancient and now unfamiliar term that describes the best of what we can be.[3] C.S. Lewis observed that courage is not merely a virtue, but the form of every virtue at the testing point and it operates at the highest point of reality in which we live.[4] It's the foundation upon which all the other virtues rest. Author and ambassador Clare Boothe Luce described courage "as the ladder upon which the other virtues mount,"[5] which restates the primacy of courage and illustrates that we achieve courage by taking measured steps.

I think I'm kind, compassionate, and caring. But hurt my feelings and what happens? My theoretical virtues become defensiveness, withdrawal, and anger. When I practice steps toward my courage, I remain calm, kind, and compassionate in the middle of an emotional storm. But without courage, my virtues and, to quote Amy Tan, all my best intentions[6] get blown away. For when courage goes, all goes. Courage, in a uniquely central manner, safeguards respect, leadership, integrity, love, tolerance, compassion, decency, harmony, safety, true justice, hope, and all of the other fine words of our existence.

For example, we all want to love and to be loved. But the astonishing truth is that without courage, we can't give love in a sustaining way and we can't get love if we're anxious and stressed. Millions marry and pledge to love each other exclusively and forever. But what happens? In our hard and busy lives, we fear that we're not receiving enough love or sufficient respect. We accidentally leave the door unlocked so the pernicious 3 NOs enter to kill our patience, affection, and caring communication. Without practice, we lack the guts to simply listen, bravely forgive, and to be kind instead of hurt. Life tests us by testing our courage; if we're found wanting, even love, that great reason for living, fades. Selfishness then defeats promises and vows, and hurt feelings and old arguments can career into bitter divorces that jeopardize our own and our children's well-being.

Courage equips us to be positive, encouraging, resolute, and affirming when fear triggers negativity, dismay, quitting, and accusing. We can then exercise the inner steel of our strengths to serve the good instead of surrendering to the grip of our anxieties. Courage requires that we not waste time by weakening ourselves or mistreating others. But for too long, we've only sensed courage as a fading echo in the backwaters of our wishful imaginations.

For courage to return to its natural habitat in the interactions of daily life, we first admit and quit our negative reactions to fear—the 3 NOs. You did this in Step Two and are thus prepared to see courage as realistically, functionally, and intimately authentic.

We summarized fear in three negative reactions. In similar fashion, courage lends itself to be usefully captured in a specific set of key human behaviors. We call these The 3 GOs.

The 3 GOs Overview

The GOs are a Rosetta Stone to courage. They decode the secret of living rightly to free us from the rule of fear. They are fundamental to contentment in a disordered world.

The 3 GOs are not simply opposites of the 3 NOs. Yet the first GO, unconditionally and positively respecting all persons (UPR), is clearly related to our first NO, disrespecting others. But we'll see that our essential courageous behaviors are far grander in scope, penetrate deeper into our identity, and produce greater sustained positive impact than the relative smallness of their negative semi-counterparts.

I recently did a videoconference call with Sean Madison.[7] An exec in a boutique manufacturing firm, he was composed and appeared lean to a point of austerity. He spoke thoughtfully. "I need help with a bad boss," he said. "He's an adrenaline junkie who pushes me like we're in a constant DEFCON 1 emergency. Yesterday, he publicly sandblasted my best contributor, who just quit. He said he wasn't leaving because of our boss—he was leaving because of me—because I didn't speak up to authority. That was pretty harsh, but probably true."

Sean was trapped in his Tier 3 behaviors while working for a Tier 2 supervisor. The mere thought of facing him made Sean freeze as if he were in a Simon Says game with real-life consequences. As he danced to the sad tune of the 3 NOs, his leadership abilities evaporated like a magician's handkerchief in a flash of fire.

"I just get paralyzed with hormonal overload," he said. "Some of my folks are putting on life preservers to jump ship like it's the fall of Rome. I know I have to do something but I'm afraid I'll mess up and make it worse."

I asked if he'd agree to stop his fearful reactions, accept me as an acting accountability partner, and do a crash course in practicing the behaviors of courage.

"Yes, since what I'm doing right now totally sucks."

We did the Biography Form and 3 NOs.

"Good," I said. "Take a deep breath. Ready to see the key verbs of courage that we're going to practice doing?"

He nodded and looked at the 3 GOs:

1. Unconditionally & Positively Respect all persons (UPR)

2. Comprehensively Self-govern/Act with Humility

3. Discern | Act | Then Train Others in the Highest Moral Action (DAT)

"Notice anything about them?" I asked.

"Yeah, it jumped right out," said Sean. "They're all impossible."

I smiled. "Tell me more."

"I mean, really, these GOs are unnatural acts. They violate human nature. No one can respect everyone. How can I respect my boss? The guy's a turd in the punchbowl. I don't think we can totally self-govern. And man, be humble? That's un-American. Doing 'the Highest Moral Action?' I bet even Gandhi flunked that."

I wrote, "UNNATURAL" on the whiteboard behind me (I'd unclicked, "Mirror my video" so the writing wasn't reversed). "You're right," I said. "Fear is intuitive. It comes naturally. It takes absolutely no training. Courage, as you said, is unnatural and counterintuitive. We only gain it through practice. You play sports?"

"Bike, softball, mountain climbing. Good stuff for a guy who grew up poor."

"So why do kids crash," I asked, "while learning to ride bikes? Why can't we hit a curve ball? Why do novice mountaineers struggle to climb?"

Sean paused. "It's natural to fail at first. We all fear failure and tend to clutch under pressure."

"Yes. And then there's also our seductive power of intuition. Kids trying to ride a bike intuitively want to pedal before they learn the counterintuitive: to balance and coast before they try to pedal. So they crash and cry. Batting, we intuitively look at the fences we're aiming at instead of first counterintuitively and unnaturally cranking our necks down to glue eyes on the ball. So we stupidly whiff and get embarrassed. Rock climbing in the Army, I instinctively hugged the cliff like it was my long-lost mother, futilely seeking a fake sense of security, instead of first counterintuitively separating from the cliff to see where and how to move. If I hadn't been on belay, I would've gone splat. The ways in which we intuitively treat people; react to common, everyday stress; respond to predictable pressures; and try to solve problems can feel intuitively right in the spur of the moment and yet be utterly wrong in reality and practice."

Sean sucked his lips inward. "Like what I've been doing with my people and boss."

Sean is just like all of us. In every interaction with people, we're given a beautiful opportunity for courage. The first of courage's abilities is our first GO, for it equips and inspires all the others.

The First GO: Unconditionally and Positively Respect All People (UPR)

"A person's a person, no matter how small."

—Dr. Seuss[8]

J. Robert Oppenheimer, an isolated child prodigy, became a tall, gaunt, chain-smoking genius-level thinker who spoke classic languages, sailed through Harvard in three years as a summa, and then for fun went to Oxford. Earning a doctorate, he frightened the faculty[9] and was rude, arrogant, judgmental, intolerant, friendless, depressed, and homicidal. As a top physicist, he was considered to head up a major national project. "But he's never run anything," said others. "He's 38 and can't handle people." "Couldn't run a hamburger stand," they said.[10] So it came as a shock when "Oppie," infamous for disliking humans, became director of the world's greatest science initiative with the world's top physicists and 125,000 people at a cost today of $24 billion dollars. It was thought that if Oppenheimer failed, as surely he would, millions would die.

But the greater shock was that he transformed himself. How did he do it? He simply found the courage to change his behaviors. He suddenly began treating rivals, critics, and everyone with "exquisite grace and sensitivity,"[11] unconditional respect, patience, attentiveness, empathy, and compassion. He became "indispensable" to the project's success. The hideously disrespectful physicist had "rapidly metamorphosed into a marvelously efficient and charismatic administrator" by practicing UPR and killing his previous negative identity.[12]

Training people to overcome fear, I'll ask them to think about someone they've always admired for their courage. I want to tell you about the person who comes to mind for me.

Grace C. ("Gracie") Collins[13] began as a cardiac floor nurse and rose through the ranks to become a senior nurse manager. Like the majority of people on Earth, she'd endured poverty and gender and racial discrimination.[14] Unlike most, she built up an inviolate respect for all persons, causing superiors to suspect that she couldn't lead or team build, much less become a senior administrator in an old hospital that was being reopened in an acutely underserved area.

"Gracie's too kind and modest," they said. "Too weak to manage people who'll lose their jobs if the new place fails." "Anyone who goes there will have longer commutes and child drop-off issues—stuff above her pay grade." "You know they'd only give it to her because she's Black," they said. So it came as a shock when Gracie, famous for quietly respecting others, became the chief nursing officer for a high-risk facility that was practically designed to quickly devolve into a hotbed of conflicts and a free-fire zone for angry, dislocated, and resentful employees.

But the greater shock was that the moment Gracie was selected, the highest-performing employees in the main facilities volunteered en masse to be reassigned to work for her. Others were surprised that some in upper management didn't see this coming. It was around this time that I'd been engaged to do Courage Training for the new hospital, and people asked, "What is it about Gracie that would motivate people to risk their jobs and take on personal discomforts?"

I needed to know who Gracie was. Had she become who she was truly supposed to be?

What meaning might this answer carry for you, the reader, and for your identity?

Gracie knew the right plays in the high-stakes game of life. Thus she didn't default to the intuitive way of working: avoid discomfort; watch out for Number One; use people to get ahead; respect those who make you feel better about yourself; and flap your wings about the need to change without actually changing.

Gracie Collins accepted that respect is counterintuitive, which leads us to UPR: UNCONDITIONALLY AND POSITIVELY RESPECT ALL PERSONS, emphasis on the *all*.

Her second master play: she had learned that universally deploying respect at all times was the prerequisite to doing the right thing, and that doing the right thing was the prerequisite to living well and leading effectively, both at work and at home.

"Without what you call UPR," she said, "I'd give in to my considerable temper, resentment and doing paybacks to anyone who hurt me. Now just imagine the impact of that kind of behavior on patient safety, teamwork, on enjoying each other and our profession! If I don't respect every person, I could slide into favoritism, which is a team-killer. But if I failed to respect all people as a matter of identity, I'd end up giving in to bias, discrimination, and racism, the torments of my life.

"As an African American woman, you know my door's wide open to being resentful and bitter. So when I was little and got steamed? My mother would ask, 'Gracie, are you focusing on the evil in others or are you working on being the righteous person you're called to be?'

"My mother cleaned the houses of bigots and never let them defeat her by giving them her dignity. She'd get busy being attentive to doing right by people and didn't waste time on getting into cruelty and meanness. She won by refusing to be like them. She'd get rid of her anger so she never brought it home to her kids, and especially to me, as I already had this thing with anger.

"But as a young nurse, I knew better—that bad people deserved some cruelty in return. One day, a bigoted patient got me so mad with his evil comments that I fouled up some charts. Later, all my energy going into hating that man and blaming him for my mistakes, I made a near-fatal medication error with a sweet child patient down the hall. It dawned on me that my mother, to raise me with my temper, had to practice respect not just with rude strangers, impolite men and racists, but with me, her own daughter. I'd seen her look at her fear and her own temper. She was very smart and I saw her work to do the opposite of the impulse. She was my permanent 'Battle Buddy' of the heart.

"So I began practicing it like putting in an IV right, or safely lifting a heavy patient. Someone would dish me disrespect and my blood would boil and I'd think of the opposite. How many times I heard a patient rudely say, 'I want a different person,' which means, 'I want a white nurse.' And I'd go cold and hot at the same time. I wanted to say, 'Mister Smith, I'm the best cardiac nurse you'll ever get and you need me to keep your sorry ass alive!' But I'd take a breath, exhale the hate and ask, what's the opposite of yelling and stomping out of his room?

"Then I'd calmly say, 'I'll be happy to get my supervisor.' I keep breathing and tell my manager that my patient wants to see her. Then I'd go about my business, cool as the underside of a pillow in winter, still feeling like a human being instead of a little hand puppet controlled by my anger. Later, I'll visit that patient and check up on him. Quietly, I said, 'Mr. Smith, can I be so bold to tell you that I felt very hurt when you asked that I be replaced?'"

"What did he say?" I asked.

"They usually say, 'I'm sorry, Miss Collins.' Sometimes they'd just glare. But I know their conscience just got a little electrical jolt, and a better medicine than that is hard to find."

Reader: we'll practice how to speak to an angry person and to address conflicts in Step Five.

"What else is part of your respecting people?" I asked.

"There's empathy, feeling what the other person feels without going down the drain over it. This happens: a patient's spouse hysterically accuses me of something. My mother would say, 'Grace honey, this poor person's hair is on fire. She's hurting, full of fear, crazy afraid that she's going to be alone for the rest of her life. She needs you to give her some understanding." Grace closed her eyes. *Take a deep cleansing breath. Use respect as a gift to a person in fear. Model what she needs: quiet courage and a dose of confidence so she doesn't make things worse for her spouse.*

"So I said, 'Ma'am, you must be so worried. I will make those corrections. We will do all we can for your husband. What else can I do to help?' Even as I'm speaking, my blood pressure drops and I'm in control of myself instead of becoming this woman's hand puppet. You see what I mean?"

"These are terrific UPR examples," I said. "Did you ever help someone you *really* disliked?"

"That's the test, isn't it? I do it all the time. The bigoted patient, the drug ODs, armed gang bangers threatening us. No one's ever in a good space when they come to us."

UPR is respect but far bigger than our common view of it. Not only does it far exceed common courtesy, minimal civility, and being polite and "nice," but it also sets the new code of how to treat all people, build relationships, install values into how we work, and strengthen our courage and character to live the way we should.

The diagram in Figure 3.1 provides a suggestion of UPR's vast power to do good.

If you doubt this, simply replace "UPR" with "DISRESPECT" and you can visualize the instantaneous reversal of each of the outer-spoked results, giving us more fear, stress, bias, conflicts and wrecked relationships and less empathy, encouragement, leadership, teamwork, and problem-solving. Remember how the virtue of courage serves as the foundation, the steps to freedom, and the central point of origin for all the other virtues? UPR plays the same role for the behaviors of courage.

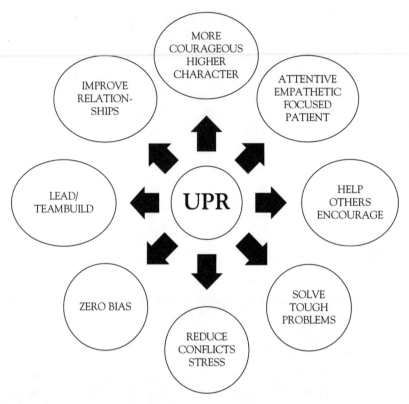

Figure 3.1   The UPR Wheel

A courageous Ms. Collins had the UPR—the guts—to demonstrate exquisite grace and sensitivity to everyone. UPR consists of many behaviors: listening when you're tired, helping someone you dislike, being calm and not giving in to your worst self even as you're being disrespected. It's not the law of the street in which I was raised where anger was met by anger and violent words simply begot more violent acts. UPR is the precise opposite of "getting even," which is a polite way to describe giving in to conflict, anger, and hate.

In the Step One Bio Form 5 we looked at questions that dealt with *unconditional respect*. Let's go into a bit more detail in the following inventory.

The First GO Inventory: Unconditional Positive Respect (UPR)

Check those that apply.

☐ I always listen very carefully to my spouse/significant other/ family members.

☐ I always respect all people—even when arguing with someone I dislike.

☐ I respectfully challenge biased or bigoted comments or behaviors.

☐ I am routinely unselfish, fair, kind, compassionate, and without bias.

☐ I consistently improve how I treat others.

☐ When I see someone act wrongly, I respectfully tell that person about it.

☐ I am always fully attentive when others speak.

☐ I know the behaviors my spouse/significant other wants me to change.

These are tough questions. Unchecked boxes identify new and bold personal behavioral objectives. We're reminded that courage and respect are rare and badly needed skills.

In this section, we will start working on those abilities.

You can now answer the Big Question on UPR. Please circle your answer on the following Likert scale.

I believe respect must be earned.

1	2	*	4	5
strongly disagree	disagree	—	agree	strongly agree

Grace demonstrated that to overcome our fears and become our best selves, we respect every human being without any conditions.

It this vein, let's dispel a common error about respect. Many think and say, "You have to earn my respect." This is because we often confuse the action of respect with the result of trust.

Trust must always be earned. It's an outcome that's easily lost when violated. We must discern who is trustworthy and we cannot and must not trust everyone. Trust requires judgment and awareness.

Respect is radically different; it's a courageous action, a calming competence that results from our courage. It is freely given to all persons, regardless of their actions, for the sake of principles, humanity, and dignity.

Now, and this is important: respect does not mean agreeing with or endorsing what another person says or does. It does mean that with courage, we can respectfully deal with disagreement instead of giving in to fear, anger, and hostility or weakly avoiding an important challenge with which we should deal.

Each of us uniquely differs from all others. Courage gives us the ability to unconditionally respect all people—despite differences, or disliking or not admiring them.

It is upon this ironclad foundation that professionals provide care to the most despicable criminals, bosses, or family members. It is upon the same basis that we can be fair and right in dialogue with all persons to explore differences, find commonalities, and intentionally develop ways to be in accord.

UPR is our universal stance of courage.

When I do UPR, regardless of how I feel, it's functionally impossible for me to discriminate against people, whoever they are, or to favor one group of people over another. When I practice UPR, however imperfectly, I'm overriding the fears, biases, and deficiencies in my character that drive me to be anxious, self-centered, indifferent, and resentful of some. When I do UPR, I build within my deepest identity the courage to honor every human being I meet.

If your answer to the Big Question on UPR was a circled "1" or "2," I invite you to take the Respect Challenge and practice respecting every person as a human being.

As a kid, I deeply feared non-Chinese people and couldn't play sports, tussle, or rap in an African American neighborhood. I was sent to a downtown YMCA to box with lads of every shade of skin except mine. My profound terror of other boys, the ring, the conditioning, the punching, and the blood exceeded my tiny English vocabulary. But the more I practiced respecting the rules of boxing and kids who were different and always better, the less I hated it and the less I feared them and the world. I got friends, I could box, and I learned how to breathe during exertion with only one lung. Toussaint Streat, my first friend and my first best friend in life, taught me how to laugh. I found I could even enjoy being with kids I didn't like. I became a peacemaker who saw no skin color. I was no longer a youth with rampant racial fears.

That's why UPR is our first GO.

When I related this to Gracie Collins, she looked up and went back in memory.

"Martin Luther King taught us, you know, in a speech, 'You don't have to see the whole staircase, just take the first step.'"[15]

We were quiet for a while. How we missed that man.

Grace spoke. "I think of him when I respect some bad character who looks down on women and has no charms for the color of my skin. I think on Dr. King and Mahatma Gandhi, but some people think that means sucking up to a smiley-faced person that doesn't deserve respect, you know what I'm saying? Is that your view on UPR?"

"I couldn't have said it better," I said.

UPR isn't transactional. I don't hold back respecting my spouse, relatives, colleagues, or a stranger and wait there, tapping my shoe until they respect me. I demonstrate Tier 4 courage and strength by not confusing respect with trust or approval. I practice honoring every person I come into contact with and keep my integrity intact by not acting like a bigot toward bigots.

We see that UPR not only works in trouble and conflict. It come fully comes to life in the routines of the day-to-day.

With UPR, we can fully utilize the Tier 4 GPS to help us eliminate the worst and leave us the best options in dealing with others.

> ## Tier 4 GPS: The First GO: Relating to People
>
> **Tier 1:** Dishonor—You're a thing, an object to use, abuse, or worse. (Driven by fear)
>
> **Tier 2:** Disrespect—You're someone I can use, exploit and forget. (Controlled by fear)
>
> **Tier 3:** Uncertainty—I'll respect you if it's easy for me. (Controlled by mood)
>
> **Tier 4:** UPR—I respect all persons equally. (Inspired by courage)

This helps us to not choose Tier 1, 2, or 3 options. In Step One, Gary and Bella saw the logic and desirability of Tier 4 behaviors of courage but weren't clear about what they might be.

What might courageous, Tier 4 behaviors look like?

As humans, we have always had an idea about how to treat each other at a Tier 4 level, for this concept can be traced back to ancient wisdom literature and the Golden Rule: "Do not do to others what you do not want done to you," and "Therefore, whatever you want others to do to you, do also to them."[16]

To absorb UPR beyond cognition, you'll need to practice, and that means having a practice partner. Recently, I've done most of my behavioral practice sessions via videoconferencing, so practice and training no longer require being in the same room.

Training begins with questions: first, think about situations or types of people that trigger you to be disrespectful. Behavior #1 is "*I always put aside work and screens to fully listen and remember what the others said.*"

If I were doing the exercise, I'd say to my practice partner. "I do a terrible job of listening to anyone who interrupts my work. So I'd like to practice improving the UPR behavior of setting aside work to fully listen."

My practice partner acts out interrupting my work and speaking rapidly about topics that invite my casual inattention (quantum physics, the Internal Revenue Code). I then practice specific behaviors: *turning* away from the screen; *focusing* on the other person visually, personally, relationally, and aurally; and *remembering* what is being said to me.

The practice partner gives me feedback (I kept glancing back at the screen, breaking eye contact, and missed the point of their message.) I try again until I get it right.

The partner then tells me what triggers them to not pay attention, and I'll play that role for them.

It's no surprise that we quickly forget what we hear. Research reveals that in 24 hours, we forget a staggering 90 percent of what we heard in a lecture.[17] To counter this unhelpful deficiency in our learning, we use dynamic, coached feedback with an accountability matrix to actually learn, remember, and imprint new human skills into muscle, mind, memory of the heart, and even into our very identity.

That's why we *practice instead of merely trying to hear.*

Practicing UPR gives us a mindset about how to treat people in all situations. It trains us to not be indifferent to people or uncaring about who they are.

We use UPR as the starting point to acquire courage.

Here's a recommended UPR 10-week dynamic practice routine (Figure 3.2). After practicing one of the UPR behaviors for a week, check it off in the column on the far left.

But first: identify the "triggers" and particular situations in which you're likely to be inattentive, indifferent, or arrogant with others. Use those triggers and situations as the fact patterns in which to practice each of the 10 UPR behaviors. Meet later with your Battle Buddy to update your behavioral accountability list.

My trigger was being interrupted at work. So my practice partner deliberately interrupted me until I got it right.

The inspirational examples of "Oppie" Oppenheimer and Gracie Collins remind us that behaviorally honoring all persons is the most fundamental and crucial competence in both a courageous individual and a courageously content person.

We spent a great deal of time on Unconditional Positive Respect because it is the very foundation of courage and the keystone of behavioral integrity. It's also because we'll need UPR to master our other GOs. Let's take a look at our second GO.

√	WEEK	UPR BEHAVIORAL PRACTICE
	1	Be fully attentive and focused when you don't feel like it.
	2	Be patient and thoughtful when you're tired and stressed.
	3	Be aware and attuned to the sensitivities and feelings of others.
	4	Govern my feelings so they don't overshadow the presence of the other person.
	5	Encourage others to act as their best selves.
	6	Respectfully give Buddy Checks; respectfully welcome and receive them.
	7	Practice giving a respectful response to a bigoted or discriminatory remark.
	8	Be faultlessly respectful, despite negative feelings, in an argument.
	9	Practice the mindset of caring for every person you meet.
	10	Practice the mindset of never dishonoring a human being.

Figure 3.2   UPR 10-week Dynamic Practice Routine

The Second GO: Comprehensively Self-govern/Act with Humility

"Until you have the inner discipline that brings calmness of mind, external facilities and conditions will never bring the joy and happiness you seek."
—Dalai Lama[18]

"It is unwise to be too certain of one's own wisdom."
—Gandhi[19]

The ancients held that virtue meant ruling over our emotions. Some moderns believe the opposite: being yourself means giving in to our feelings and disregarding our virtues.

By entering the far country of the GOs, you're voting to actively test both propositions and, having practiced UPR, you're ready to meet our second GO.

As you take in the counterintuitive expression, COMPREHEN-SIVELY SELF-GOVERN, you meet the formidable words, ACT WITH HUMILITY. You might suspect you're in science fiction territory instead of entering the deeper reality of the behaviors of courage.

I've linked self-governance and humility because both are innovative apps. They further equip us on the road to our good courage, a consistent integrity, and an identity grounded in a Kevlar-tough strength of character. In our individualistic times, exercising self-control and defeating arrogance represent heroic deeds.

Dutch social psychologist Geert Hofstede studied cultural *collectivism* in which the value of the group outweighs the importance of the individual. Collectivism is marked by tight family bonding, group safety, and loyalty to the larger body, and pride resides in the clan. Latin American nations topped the list of collective societies.

Its cultural counterpart is *individualism*. Here, the person is more important than the group, individuals are loosely linked to each other, each pursues personal economic success, and pride is possessed by each isolated person. Five Western nations scored highest in individualism and it comes as no shock that the United States leads the pack.[20]

"North Americans seem to be the kings and queens of overestimation," said Cornell University's David Dunning. "In places like Japan, Korea, or China, this phenomenon evaporates" because the East values self-improvement while the West values self-esteem.[21]

International behavioral researchers found that Americans are universally seen as being so self-centered that they meet the definition of pathological narcissism in the *DSM-V*, the accepted manual for the interpretation of mental disorders. People in this category are "grandiose... immodest, self-centered, entitled, exploitative, dishonest, noncompliant, and callous"[22]—the very opposites of an unpretentious individual or a courageous leader.

Humility born of courage is a potent antidote to an ego without walls. Humility, from the Latin, *humilis*, means *to be grounded*.

My law school mentor, Professor Edgar Bodenheimer, was admired for his intellectual brilliance but was beloved for his modesty. Never a competitor in the Low Games of the Self, Edgar, a short-statured gentleman who had stood tall against the Nazis, won our hearts with his strong, steady, patient, and quiet nature. That quality—more than the flamboyantly amusing profs with outsized chest-pounding personalities—imprinted his moral teaching into our memories.

Sensing the hot fires of our pushy law student pride, Professor Bodenheimer paraphrased St. Augustine, "It is humility that makes the selfish into angels. It seems to me that you students would save much mental energy by not thinking so much about yourself. Arrogance demands so much energy and requires you to constantly replace your batteries."

When headline-seeking CEOs became showtime rock stars, humility couldn't find a seat in the theater. Then Jim Collins' profitability studies in *Good to Great* revealed that the best CEOs of the most profitable Fortune 500s were "Level 5 leaders" who were ambitious for their companies' ethical success but were humble about themselves. "Compared to high-profile leaders with big personalities who make headlines and become celebrities, the good-to-great leaders seem to have come from Mars.[23] *Self-effacing, quiet, reserved, even shy*— these leaders are a paradoxical blend of personal humility and professional will. . . [they] display a compelling modesty, are self-effacing and understated. . . [while] leaders with gargantuan personal egos. . . contributed to the demise or continued mediocrity of the company."[24]

As a consequence of a practiced personal humility, they were indifferent to compensation packages and avoided attention from others and the media.

What? *Personally humble? Self-effacing? Indifferent to money and perks? I need humility to make huge, sustainable profits in Ted Turner's game of life? Are you kidding?* But Collins wasn't joking and instead had hit another literary home run. For the next decade organizations and the leadership guild energetically talked about Level 5 leaders. But while excited about Level 5 leader achievements, the guild didn't train execs or family members in the behaviors of courage, respect, self-governance, or humility that had generated the record-setting outcomes. Most decided to ditch the humility but keep the cannoli and the money.[25]

Research reveals that humility not only accelerates performance, improves competence, and helps make record profits, but it also produces significant personal pluses. It sustains our most important relationships, reduces anxiety and stress, advances trust, improves our mental and physical health,[26] and increases positive emotions. Students who demonstrate humility are more likely to seek advice and input and learn faster than more arrogant students who are too proud to accept feedback. Thus, humility improves our ability to learn and to perform academically.

Studies found that humility was a better indicator of future work performance than IQ. In my experience, practiced humility is a prerequisite to the exercise of self-regulation and self-governance.

Anna Katherina Schaffner, PhD, in her study of humility in leaders, concluded that "these leaders believe in human development. *They do not crave credit, nor do they constantly need to show how great they are or undermine others to feel powerful. They are instead relentlessly trying to improve and learn from their failures* [italics added for emphasis].[27] By modeling humility, they create a humble working culture in their organizations.

Bradley Owens says that humble leaders are essentially self-transcendent. Humble leaders "*have successfully tempered or tamed the ego and embraced a leadership perspective that seeks to elevate everyone* [italics added for emphasis]. They are teachable, eager to learn, willing to see themselves accurately, and able to praise those around them. They foster in their workforce hope, efficacy, resilience, and optimism."[28]

As we inhale this powerful data, please remember that we don't acquire courage to improve results. We do it to improve how we treat others. This is the fundamental distinction between a virtue, which has moral significance, and a skill, which is morally neutral.

But wait, there's more: the very essence of humility also requires the courage to see ourselves truthfully, candidly, and with a steady eye on our imperfections so we can improve.

You may now wish to sniff smelling salts to recover consciousness and rise from the canvas after being knocked flat by the impact of our second GO. CNN founder Ted Turner, who said life is a game and money is how you keep score, added, "I love CNN and I love the Cartoon Network, I mean, I thought these things up. . . I'd be perfect if only I had a little humility."[29]

To counter a popular scorning of humility, consider Trappist monk Thomas Merton, author of 50 books and the *Seven Storey Mountain*, who concluded from a spiritual life with physical labor that "pride makes us artificial. Humility makes us real." "Humility," said French philosopher Simone Weil, is "attentive patience." These are the notes of an identity in courage that reduces our naturally powerful, inborn, and insatiable love of Me.

This expands to "cultural humility," a term developed by Hook, Owen, Davis, and Utsey to describe viewing other cultural groups without prejudgment—*prejudice*. If I lack cultural humility, I feed my sense of superiority over other groups, devalue the abilities of those from diverse cultures while thinking too highly of my own talents.[30]

When we gain courage and humility to benefit others, this is courage gained and humility realized. But when the practice of courage leads to the self-serving pride of achievement ("Look how courageous and humble I am!"[31]), this becomes courage lost.

Dramatically, humility is the forgotten element of courage. For others have confused humility with shame, low confidence, uncertainty, submissiveness, self-degradation, or craven timidity. Instead, humility has guts. Courageous humility projects quiet self-assurance, comfort in one's skin, an absence of any need to demand attention or to show off, and a commitment to principles and an orientation toward others. There is no haughtiness, vanity, or pridefulness.

In America, the planet's most individualistic, self-focused, and ego-promoting culture, acting with humility wins the prize as our most counterintuitive behavior.

Sean Madison said that the 3 NOs shared the happy status of being impossible to do. He must have been thinking about humility. Luckily, humility is a renewable resource.

Practicing humility strengthens our skills of UPR, self-governance, ethical diversity, and authentic multiculturalism. These moral muscles are the strong and principled countermeasures to our ancient and instinctive tendencies for bias, discrimination, bigotry, and racism.

Benjamin Isaac, in *The Invention of Racism in Classical Antiquity*, clearly states that ancient cultures actively and consistently discriminated by race as well as by ethnicity, gender, and culture and employed, in support of their biases, the familiar and awful mechanisms of war, conquest, enslavement, subjugation, and annihilation.[32]

At ground level, in every personal interaction, and particularly in our current social state, the dynamic and counterintuitive practice of humility can greatly help us all.

Using the Tier 4 GPS tool, we clearly see Tier 1 and 2 individuals demonstrating rampant narcissism and egos run amok, while our Tier 4 person is consistently other-directed, not self-absorbed, quick to help others, and uninterested in recognition and acclaim.

Under self-governance, we need humility to rein in our personal wants and impulses if we're to authentically consider the needs of others and those of our communities. But what does it mean to actually own self-governance? What specifically does this relate to as we grow our courage?

Four out of 10 Americans make New Year's resolutions yet only 9 percent follow through on them.[33] So it's not headline news that we often eat unhealthfully, exercise insufficiently, drink unwisely, and endure unhealthy levels of anxiety, sadness, and depression while suffering existentially due to conditions we cannot control and which we seek to address, with grand futility, through blame and anger.

But research proves we can change unhealthy habits—you're doing that right now with the 3 NOs. One of the most effective methods to produce change is the use of routine accountability.[34] This aligns with the ancient wisdom of "iron sharpening iron" and the *Analects'* instruction to welcome honest feedback.[35] In the journey to be your best self, recruiting a Work Battle Buddy places you miles ahead of those who have friends but lack authentic comrades.

If we forgo accountability while hoping for good things to result, we're living in the land of wishful thinking. If we expect things to simply happen, we've crossed the border into magical thinking. When we set a self-improvement goal, we've entered the ancient battleground between self-control and self-indulgence, and between willpower and irresistible temptation.

The ancient Greeks defined "desire" with brutal honesty; *epithumia* means "to focus on our passionate urges and hungers." David Hume, the Enlightenment empirical philosopher, thought impulses were uncontrollable and wrote, "Reason is the slave of the passions."[36]

Current science provides a ray of hope by adding, "well, not always." So can our second GO, Comprehensively Self-govern, equip us to rule our passions and midnight urges?

Let's say at first that *control* is the use of power to dictate how others behave and to impose behavioral limits on ourselves. When we choose a specific goal (lose weight, improve heart health, choose better friends, or look and be more fit), our concept of control becomes *willpower*.

Studies reveal that we consistently overestimate our ability to resist urges and that the most optimistic about the strength of their willpower usually fail first.[37] (We unrealistically expect that we can accomplish our hardest challenges without the courage they require. Similarly, we expect employees to be self-initiating and managers to be selfless without training in self-governance.)

But we default to willpower as the answer; we might more honestly call it *wishpower*.

For most, the "power" of our will dead-ends into the decision: *I quit*. Wishpower is a maze in which few find the cheese and most are still searching for the exit.

Courage operates in a different space. Self-governance is not our familiar New Year's Resolution, which belongs in the nearby bucket of self-control. When I overeat or smoke and drink excessively, the underlying driver is anxiety about some immediate situation. When Jessica, our daughter, died of heart disease, I experienced an acute agony that surpassed all previous suffering. Knowing it was destructive, instead of comforting Diane, I tried to self-medicate with alcohol. Hating my weakness, I tried to stop.

But I learned an important lesson: fear without courage defeats willpower and even love. I saw that I was more afraid of pain than I was loving to Diane in her unspeakable loss. I needed something deeper than merely stopping an undesirable action. I needed courage.

Self-governance doesn't aim at tactical objectives such as weight, health, or needed skills; it targets the anxiety and fear that drive all dysfunctional habits. As we continue to acquire the 3 GOs to counter our reactions to fear, we can then use our newly gained courage to focus on changing particular habits.

Our need for self-governance is evident in the heavily referenced topic of. . . obesity. Obesity is associated with a wide range of serious health risks and a reduction of quality of life.[38] We spend $72 billion a year on dieting and health plans, a sum that doesn't include the costs of fitness, gyms, and supplements.[39] Impressively, 42 percent of Americans try to lose weight but sadly, 49 percent of us remain overweight. Our stats are trending upward in a downward spiral of national health.[40] After learning that they'd die if they didn't diet, exercise, or stop smoking, only 14 percent of last-chance cardiac patients made the change.[41] This statistic is alarming, but the reality is that it reflects on all of us when we struggle and then fail to overcome our resistance to change.

Self-governance, like courage and character, is most evident when we are tested. Let's meet another client.

When Caleb P. Novak[42] of the Yukon was nine, he rode a big brown roan with a snaffle bit, twirled a lariat, jangled carpenter's tools on his belt. And sang to his horse. If you dropped the adult Caleb into the wilds and came back three months later, you'd find that he'd built a town with a library, a water tower, a train depot. And a sweet shop. He'd recently returned from three months of engineering on Azerbaijan's Baku-Tbilisi pipeline to learn that his wife Hedy had moved a guy into their bedroom, changed her name to "Luna," and no longer wished to be married to someone with his travel schedule. She'd brutally rebuffed his efforts to reconcile or go to counseling, as well as his offer to quit his profession. The diligent Caleb was now too depressed to work, so he quit his job—hoping that Luna would return. I had met Caleb years before when I needed to learn basics about innovative and renewable energy engineering.

"I'm broken," he said on videoconference. He looked bad, explaining events. "She loved me, meets a guy in the gym and she's done. I'm stuck in my head about hurting the guy and screaming at Hedy, at Luna, to wake up. I can't sleep, eat, exercise, or think straight. I drink like a fish and it doesn't help except for the all-day headaches. Back when my group was in a conflict, you gave us a talk on self-control. I want you to walk me through it again."

The Dalai Lama called life a gift—but only if we can manage it. Caleb Novak is hurt, angry, and depressed and is finding out that food and alcohol aren't morally neutral.[43]

"Caleb, alcohol taught me that it's a poison more than a pain-killer. Self-governance is better than self-control.

"Here's why: we *resist* control because it's imposed, even if it's on our own initiative. Governance is an ability and a competence; it represents a form of ownership and mastery. We *own* self-regulation.

It starts by looking at a courageous Tier 4 Mindset and doing a quick Assessment. Then we'll practice three behaviors. Are you up for that?"

He nodded.

"Mindset isn't merely to suppress drinking or to stop some other form of self-trickery. It's to practice ruling yourself so you can be who you're supposed to be, so you can live at a higher level of life. Self-governance means fearlessly working on yourself, so you can tackle the real problem—something that you can actually control. What do you think that is?"

"Man, if I knew that, I wouldn't have bothered you."

"Hey, Caleb, I'm glad you called. What are the real, genuine things to you? And try to go deeper than even Luna, your daughter, your marriage, your family. Like, it's knowing that regardless of how bad things get, I won't fold to fear, I won't quit doing things right, and I won't take my problems out on myself or on others."

Pause. "Crap, Gus, maybe that's it."

"I think it's a courage standard we could all start with. Caleb, what's the worst mindset—mental attitude—you could have right now?"

"Probably the one I've got."

"And the best one?"

"I don't know."

"The term, 'Tier 4,' means courage. The Tier 4 Mindset is to be stronger than our weaknesses and not to go it alone—get a Battle Buddy. That's in the center of our self-governance and at the heart of proven, long-term, successful weight-loss and alcohol recovery programs.

"Next comes the assessment: if it's really bad right now, get therapy. What do you think about getting a Battle Buddy and going to therapy or a support group?"

"Battle Buddy sounds good. Forget a support group. Therapy sounds like digging out root canals. I don't know. Maybe I need it."

"We'll figure it out. Let's look at this Inventory."

Reader, please join us in checking the items that apply to you.

The Second GO Inventory: Comprehensively Self-govern/ Act with Humility

Check those that apply.

Basic Self-governance to Live Well[44]

☐ I practice a Mindset of courageous transformation instead of willpower and wishpower.

☐ I've recruited reliable Battle Buddies into my daily accountability network.[45]

☐ I'm on a healthier, nutrient-dense diet of lowered sugars, saturated fats, and sodium.[46]

☐ I'm exercising safely at least 30 minutes every other day.

☐ I get up and move every 30–60 minutes.[47]

☐ I am in a healthy sleep hygiene routine.[48]

☐ I don't focus or spend time on my unrealistic worries.

☐ I don't give in to complaining and self-pity.

☐ I reduce stress: slow diaphragmatic (belly) breathing; count to 10; change physical space.[49]

Humility

- ☐ I treat all people as being at least as important as I think I am.
- ☐ My mindset is other-directed and not self-absorbed.
- ☐ I consistently see and then improve my deepest faults in every situation.
- ☐ I graciously accept and take to heart all criticism and negative feedback.
- ☐ I have an active Battle Buddy and am a Battle Buddy to others.

Grit and Gratitude in Self-care

- ☐ I daily express gratitude for the good things in my life.
- ☐ I focus on my strengths and courage and don't listen to negative self-talk.
- ☐ I spend time with positive and healthy people with whom I'm at my best.
- ☐ I celebrate (modestly) my commitment to live well with Battle Buddies and friends.
- ☐ I don't become self-critical if I fall off my commitments; I start fresh, again.
- ☐ I don't lie to or make global judgments about myself if I fall off the plan.
- ☐ I celebrate at the end of every week with one meal that's for pleasure (no gluttony).

Facing Addiction and Bad Habits

- ☐ I've stopped smoking, heavy drinking/drug use, by clinical and/or spiritual help.[50]
- ☐ I'm curtailing non-work screen time.
- ☐ I'm reducing wasting time at work.
- ☐ I'm not defaulting to the 3 NOs.

> **Courage In Self-Care**
>
> ☐ I'm practicing UPR.
> ☐ I'm working on specific challenges (see the following Specific Challenges box).

Each unchecked item offers you the chance to practice new skills. You can insert them into the Comprehensive Self-governance Behavioral Practice schedule, which we'll see shortly.

"Hey," said Caleb, "this is awful. I'm not checking any of the good boxes and checking too many of the negative ones—I'm constantly worrying and punting."

"No, you're not—you're figuring out the real game. You now know what your worries are saying. My worries whisper, 'This is scary; you're weak, you can't cope; quit now.' That's fear using an internal bullhorn brain to pitch lies to your psyche. Best-selling author Tim Keller tells us to stop listening to that so *we* can speak truth and reality to *ourselves*.[51] I call this *Self-talk*. My Self-talk is, 'Stop sniveling and feeling sorry for yourself! Find your guts. You love courage and dislike cowardice. Act courageously. Govern you! Be who you're supposed to be!'"

Silence.

"Caleb, what do you do when a bronc throws you?"

"Partner, now you're using my words against me. Well, heck, you get back on."

"There you go. And why do that?"

"To not be a coward even though, right now, I kind of feel that I am."

"And, Caleb, I think it's to model courage for those around you. And then, when we're tall in the saddle on a fine summer day, we still govern ourselves so we don't get cocky and start thinking that we're above others or that we're Grade A stock."

Caleb's situation was so dire that he quickly admitted his struggle with self-governance, easily hurdling the denial common to most males I know. At the outset, Caleb agreed that he wouldn't physically threaten or hurt anyone, including himself. He agreed to get a therapist and accepted ideas about how to select one wisely. He got it that self-governance is not using wishpower in a sorry attempt to survive this crisis as you wait for the next one. It's to courageously become your best self by practicing the governance of our anxious impulses so that we have space to take our best actions. He saw that self-discipline, self-control, and wishpower carried the unwelcome aromas of pressure, guilt, and failure. Self-governance is restoring our sovereign authority over ourselves.

Caleb became specific: he was drinking too much alcohol and coffee, was aimlessly schmoozing on internet news, entertaining fantasies of doing harm, degrading his body, and starving on junk food while nourishing the 3 NOs as if they were his children.

He would now follow these steps.

1. *Identify your behavioral objectives:* Flex your strength: What behaviors do I need to stop and start to be stronger than my weaknesses? How is my humility?

2. *Prepare for temptations:* What situations or triggers prompt me to become weak? When weak, I have a plan (get with strong people and move fast to better situations). When do I find myself believing my way or my person is better than others'?

3. *Don't let anxiety control your actions:* Face your temptations and fears (*Get back on the horse*) with Battle Buddies who have your interests at heart. Stop selfish ideas by thinking of what it's like to walk in the other person's shoes, such as Luna. You're part of Luna's current situation.

Author Viktor Frankl, who faced a continuing catastrophe, wrote that everything can be taken from us except one precious idea: *"the last of the human freedoms—to choose one's attitude in any given set of circumstances, to choose one's own way."*[52] Despite the desire to get even with others, he flatly refused to give in to anger and hatred.

Self-governance begins with the positive mindset of courage.

The following nonclinical self-care behaviors for particular challenges remind us that courage is moral action. It's neither inaction nor quitting; it's the courage to decisively govern the self and to model it for others. In our self-maintenance, we too frequently quit before we start. West Point teaches young future leaders that doing something is better than being paralyzed by inaction. Command Sergeant Major

Kihara, observing my enjoyment of indecision, said, "Lee, the road of life is filled by very flat squirrels that couldn't make up their minds."

Taking courageous action is superior to habituated paralysis.

These self-care actions can correlate with items in the Self-governance/Act with Humility Inventory.

> ### Specific Challenges
>
> - **You're depressed:** Practice taking small, healthy, and positive movements for 30 seconds, and then a minute; build up to exercise and contact a Battle Buddy to take a short walk together. Look for sunlight or use Seasonal Affective Disorder illumination.
> - **You're caught in self-pity:** Practice helping others instead of complaining and giving thanks for the courage you're gaining and for small favors, and then give thanks for the bigger ones.
> - **You're fatigued:** Cut back nonessential, draining activities to recover energy; practice good sleep hygiene.
> - **You're angry:** Renew your pledge to not give in to anger. Redo your Second NO process with Battle Buddies.
> - **You have a bad diet:** Start by replacing one junk food item with something healthy. Eat healthy vegetables/proteins/foods slowly, with appreciation, at the right times.

Here is your nine-week behavioral practice schedule (Figure 3.3). As always, it's strongly recommended that you don't do this alone. Partner up with a strong Battle Buddy who sees your behaviors on a regular basis and will give you reliably candid feedback.[53] When you start a new week's behaviors, please continue to practice the behaviors of the preceding weeks.

Battle Buddies work differently with you in the 3 GOs than they do with the NOs. They affirmatively promote the GOs by catching you doing the right thing—and you do the same for them. Ken Blanchard wrote a whole book on this.[54] So the Battle Buddy looks for positive and courageous behaviors and verbally acknowledges them, doing this as soon as is appropriate.

Caleb spent a week finding a competent therapist and a Battle Buddy. He spent three tough months in counseling while following the weekly schedule to practice the Comprehensive Self-governance Inventory behaviors. He found that (a) his Battle Buddy began to see his own issues and bravely cleaned up his own marriage, and (b) by cutting down on sugar—no colas, sweetened drinks, flavored yogurts with high sugar content—he'd lost 40 pounds. He was back in the gym, got up from his desk every 30 minutes, and said his horses are enjoying carrying a lighter Caleb P. Novak.

He told himself that if Luna could deliver a baby, then he could stop acting like one. He took a year to pull himself up from the pit. He did the heavy lifting of forgiving Luna, despite the divorce, and is demonstrating UPR to her boyfriends.

"Governing me brought back my life and my relationship with my daughter." After a long break, he's in a new and stronger relationship; the two have taken jobs that require less time apart from each other.

Most of us, like Caleb, are endowed with basic intelligence. But unlike him, many must discover in hard and painful ways that intelligence and experience don't equate to the courage of self-governance. We need that ability to thrive in a difficult world that mercilessly markets to our weaknesses and begs us to become shamelessly self-indulgent. Caleb's now helping guys in his men's support group to exercise better behaviors so they can be better and stronger people for the people in their lives.

Caleb had learned that practicing UPR toward the people who troubled him fortified his self-governance. And that UPR and self-governance strengthen an ability he didn't even think of as a measure of human competence: Humility.

Practicing self-governance and acting with humility, you're equipped for our third and final GO: Discern, Act, and Train Others in the Highest Moral Action.

√	WEEK	
	1	I practice a mindset of being other-directed and not self-absorbed as evidenced by my treatment of other people as being at least as important as I think I am.
	2	I consistently see and then improve my deepest faults in every situation.
	3	I graciously accept and take to heart all criticism and negative feedback.
	4	I replace junk food and poor sleep with healthy food, exercise, and good sleep hygiene.
	5	I govern my emotions even when highly stressed or anxious.
	6	I learn from my mistakes and do not repeat them.
	7	I govern my negative feelings that I've guarded for particular groups and people; I practice being positive instead of negative.
	8	I change the behaviors my spouse/S.O. most wishes me to change. I stop smoking, alcohol/drugs, and screens, and get required professional help.
	9	Spiritual Practices: gratitude & forgiveness. Reflect daily on the good things of life. Practice forgiving in small ways. Courageously forgive in larger ways.

Figure 3.3   Comprehensive Self-governance/Act with Humility Behavioral Practice

The Third GO: Discern | Act | Train Others in the Highest Moral Action "DAT"

"The time is always right to do the right thing."

—*Dr. Martin Luther King Jr.*[55]

A small part of courage is discerning that problems are the first forms of our best answers. As a deputy district attorney wrestling with trial tactics, I asked the help of my law school mentor, Professor Emeritus Edgar Bodenheimer. I have previously described Edgar's humility which, contrary to his hopes, had drawn rave reviews. He generously set down his pen and we left the quiet law school library for the shaded stillness of the creekside courtyard. Nearby was Lisa Reinertson's striking terracotta statue of Dr. Martin Luther King Jr., for whom our school is named. His life-size figure purposefully strides forward to answer his calling.

Edgar waited with a scholar's ageless eyes.

"The victim's a young girl," I said. "Small, vulnerable, an abandoned street kid, too traumatized to speak, much less testify. She's terrified of even seeing the defendant again. He's a total monster." I paused, wanting him to get it. "I actually hate him. I think about how you must've hated those Nazi defendants."

Edgar had escaped Hitler's holocaust before Nazi Germany murdered 21 million people; six million were Jews, including every member of his family. At the end of World War II, Edgar ironically became a Nuremberg prosecutor, trying Nazi leaders for epic crimes against humanity. Later, he joined the faculty of King Hall, University of California at Davis.

Now he was silent, as if an unprepared student had suggested the wrong case law to an easy question.

"There was," he said softly, "a man who had three unsurpassed abilities." Edgar, a giant in jurisprudence, was not physically tall. He looked up, eyes sharp, illuminated in memory.

"Hitler's talents were *fear, anger* and *hate*. He used them to set fire to the world, to feed his malignant heart and to destroy innocents. I escaped to America to teach the unchanging moral principles of natural law and human conduct with, shall we say, new meaning."

He smiled as if we were discussing the pruning of roses. "I was summoned to Nuremberg to practice those moral principles in a grand test for the world. Was not my task to align the reality of my life with the theory of my lectures?

"And so, prosecuting his henchmen at Nuremberg, remembering the endless dead, I burned with fear, anger, and hate—I was *becoming* the character of *Herr Hitler*. Something stopped me at the tall doors of the *Justizpalast. What of my love for virtue ethics?*"

I was holding my breath.

"I said to myself, 'Edgar, you have an important job. Do not imitate the actions of criminals. You must know and then do *the most right thing* despite feelings, regardless of outcome. You will respect those that hate you and not permit their brokenness to break you."

Edgar was discussing his past as a way to ask who I was.

He patted me. "You will use your energy correctly. I am certain you will be all right."

I'd respected thousands of criminal defendants in military courts and civilian trials. But this one was different. Our precious, one-year-old daughter had just died from heart disease; I was broken, twisted by loss, my courage insufficient to keep my backbone from melting into moral mush, and I had just recovered from drinking without a hint of self-regulation. I detested this defendant who'd broken the heart and life of another innocent girl. I had become, per Emma Pattee, another freaked-out Neanderthal ready to fight.

I felt justified and even noble by loathing him, as if hatred and internal screaming would restore the wounded and heal the living. But sitting with Edgar Bodenheimer, I'd experienced our Third GO. He'd recognized his instinctive reactions to human wrongs, discerned how to live out his high principles, and in that manner, conducted himself in the trial.

He'd taught me to do the same through my own long jury trial with hundreds of moving parts, great stakes, and surging emotions that made my heart pound. I stopped bleeding off energy into anger and depression. I listened and thought more effectively and asked more insightful questions so witnesses could testify more bravely. A clarity and new possibilities returned to the courtroom and even the world. I treated the defendant with what I'd come to call UPR—the respect due to all human beings in all circumstances. Not to win, although I fervently sought it, but to act rightly.[56]

Whether we're in Courtroom 600 of the Palace of Justice's Nuremberg trials, or Courtroom 29 of the Sacramento County Superior Court, or in our own difficult version of Orwell's Room 101 in *1984*, it is the right time to do the right thing, regardless of the outcome.

As few of us face tyrants or criminals for a living, do we really need to put energy into doing the right thing? Further, can we actually agree on things that we consider to be universally right?

Moral relativism sees the world differently, holding to "the idea that there is no universal or absolute set of moral principles. It's a version of morality that advocates 'to each her own'. . . 'When in Rome, do as the Romans do.'"[57] Executives I've coached and trained and graduate students I've taught have similarly stated, "Morality probably depends on circumstances"; "We're all different"; "Live and let live"; "We can't impose our standards on others"; "We can do anything as long as it doesn't harm others"; and the thunderbolt query of relativism, "Who am I to judge what others do?"

But surveys reveal that we continuously judge others: 90 percent of moms and 85 percent of dads feel judged; half feel they're being judged nearly all the time;[58] 80 percent of Americans make judgments about others based on looks; 41 percent of Millennials, 28 percent of Gen Xers, and 20 percent of Baby Boomers, in pure *schadenfreude*, feel better about themselves when someone else looks bad.[59] Forty percent of American grocery shoppers use self-checkout to avoid others judging their purchases.[60]

In the last year, 82 percent of Americans disapproved of how Congress does its job.[61] So we ask, "Who am I to judge" and answer it with a resounding, *all of us!* We say we cannot impose standards on others, and yet we do so every day if not every hour, with a focus on looks, which are temporary, instead of on courage, which profoundly determines our fates. So is there a universal, human right and wrong? Or does it transform its nature in the winds of society and culture?

In the humility section we considered Hofstede's cultural studies (Hofstede, 2006).[62] Wharton School's Robert J. House, referencing that work, led Project GLOBE[63] to measure differences in leadership cultures. Its quantitative instruments, international coordinating body, 170 indigenous researchers in 62 world cultures, and survey of 17,000 middle managers in nearly a thousand organizations qualified it as a valid UN international study.

Instead of finding differing principles, GLOBE discovered human commonalities in values.[64] It clearly revealed qualities of courage and character, as captured in Figure 3.4.[65]

This parallels Stanford's profitability research (Collins, 1994; 2001), which found the reasons that a few Fortune 500 companies made 1500 percent more in profits than the market for a century. Expecting the answer to be brains, risk, innovation, or technology, they found it to be the courage and humility in a small number of effective leaders. No subsequent studies have invalidated the Stanford or Project GLOBE's findings.[66] These scientific studies haven't named moral idealism the victor, but they prepare us to see the validity of our Third GO on our journey to courage.

ADMIRED ("RIGHT?")	NOT ADMIRED ("WRONG?")
Relational	Egocentric
Encouraging	Dictatorial
Honest	Ruthless
Trustworthy	Not trustworthy (added by author)
Dependable	Unpredictable
Communicative	Asocial/Loner
Cooperative	Uncooperative
Positive	Irritable

Figure 3.4   Project GLOBE Leadership Characteristics
Source: Table by the author.

The *Playbook*, consistent with the preceding uncontested data, is premised on the belief that across America's many subcultures and its conflicts, most of us would agree with the following (Figure 3.5):

Most of us would rather be:	Instead of:
Courageous	Fearful
Respectful	Biased
Self-governed	Inconsistent
Humble	Self-absorbed
Doing the right thing	Not doing the right thing
Admiring courageous individuals	Admiring cowardly and selfish individuals
Able to know the right thing to do	Unable to know the right thing to do
Able to do the right thing even when anxious	Unable to do the right thing because of fear

Figure 3.5   Observations

Twentieth-century social scientists Jean Piaget and Lawrence Kohlberg researched stages of moral development. University of Minnesota Professor and moral psychologist James Rest helped found the Center for Ethical Development and followed up Kohlberg's work.

Rest identified Four Components of Moral Behavior. Scan the stages below and check where you are right now.

Stage 1: Moral Sensitivity: I see specific courses of action and their effect on others.

Stage 2: Moral Judgment: I judge which action is right and decide what to do.

Stage 3: Moral Motivation: I choose moral values over personal values.

Stage 4: Moral Character: I have the courage and strength to carry out the moral intention.[67]

Rest identified that our greatest challenge and toughest moral battleground is rising above our natural and powerful self-interest. To do that, we need the independent self-regulation of Stage 4 to actually own the moral courage to do the right thing.[68] *The Playbook* brings us a process to do this in our Third GO:

Our Third GO, like the number of primary colors, has three parts:

I. *Discern the Highest Moral Action* despite feelings, anxiety, biases or previous history

II. *Act—Do—the Highest Moral Action*—regardless of risk to self or outcome

III. *Train others in discerning and doing the Highest Moral Action*

How might you use our Third GO's three parts of DISCERN, ACT, and TRAIN? We begin with Discern.

I. *Discern the Highest Moral Action despite feelings, anxiety, bias, or previous history.*

"He who knows others is clever; he who knows himself has discernment."

—*Laozi*[69]

In courage, discernment means to reason in the moral frame to know what is most right. The roots of this key human action come from a host of words in three languages which mean to *sort, sift, separate, and choose the truth. . . and decide on the indisputable.*[70] Accordingly, in Tier 4, we eliminated lesser choices to see "the most right thing."

Since writing *Courage: The Backbone of Leadership*, my work with more diverse people and organizations has led to framing "the most right thing" as a practiced concept I call the Highest Moral Action (HMA).

Courageous Discernment of the HMA has four considerations:

- Consult the conscience
- Question your prejudices and personal needs
- Consult with Wise Friends
- Morally reason

Consult the Conscience

"The conscience," wrote author Carlo Collodi, "is that still small voice that people won't listen to."[71] Conscience, per the Oxford English Dictionary, is a *"person's moral sense of right and wrong, viewed as acting as a guide to one's behaviour."* The American version says it is "an inner feeling or voice viewed as acting as a guide to the rightness or wrongness of one's behavior."[72] The word comes from Anglo-French *science, cience,* from the Latin *scientia,* which means knowledge, awareness, and understanding; and from the Latin *conscient, consciens,* to be conscious of guilt.[73] There are many complex and deeply meaningful words to describe the small, inner voice that has proven to be one of my most reliable companions.

Consulting conscience is a radical step, for it leads us to not attempt reasoning based on feelings, fear, and the habits of negative history without first framing thought in what is right.

Research at Yale by Professor Paul Bloom and Karen Wynn, his wife, led to a startling conclusion: "We are *naturally moral beings* (emphasis added), but our environments can enhance—or, sadly, degrade—this innate moral sense.[74] Thus, contrary to the thinking of many in an age of sensitivity, we may not be primarily "emotional creatures," and when we ignore our conscience, we pay a cost in many ways.

We can strengthen conscience by simply thinking about what is right. MIT and Duke Professor Daniel Ariely's experiments at UCLA, MIT, and Carnegie-Mellon found that given the opportunity to cheat, over 70 percent of our students did so.

When students in identically formed cohorts were reminded of honor-related rules before an exam, Ariely was surprised *that cheating dropped to zero*.[75] It is upon this theory that the best institutions emphasize doing the right thing before projects are initiated. It is a reason for *The Playbook*.

In my generation, many relied on conscience, the "referee of the soul," to grant us a steady authority to not cave in to temptation. My generation may be the last link to this practice. When Edgar Bodenheimer related his struggle with self-governance, my conscience said, *Do not hate your defendant*.

I believe a practiced conscience can indicate the Highest Moral Action.

Question Your Prejudices and Personal Needs

"Prejudice," wrote Maya Angelou, "is a burden that confuses the past, threatens the future, and renders the present inaccessible."[76] Prejudice means forming a prejudgment that harms others. Research has made it very clear that we begin judging others at infancy and stick with it until it becomes a deeply ingrained habit. Overcoming our built-in and acquired biases takes practice biases.

We tend to have many personal needs. Purposefully setting them aside to clearly see what's happening to people around us is an integral part of advancing our humanity. Because you've stopped the Three NOs, this will be easier now than it might have been earlier.

In the second element of Discernment, we begin by candidly listing the prejudgments to which we default in a given situation and identifying our deep and superficial personal needs that would cloud our good judgment. We then practice (1) frankly acknowledging their existence and their power to misdirect us, and (2) setting them aside as we discern.

Consult and Imitate Wise Friends

Neighbors can be helpful, but a wise friend's counsel and modeling are priceless. As a kid I copied my pal Toussaint Streat and imitated Coach Tony. In high school, my principled English teacher, Mrs. Marshall, consulted with my coaches and employed their advice to help me overcome my fear of writing. In the Army I tried to measure up to Infantry NCOs and officers and leaders Theodore L. Dobol, Charles A. Murray, and H. Norman Schwarzkopf. Doing criminal jury trials, I imitated the deeply discerning Edgar Bodenheimer.

We likewise can build selfless relationships with those who are wise. Who are they? They're not self-absorbed and don't deny their weaknesses. They don't do the 3 NOs. They care about people instead of exploiting them; honor all persons; govern their emotions; take responsibility; don't seek credit; learn from their mistakes; and don't mess up their lives with Tier 1, 2, and 3 habits. They strive to morally reason, listen to their conscience, and do the most right thing. They find and cultivate wise friends. Oh, and, regardless of transient circumstances and even deep losses, they're truly happy.

Morally Reason to Identify the Highest Moral Action

Logic and reason are required in education but have been used to justify moral outrages and to harm and exploit others.[77] Intelligent criminals offer well-reasoned answers for their crimes. Nazi Germany was "Europe's most cultivated, best-educated country (with) the world's. . . highest literacy rate and best universities" and annually published more books than any country in the world.[78] Later, well-educated Germans gave logical reasons for supporting Hitler and Nazism.[79]

In figuring out what action to take, it's important to accept an uncomfortable truth: logic, reason, and critical thinking—though they be vastly powerful and deeply influential—are morally neutral. That glaring neutrality means that they are and have been employed to produce disastrously inhumane decisions and outcomes.

Each of these qualities logically uses evidence. But reflect for a moment on the fact they organically lack a filter that requires that the evidence and its use be ethical or moral. This invites the worst of our biases and our politics.

Discernment is radically different from our daily and academic manners of thought. As their cousin, it begins with logic and reason but then exceeds both to become *moral critical thinking.* Importantly, discernment seeks to identify the HMA. It takes courage to do this and character to do it consistently. Discernment is a challenging and pure form of truth-seeking.

More complex institutional issues require consultation with varied wise counsel. For example, hospital ethics committees are multidisciplinary bodies that use a discernment process to make difficult holistic medical recommendations. They consider the patient, family, therapies, legal issues, and guiding policies. Many voices are considered to determine the HMA.

> II. *Do the Highest Moral Action regardless of risk to self-interest or outcome.*

"Always do the right thing no matter what others say. It is you, not them, who have to face the consequences."[80]

—*Leon Brown, professional ball player*

For a few years, I gave a two-week Courage Training Intensive at Colorado State University. The first cohort included talented graduate students from all over the country and from foreign countries, dominated by Africa. The year 2021 marked the tenth anniversary of that class and a few traveled to visit me.

"We're still using takeaways from your course," said Christie Jorgenson,[81] an overseas environmental services technology leader and faculty member. "I was teaching grad students on an environmental survey project. Some students fudged data to meet their hypotheses. I used Buddy Checks and they stopped. Except for one guy. I said I'd have to fail him if he kept cheating."

"There's always one," said Seth Crooks (actual name), also in environmental sciences.

Christine continued, "He says to me, 'It's your word against mine. Go for it. I'm not afraid of you. The department chair likes me. She won't hurt me. She will get rid of *you.*'

"I got that hormonal zing of fear you trained us to expect. Like, I *would* be in trouble with the chair. So I did the breathing, UPR, was Warm, Open, Welcoming, exhaled fear and inhaled courage [we'll learn this in the next Step]. This student is a big guy who tries charm and then pushes his size on you. I kept calm and told him we all had to do the right thing. He snorted at me and kept fabricating data.

"I remembered, *Discern the Highest Moral Action despite feelings, anxiety, bias, or history of habits.* I had a lot of feelings, all negative, including anger against a big bully. I breathed them away and moved to *Do the Highest Moral Action regardless of risk to self or outcome.*

"Christie," said Seth, "I'll repeat what I told you before—you did good!"

"I'm proud of you, too, Christie," I said.

"Thanks, guys," she said. "I had to fail him. The department chair called me to say 'It looks bad to fail a graduate student. It is worse for our reputation if the reasons got out. Give him a passing grade. I will take care of any possible complications.'"

"Gus," said Christie, "You taught us to not be surprised when people lie to get their way. But I was just shocked. I said, 'I must not have been clear. This student used falsified data from the start. His work is fabricated, false, made-up. It's not science, it's fiction.'

"The student got his degree and a job. The chair didn't renew my faculty contract. I felt sorry for myself until I realized that I couldn't work for her or a dishonest program. So what hurt was that zing to my pride. I'd done the HMA, a couple times, where my natural instinct would've been to let cheating happen. But I didn't train others."

"You just trained me," said Seth.

"And me, and others in your new and better job," I added. "Thank you for a great story about courage. Regardless of short-term outcomes, because it's courageous, it's still positive. It's also an unforgettable inspiration for everyone who hears it. You freed yourself from fear, an unhealthy place, and now have a much better job with a good boss and colleagues."

"My only worry," she said, "is that I didn't do enough about a university that allows the use of fictional 'science.'"

"You did," I said, "more than anyone else in that setting. Sadly, cheating is a carry-through habit that goes from universities into the scientific community. You did good."[82]

Knowing the right thing to do is easier than *doing* it. Christie had done even more than mere *knowing*; she had first overcome the even greater challenge of courageously acknowledging—now rare in our culture—that there even *existed* a better and right thing to do. For Dr. Paul Brand finds that Americans will do almost anything to avoid even the slightest pain. Author Lolly Daskal discovered that "most of us will do anything to avoid facing ourselves."[83] Thus, Kerry Patterson reports that 95 percent of us avoid conflict—we run from fear.[84] Few of us discern, meaning that only a minority are actually doing the HMA.

Acting rightly sounds like jumping out of an airplane at night with a hundred pounds on your back, but once you know that it hurts you and others to do a thing incorrectly, and once you've discerned the right action, it can become as simple and straightforward as getting out of bed in the morning. It's a practiced behavior.

Let's get to the basics of DOING by answering FAQs about doing the HMA:

"*But doesn't doing the 'right thing' take away from results?*" We fear failure and focus on our losses, but when we improve the self and others by focusing and doing the right thing. We saw that profitability research reported that the Fortune 500 companies that did the right thing in business produced 1500 percent more in earnings than did the general market over nearly a hundred years. A parallel study on government agencies and nonprofits generated the same results.[85] The uncontested scientific evidence is that doing the right thing multiplies results. The habit of doing the right thing generates better outcomes than selfishness, but that is not why courageous people do it. Then what drives them?

The world-shaking answer is that they act with integrity *because* it's the right thing to do.

"*How can you expect anyone to do the right thing **regardless of risk to self-interest or outcome**? Isn't that an oxymoron?*" Christie Jorgensen's peers worried for her when she spoke respectfully to the cheating grad student. She felt anxiety but did not act anxiously during her forthright dialogues with him and the department chair. But when the brief emotional storm passed, she felt stronger and more confident than before, and the zing of anxiety was a memory. Some of Christie's colleagues can now imagine being as courageous as she.

If you don't have the habit of doing this, first attempts can produce doubt and short-term results can stink (management doesn't do anything, bad conduct continues, you get fired). But addressing errors, whatever the outcome, morally aids people in need. It strengthens our most crucial competence of courage; advances character; elevates organizational culture, however minutely; and inspires others to find the courage so they can be their best selves. We then, like Samwise Gamgee, find ourselves with a newfound strength that neither despair nor weariness nor endless barren miles can subdue.

Problems multiply like viruses. How can addressing them while many remain silent actually serve our "self-interest"? The benefit is initially invisible, for it takes place in the deepest and most real way by giving us an internal courage. We see that short-term and strategic results and happiness aren't the motivation; they are but logical by-products of living rightly.

"*Aren't we supposed to pick our battles? We can't physically fight every battle.*" A Trigger Bill saying from the Old West is, "All fires are the same size at the start,"[86] which joins Benjamin Franklin's *Almanack* aphorism, "A stitch in time saves nine."[87] In other words, *act*.

Our anxieties translate the term, "picking battles," into nervous inaction. Discernment, conscience, and wise friends join experience to (a) engage quickly in moral dilemmas that arise within your reach; (b) begin small, to gain experience for larger and more complex issues; (c) focus on what you can directly affect and don't be disabled by the vast and perpetual problems of humanity.

"*What if we don't have time to discern and just have to react?*" Discerned action helps us navigate between impulsive avoidance and aggressive overreaction. Part of courage is having excellent situational awareness and sufficient wisdom to know that people and events usually surprise us if we're mentally, emotionally, and spiritually unprepared.[88] Courageous individuals think ahead to anticipate, plan, and be prepared for the unexpected. This begins by being aware of your environment with a calmness that knows no nervousness.

If you know you're going into a volatile situation, you can estimate that three things might happen (good, bad, or worse), and you can prepare for each.

Unfamiliar things seem to move too fast; this is evident in tennis and in war. The more you plan, the more time will slow down for you to discern the HMA in a time-sensitive situation.

The entire theme of courage is that it is acquired by practice. The more you practice, the easier it is, to quote camping leader Frank Cheley, "to act spontaneously in the right."[89]

"Isn't it okay to run away to fight another day?" This is a statement best applied to war, physical combat, and facing certain street crimes. In war, fighting withdrawals are a recognized tactic. But in moral human relations, it becomes cowardice. We make too much of our fears and allow them to defeat our courage before we even step onto the field of play.

"What if I'm just not that courageous?" None of us are. Want to bike or play the piano? Practice it. Want to be more courageous? Practice its behaviors. We all need more courage.

III. *Train Others to Do the Highest Moral Action.*

"Starbucks is not an advertiser. . . in fact we spend very little money on marketing and more money on training our people than advertising."[90]

—*Howard Schultz, former chairman and CEO, Starbucks*

It's natural to hoard special knowledge for ourselves. But if we squirrel away the behaviors of courage and of character competence for our own use, we instantly defeat their purpose. Not sharing courageous ability is akin to a physician withholding needed pain medications—it's organically incorrect. We gain courage not to edify or advance ourselves; we do so to equip others to also be courageous. Courage is a relational, social, communal, and human resource. Kept to ourselves, it's now something, but it's no longer courage.

So how do we train others? There are countless ways.

A reminder: teaching or training someone else in a new skill soon after you've learned it imprints the learning into your memory. With courage, it imprints into your character.[91]

Ask questions. Ask someone how they did in a difficult situation. Do you wish you could've done something different? What might that look like? What would the most courageous person you know have done? What good might've come from that? What stopped you from doing a similar thing? What was the result of not doing it? How did *not* doing it have an impact on you and others? We'll see more of asking OEQs, Open Ended Questions, in Step Four.

Storytelling. Christie used the classic method: tell stories of how we overcame fear, stopped a NO, did a GO, discerned and did the HMA, and how you felt after reflection. This differs from gossip, the point of which is to make someone look bad. Christie didn't use any names and didn't name the university; she made the Tier 4 Mindfulness pivot from blaming others to correcting her own fears. She then advocated doing the right thing in the face of risks. Not long before, she saw herself as a person who was incapable of becoming who she was supposed to be—her admirably courageous self.

Buddy Checking. You can ask open-ended questions of people in your accountability network. You see your Buddy is struggling so you ask questions and walk alongside that person. Ask if they'd like some thoughts or tips from you; ask them for inputs on matters with which you quietly struggle. Help sustain courage improvement for both of you. Expand your Buddy Check network to enlist more courage, strength, and wisdom into your circle.

Get trained. Become a dynamic skills trainer. I secretly hated public speaking. I hired ExecuProv in Santa Ana, California,[92] to train me as a trainer, public speaker, and communicator, and to then train my trainers in prosecution, health care, and at West Point. To train me, Cherie Kerr, ExecuProv's CEO, filmed me. "How could you have improved that specific part?" she asked. She leveraged my answer to add, from language, body movement, and mostly, my difficulty in smiling; I was a frowner. I realized I knew very little about public speaking and had much to change in a lifelong process of improvement.

Training. Use *The Playbook*'s Five Steps to walk someone through a courage training for their particular challenge.

Read *The Courage Playbook* in a study group of Battle Buddies, family, friends, and coworkers and follow the Five Steps as a community both for practice and for an enjoyable and comradely accountability.

Our Third GO Inventory: Discern the HMA | Do the HMA | Train in the HMA

Third GO Inventory

Check those that apply to you.

☐ I heed my conscience, "the referee of my soul," about doing the right thing.

☐ I consider my definition of "moral." What are immutable human values?

☐ I practice discerning the Highest Moral Action.

☐ I consult wise people about the HMA and about how to do it.

☐ I practice doing the HMA.

☐ I have begun encouraging others to figure out the highest right and then to do it.

☐ I get it that Discerning, Doing, and Training in the HMA is a lifelong process.

As always, it's best if you do the following month-long practice (Figure 3.6) with a strong Battle Buddy who sees your behaviors on a regular basis and will give you reliably candid feedback. As you start a new week's behaviors, continue to practice the behaviors of the preceding weeks.

We all recognize the evils of injustice and the automatic, avoidant reflex of looking the other way. Thus, personally, we are to stop avoiding and instead practice doing the right thing when we witness unjust behaviors. Acting rightly has always been essential to the well-being and even safety of others. Because it is now increasingly rare, doing the HMA has become more vital.

Our Third GO reminds us that we have choices.

Discerning the Highest Moral Action despite feelings; doing the HMA despite risks; and training others in the HMA without biases

√	WEEKS	
	1	I practice listening to my conscience before I speak, act, or decide.
	2	I practice doing the Highest Moral Action | I log my HM Actions and outcomes.
	3	I review my Highest Moral Actions log | I record Lessons Learned.
	4	I improve doing 1–3 | I encourage others to discern and do the HMA.

Figure 3.6   Discern HMA | Do HMA | Train Others to Do the HMA

is a fitting capstone for the 3 GOs. It also adds to the abilities, human competence, moral contentment, and happiness of others and yourself.

Many of us struggle to say what we mean and instead foul up the content and the delivery. We can also unintentionally convey the wrong emotional message. It's one of the big reasons most of us choose to avoid conflict.

That's why we have Steps Four and Five.

Think of the 3 GOs as the basic operating principles in humanity's game of courage. Our ability to apply them shapes the nature of our narrative, affects the lifelines of our story, and informs our identity.

In our next two Steps, we'll use the GOs in lifelike situations with basic and conflict communication plays.

PART

II

Courage with Others

"We cannot solve our problems with the same level of thinking that created them."

—*Albert Einstein*[1]

EINSTEIN MERELY FIGURED out the theory of relativity; you're solving the larger question of who you're going to become. You have deleted negative bugs from your hard drive; on a now-clean disc you can apply principles of courage in doing what occupies most of our waking hours—communicate. To be more accurate, I should say: we *attempt* to communicate.

Communication works better when we do it intentionally instead of casually tossing words about like they were someone else's money. Well-capitalized companies are at existential risk when they must rely on search engines to find the right words to lead and treat people as people instead of things. Pro football teams tank because owners fall into corporate-speak and miscommunicate with general managers as GMs misfire with head coaches, and coaches are too stressed to listen to their players. Then come families, needy friends, and the media.

That's why teams, politicians, and organizations hire public relations professionals to speak for them.

In a context of courage, are there Plays to connect people, keep them linked and cut down the natural sparking of conflicts? When discord happens anyway—after all, we are talking about people—are there courageous communication Plays to help us address them in practical ways?

Rather than sparking discord and aggravating existing antagonism, are there ways that we can lessen the chance of conflicts before they erupt? Instead of accelerating the damage produced by conflict, can we lessen their harm once they've begun? Instead of retreating in sullen anger and hostility, can we repair broken relationships and strengthen others in the aftermath of conflict?[2] This is Courageous Communication, or CourCom. It is a new level of thinking to solve a problem of our own making.

It relies on one premise and two Playsets.

The premise and operating assumption is that we always start and end with Unconditional Positive Respect.

Our first Playset is Basic CourCom. This enables us to become spellbound listeners, solve problems effectively, and not do harm in everyday interactions.

Our second Playset is CourCom for Conflicts. Here, even in a dumpster fire, we can synch up with the other person to truly connect when it really counts.

4

Step Four: Playsets for Basic CourCom

CALEB NOVAK'S NOT feeling it. He texted: talk now. We conferenced by video.

"I don't hate my ex. I quit alcohol and junk food. I don't criticize myself or feel sorry for myself. I'm working. I'm cool with my daughter and have a girlfriend. But it's still a big hassle."

"What's wrong, Caleb?"

"Danielle, the girlfriend, doesn't make sense. We, we argue all the time."

Let's remember that we spend 80% of our waking hours communicating[1] and that we get more training on bike assembly than we do on how to talk to each other. So we fail to listen, get distracted, misspeak, misunderstand, bruise sensitive feelings, cause relationship crises, job loss, social failures, and far worse. We're like a living documentary on How Not to Chat.

You may conclude that we lack a reliable way to talk to each other about real stuff. Studies show that most of our work outcomes, marriages, and relationships fail because of poor communication while effective communication drives most of our successes.[2]

123

Despite evidence about the centrality of communication, we seldom think out what effective dialogue actually looks like. In our daily football-like scrimmages, we forget the plays, misread signals, fumble handoffs, make verbal errors, cause injuries, and get hurt while trying to discuss heavy stuff like where to eat, what to do, who does what when, whom to see, whom to avoid. Then come the win-or-go-home playoffs: pets, expenses, sex, entertainment, screens, games, cohabiting, families, children, marriage, and friends who seem to live on your couch.

Caleb continued, "She says I don't talk to her, work too much, and watch too much TV. She doesn't like how I eat. It sucks."

"I'm sorry to hear that. Caleb, do you remember your Tier 4 Pivot?"

He flipped through his journal and read, "Courage starts with me. Don't burn up my energy trying to change the other person. Improve myself first, to do the right thing."

"You did that in a cool way with your ex. What would that look like with Danielle?"

"I guess I'd talk more. Not get salty. I tried that and she still trashes me."

"I think you're ready to practice three Basic CourCom Plays."

"Will they fix all my problems?"

"Probably not. But they'll stop you from creating new ones. We need practical relational Plays that will safely allow us to engage in the simple hazards of routine conversations.

Three Basic CourCom Plays for Common Situations

1. The CLEAR Communication Model: The Swiss Army knife of relating to people.
2. Encourage Others: Giving what we all require to do better at everything.
3. Ask Challenges: Using the power of open-ended questions to help everyone.

The First Basic CourCom Play: CLEAR—The Central CourCom Model

"The single biggest problem in communication is the illusion that it has taken place."

—George Bernard Shaw[3]

Effective dialogue begins with the Swiss Army knife of communication: the CLEAR Play.[4]

CLEAR eliminates our common dialogue errors and ensures that we then do it right. It's no big deal, but CLEAR can simply prevent hurt feelings, resentments, broken relationships, and conflicts.

It invites true UPR, thoughtfulness and intimacy, builds trust, deepens love, and creates meaning. It lets you do the HMA 20 times a day for those that matter most to you—and to those you don't even like.

"Caleb, CLEAR is an acronym of five vital parts. Each builds your courage. Are you still using UPR at work?"

He nodded.

"Are you using UPR with Danielle?" He shook his head.

"Well, you're halfway there. Before trying one of the most dangerous, gut-twisting, heart-pounding, and death-defying stunts in the world—talking to your significant other—don't let a word escape your mouth before you turn on your UPR.

"Caleb, I can't overemphasize the need to actively use it. Whenever I or anyone else uses CLEAR, or any communication without UPR, it's a fail. Unconditional Positive Respect is the way that courage wraps around everything we do.

"Then you can use CLEAR to authentically connect with Danielle and be better understood yourself without setting fires. You can enjoy being with her.

"It opens and closes on Collegiality and the Relationship.

"In the middle are the core elements: Listen, Empathy, and Ask Questions."

> ## CLEAR—The Central CourCom Model
>
> **C:** Collegiality, open with UPR. Prepare to communicate positively.
>
> **L:** *Listen actively. Be a sincere, attentive, spellbound listener.*
>
> **E:** *Empathy. Capture the other person's feelings as if they are **the most important person in the world.***
>
> **A:** *Ask open-ended questions to fully understand the other person in important moments.*
>
> **R:** Close on the Relationship that connects you.

"CLEAR is really useful when I feel that gravitational pull to seek comfort and approval instead of improving myself and how I connect to people. It reduces the chance of sparring and resentment. It improves life and is probably an excellent shampoo and floor wax."

"Well, bring it on, partner," he said. "I always needed a better floor wax."

- "The 'C' in CLEAR is for *Collegiality*—caring, cooperation, comradeship. Start with UPR and *open on Collegial Caring*. You're WOW: warm, open, and welcoming. Don't 'fake it 'til you make it'—a regrettable expression that demeans how we acquire skills. Imagine 'faking' during CPR training or truck driving lessons. Practice being totally present even if your mind wants to go north to Alaska. Don't be a downer for your daughter or Danielle. You're warm and open."

Caleb wrote as he said, "UPR. Open on Collegiality. WOW. Don't be a downer."

- "Next, 'L' is for *Listen*. It's not listening to a podcast; it's being a *Spellbound Listener, totally focused, undistracted, no screens*. No 'I'm kind of paying attention,' like you're schmoozing in a car wash; this is an all-out, *total attentiveness*.

"Focus to get the gist, her meaning, and you remember the details. You have to do this. It means intentionally deploying every antenna and switching on all your receivers. Danielle says five things and adds, 'I love it when you give me a foot rub,' and you were actually listening. So you lock it into your memory. With lots of details and events for the calendar, write it down in the moment and you'll remember to do what she loves instead of hurt her by actually not knowing her.

"Our daughter gave my wife a small, fill-in-the-blanks book called *50 Things About My Mother: A Celebration.*[5] Her entries in the book showed that she really loved her mom because she'd been always alert to who she really was and what she loved and valued in life. She knew big facts and small details of her life. You can do the same thing for Danielle."

Caleb took notes. "Okay, got it. Man, this is not easy. What's the 'E' for?"

- "**E**' is for Empathy. Practice *being aware of and sensitive to how others feel*, especially your daughter and Danielle. Emotions count, right?"

"I kind of get that feeling."

"Even when the other person doesn't spell it out, figure it out. Empathy's like reading trail signs. Read her signs like you read the guys at work—is she in a good space? Treat the other person as TMIPITW— the most important person in the world—like the best engineer or bronc buster on the planet. Be keyed in and don't detach because there are 'too many feelings.'

"Courageous Empathy means not fearing Danielle's emotions. Doing this is an acquired skill."

"Funny. Danielle says I don't have empathy. How long will it take for me to pick it up?"

"Caleb, look at me. What am I feeling right now?"

"Hell, man, I don't know. Oh, I got it—you got that smile that says you think I know how to do it."

"See? You just used empathy. It's not mind reading or a magic trick. We used to think it was an inherited trait but research confirmed it's a learnable and acquired ability.[6] What's our next letter?"

"'A.' Antelope or armadillo. I'd guess armadillo." He made me laugh.

- "**A** is *Ask Open-ended Questions*. Relate your questions to what she just said. If Danielle says, 'I'd like to do something different,' don't say, 'When can I go the gym?' Ask, 'What sort of things are you thinking of?' 'What would you find pleasing and fun?'"

"Oh, those are good," he said, fingers flying on a smart pad.

- "'R' means you don't just turn and walk away; you intentionally close the dialogue on the Relationship. You're extremely thankful for her, intent on enjoying her company. If you get casual about this, you could accidentally treat her like furniture.

"Listen, Empathy, Ask, flanked by opening and closing on relationship. I want you to check out the tip sheet as we review the CLEAR process."

Caleb thoughtfully went through the list. Reader, please do the same.

CLEAR Tip Sheet

- Intentionally open conversations with UPR and truly prepare to listen.
- Practice active, spellbound listening to catch the gist and details.
- Practice using empathy to emotionally receive where the other person is.
- Use CLEAR in everyday communication at work and in your personal life.
- Welcome feedback from others on your effectiveness in listening and understanding.
- Practice being warm, open, and welcoming, particularly when you don't feel WOW.
- Strive to improve your overall listening in all situations.
- Strive to improve your memory of what others say to you.
- Use a memory tool, like your calendar, to take notes on what people tell you.
- Intentionally and warmly, i.e. courageously, close conversations on the relationship.

"What's next?" he asked.

"Let's practice. You get to play Danielle and I'll be you. Say something that'll fluster me. I suggest you record this."

I put on a baseball cap backwards, slouched, and turned sideways, exuding boredom.

His voice tight, as he thought Danielle had spoken to him, he said, "Caleb. You never talk to me."

Playing Caleb, I demonstrated UPR, Collegiality with WOW, Listen, and Empathy, by:

- **UPR:** I sat up, faced him, removed the cap and calmly looked him in the eye.
- **WOW:** My demeanor was warm and open, without frowning in concentration or worrying that I was going to blow it.
- **Listen:** Showing I'd actually heard, I said, "Danielle, you're right. I need to do that."
- **Empathy:** My intent, manner, and eyes said: *I really get it that this is important to you.*
- **Ask:** Ask open-ended questions, such as "When does my silence hurt the most?"
- **Relationship:** Close on your relationship. Looking her in the eye, "Danielle, thanks for this. You're important to me."

Caleb shook his head. "Lots of moving parts. I'll have trouble remembering them."

"He says humbly after leading non-English-speaking multinational crews to erect conversion towers, install catalytic chambers, put in thousands of kilometers of large-diameter pipe, and build massive storage tanks in a hostile desert without a fatality."

"I respectfully withdraw my comment," he said.

"CLEAR's a sandwich with three fillings—listen, empathy, and ask—with a piece of bread to open on, and one to close on, the relationship. You can switch the order of the fillings and ask and then listen with empathy. CLEAR's the all-purpose Play to use with everyone."

"She'll probably say, 'What the heck are you doing?'"

"And, you would answer her by saying. . .?"

"Uh, I'm, I'm, trying to respect you, talk to you. More. Uh, really."

"That's right. Try that again. Take a deep, slow breath. Use her name."

"Danielle, I get it. I'll do more talking. I'm trying to do that, right now."

"Great! When the chat's over, be WOW again. Enjoy her company, Caleb. Remember that you really care for her and that it's your job in life to improve how you treat people. It's pure reality that your life would really suck without her."

"True enough. But there'll still be friction."

"Friction's normal. It doesn't mean failure, it means you're in the game. Practice your Tier 4 Mindfulness Pivot to improve yourself and not dump on her. Even if she does it to you. Be who you're supposed to be, a better, more admirable person, strong and courageous, less male, more man."

"Wait. What's the difference?"

"A male is an undeveloped man. He's anxious about emotions, worries that he has feelings, and lets them control his actions and decisions. He flees discomfort to his hideouts, avoids conflict, and relies on a wishbone instead of strengthening his backbone. He's selfish and makes things about his needs and pleasures. He uses people. He's edgy when he's not exploiting people and feels guilty when he does. He switches opinions to get along. Boasts about backing diversity and scorns people who don't agree with him. He lacks a coherent and stable identity.

"A man absolutely refuses to just be a mere male. He commits to being other-directed and not self-absorbed. He honors all people, especially when he doesn't feel like it. Self-governs. Discerns and does the Highest Moral Action despite unpopularity or job loss. Trains others to also act in courage instead of in fear. He takes pleasure in doing the right thing and in serving. He doesn't do this for credit, but instead gives it to others. He feels sick when he doesn't do the HMA. He burns his own interests to protect principles and help others. He's courageous, so he's a brave and trusted leader, and follower, in every situation."

"Tell me you teach this to school kids."

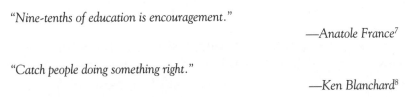

√	WEEKS	
	1	I open dialogue with UPR, WOW, care, and collegiality and close on the relationship.
	2	I listen spellbound, catching the gist and details of the other person's communication.
	3	I ask open-ended questions to understand more fully, and avidly listen to responses.
	4	I use Courageous Empathy to understand the other person; I close on our relationship.

Figure 4.1   CLEAR Behavioral Practice—The First, Basic CourCom Play

"Whenever I can. Courage is universal. We all need it. Here's a CLEAR practice cycle (Figure 4.1). As you start a new week's behaviors, practice the skills of the preceding weeks. You're going to make Danielle very happy and won't feel bad, yourself."

CLEAR is your basic all-purpose Play. We now move to something we all need.

The Second Basic CourCom Play: Encourage Others

"Nine-tenths of education is encouragement."

—Anatole France[7]

"Catch people doing something right."

—Ken Blanchard[8]

"I love this word," said nursing leader Gracie Collins. "Did you know 'encouragement' is from the Middle French, *encoragier*, to give courage, to make strong, to hearten? There are few better verbs in our world of doubts and anxieties. In health care, we fight death itself and help the dying, pandemic patients, victims of domestic violence, gunshot and stabbing victims, cancer patients, car wreck survivors, the mentally beset. We deeply need to be daily inspired with courage, spirit, and hope, to be given courage by those who know how truly vital it is. Some think leadership is brains or education, but it's really doing the right thing so you can be trusted—then you can give courage to your people, to hearten them. So few in our world know how to actually do that."

Gallup finds that over half of Americans are disengaged at work and are only showing up to get paychecks. Of our 100 million workers, a minority of 33% actually do the work; 16% are actively hostile to their workplaces and "destroy what the most engaged actually build." The vast majority—85%—are demotivated by our common and pervasive low quality of leadership.[9]

But Kouzes and Posner's research offers us good news. They found that 98% of us said that with encouragement, *we'd perform at a higher level* (emphasis added).[10]

It's astonishing to find 98% of us agreeing on anything. On that note, we meet our second CourCom Play, ENCOURAGE OTHERS.

The courageous person recognizes that encouraging the HMA inspires people to be their best with self, others and customers. This, in turn, improves performance and results—for with courage, the word "undoable" loses its first two letters.

But is encouragement really essential for us to do what we'd otherwise avoid?

Consider research that was done on a cohort of highly fit American Soldiers.

After two months of unmitigated hardship with insufficient rest, sleep, or food, they faced a final, tough, high-speed, pass/fail qualification forced equipment march in a program in which most fail. The cohort was halved. Group 1 was told, "It's a 20-kilometer forced ruck march with routine distance checks." Group 2 got a shorter message: "This is the march you heard about."

The groups were assessed for speed, injuries, and failures. Blood draws were then taken from the tired Soldiers to measure stress hormones, such as cortisol and prolactin.[11]

Group 1, which knew the task and heard progress checks, far outperformed Group 2, which was slower, had twice as many injuries, and a significant number who dropped out.

"The highest (stress) was found in the group that knew the least about the march. The lowest levels were found in the group that knew exactly how far they would be going and received regular progress reports."[12] Merely knowing the length of the march with a few progress reports dramatically elevated spirits, morale, performance, safety, health, and unity.

Knowing about the size of a task is but a small expression of common consideration. We give others courage by exhibiting positive mental toughness in the face of uncertainty—when no one knows the dimensions of a task. Less than a half a percent of Americans serve in the active military to sweat out painful, high-speed, where-the-blazes-are-we-going full-ruck marches to constantly endure the unknown. From them, we can see that it's vital to our well-being and that of others to give strength to others so they can avoid being flustered or defeated by predictable stresses.

Encouragement simply begins by modeling courage. This establishes the necessary trust so you can intentionally help, train, and develop others. True encouragement can be more robust and inspirational than giving essential feedback, merit-based promotions and bonuses, affirmations, team recognitions, award celebrations, promotion ceremonies, and self-esteem initiatives.

Research here is as surprising as the evidence that doing the right thing and practicing humility produce greater profits. Wait—did I just say that encouragement outweighs money and bonus rewards? Motivation expert Daniel Pink[13] found that encouraging autonomy in work, technical mastery, and finding a deeper purpose than self-interest were better motivators than money. Once again, doing the right thing for its own sake rises above self-interest.

I've heard hundreds of execs say that the thrills of new promotions, larger staffs, and more compensation don't last. What sank into their hearts wasn't money, more time off, or a new corner office. Deeper and more meaningful impact occurs when someone thanked them while courageously encouraging them to improve.

Encourage Others Tip Sheet

- Encouragement is personal, relational, meaningful, and real.
- When appropriate, offer encouragement that is actionable instead of theoretical.
- Practice recognizing effort and diligence instead of giving mechanical "cheerleading."
- Practice recognizing others for doing the right thing more than for their achievement.
- Encourage by giving routine "advice and counsel" instead of "feedback."[14]
- Keep encouraging others even if doesn't seem to produce quick results.
- Give true, heartfelt thanks when people do UPR, self-government, and DAT.
- Encourage all people to act rightly without playing favorites.
- Give courage to others when you're tired and they're discouraged.

Examples

Encouragement is vital in business and essential in families. Following are two examples.

Encouraging a Teen   David Kai[15] is a married, empty-nester who works in produce. A teacher he knew approached him.

"David, I have a 14-year-old student named Josh (not his real name). He doesn't study, refuses to speak in class, has a 1.5 GPA, might be learning disabled, and has no friends but tries to hang out with the drug dealers. His parents are phantoms. He needs a volunteer tutor. Like you, a volunteer soccer coach."

David didn't need to raise a fourth kid. But there was Josh, a silent, rail-thin kid who looked to be about 12 with the sad demeanor of the loneliest teen in the world. David's conscience stirred him. After reflecting, he agreed.

"I'm happy to be your tutor," said David. Three days a week, he drove 40 minutes to Josh's apartment to warmly encourage the boy as he walked him through the homework. "Josh, I appreciate your studying with me." "I'm proud of your effort."

Josh learned study skills and how to lift weights, and he played David in tough one-on-one basketball.

"When I look at you," said David, "I see a young man ready to emerge and become what he's supposed to be. A man of courage and strength who's studying and can do things in the world so he can then help others."

Weeks passed without Josh speaking. Then, Josh opened the paper and pointed to a movie in the entertainment section. David nodded and they went to see a film about a dad rescuing his teen son during a weather apocalypse. "If you needed help, I'd come get you," said David. "Teachers say you're doing better. Way to go! Josh, I'm sticking with you."

A month later, Josh mumbled something. "What did you say, Josh?" The boy shook his head. Much later, as David said good-bye for the day, Josh said, just above audible range, "I'm not worth this."

"You are worth it to me," said David softly, placing his hand on the boy's shoulder.

David's encouragement was more in positive, unflagging actions than in words. David stuck with Josh through to his graduation from high school, at which point Josh joined the Marines, made multiple combat deployments, and was quickly promoted. The years of encouragement resulted in a young man who has found his good, strong, and humorous voice and who knows himself. Josh is an independent and hardworking manager who seeks to do the Highest Moral Action and now offers love and encouragement to his wife and young daughters.

Encouraging Others at Work   Chief Nursing Officer Gracie Collins faces the daunting challenges of an overfull ICU and ER, nursing staff burnout, staff losses, dwindling revenue, and hostile board members.

Gracie knew the fundamentals of CLEAR—collegiality, avid listening, empathy, asking questions to understand, and focusing on the relationship—better than I did. How did she encourage others?

While many managers were glued to their chairs and laptops in their offices, as a leader, Gracie spent most of her day solving problems with her people on the floor. With a long list of skills to encourage, she lauded decisions and actions in which they increased teamwork, the 5 Cs: communication, cooperation, consultation, coordination, coaching, mutual support, problem solving, and helping and encouraging each other. She coached them with difficult decisions and she was highly trusted and even loved.

"Some managers," she said, "try to buy and bribe performance and hit people with a stick if they miss patient care targets. I just never see that working. People worry about what the boss thinks. Work is hard. People don't need criticism. They need strong hearts and spirits to do it."

"What happens," she said to an employee who was given to negativity, "when you don't encourage people? They get lonely and sad and they die a little inside. I don't think encouragement is saying, 'Good job, girl, for doing your job!' Repeat that a lot, and it means nothing, you know what I'm saying? But when you tell Marvin he did the right thing, the loneliness, sadness, dying inside, they all go away because you just sparked his courage."

Can people really change? Can encouragement facilitate that forward motion?

If you think the answers are Yes and Yes, Figure 4.2 offers some tips for encouraging well.

We're ready for our next and final Basic CourCom.

√	WEEKS	
	1	I practice giving courage to others to do the right thing.
	2	I practice encouraging others for doing the HMA more than for "good jobs."
	3	I now routinely catch people doing the right thing and thank them.
	4	I let people know that I'm proud of their courage and character.

Figure 4.2   Encourage Others Behavioral Practice

The Third Basic CourCom Play: Ask Challenges

"Good questions outrank easy answers."
—Paul Samuelson, Nobel Laureate in Economics[16]

It's natural for us to tell people the answer. But something almost magical happens when we ask people what they really think. Asking has the power of authentically connecting and inviting them into a trusting relationship. Telling tends to limit others and our choices. Asking expands everyone's options. Asking can invite advice, which is usually about tasks, and result in counsel, which is about who the person is and wishes to be.

We deeply value autonomy and agency, which often results from asking a particular type of question. Gracie used this tool—the Open-ended Question, or OEQ—to help her employees independently solve problems instead of calling, "Gracie!"

OEQs encourage the use of asking questions and advance functional lifetime learning.

OEQs stimulate positive, creative, and innovative thinking. The great parents I've observed use this type of question to reinforce their children's independent problem solving. They look forward to seeing what their children come up with upon which they can then offer wise thoughts

The opposite of OEQs are closed questions which limit the other person to saying, "yes, no, or maybe" or to a restricted number of other answers. Closed questions can be leading and manipulative: "Did you like my cooking?" "How much do you love me?" They're used in marketing to get good survey responses: "What part of my product did you like the most?" Or, like hostile accusations, "You call that a finished work product!?"—it's not really a question.

By contrast, open-ended questions are based on UPR and can express doing the HMA.

We ask OEQs from a mindset of curiosity and a true desire to know what the other person is thinking. At work, it creates safety, enhances effectiveness, and builds teams in ways that instructing, correcting, criticizing, and telling cannot. In building relationships, the candid curiosity of one party can provide a wide portal to understanding and connecting with the other person.

BAFF, Boss Asks for Feedback, is a powerful OEQ Play to respect the agency in others, invite trust, and model courage. It pertains to all of us, whether we're a boss or not. Courage is quickly inspirational when we ask others for candid feedback on how we're doing. The OEQ is also an encouraging approach to handling life's daily communication needs. It helps move us in a steadily positive direction. Your first OEQs, similar to your first attempts to balance an unruly bike, might feel unnatural and not cause the Olympic Committee to come calling.

That's okay, you'll master them by practicing. (Then, they will call.)

Let's take that one step further with our third basic CourCom Play, ASK CHALLENGES.

It uses the sincere OEQ for a different purpose.

We use Ask Challenges to understand what's happening when someone could use guidance, or when a situation needs improvement. If that person is getting tired, encouragement is probably needed. If they are struggling with a role or task, effective assistance might be the solution.

In Step Two, we observed a fire department admit and stop the 3 NOs. In a planned role play, Fitz, a strong battalion chief, saw a firefighter who appeared to be slacking. Fitz defaulted to anger and a closed question that, of course, is not really a question: "WHAT THE HELL ARE YOU DOING!?" The firefighter jumped at the violent accusation, the audience flinched, and birds may have fallen from trees.

To model stopping his obvious NO of anger, Fitz then did a role-play redo in which he asks a better, performance-related query: "How can I help you not repeat that?" The calmer attitude and the use of an actual question represented an impressive change.

But the question "How can I help you not repeat that?" isn't a true OEQ nor, as we'll see, is it a true Ask Challenges. Can you see why?

First, Fitz's redo question forces the firefighter into accepting that he was goofing off.

What if he wasn't? In the scenario, the firefighter was looking at his phone. He could've been playing the *Kirby and the Forgotten Land* or *Minecraft* video games,[17] listening to a podcast about a new technique in throwing a fire ladder, or giving instructions to someone who's trying to douse a burning stove. Second, the question limits the listener to accepting help only from Fitz about improvement and eliminates any of the firefighter's self-initiating or innovative ideas on the subject and, as noted, improvement might not even be the issue.

An Ask Challenge in that situation—with UPR and real curiosity—could be as easy as, "Hi, Brad, how goes your day?" It's warm, open, welcoming and presumes nothing's askew. It gives good faith instead of expressing malign suspicions; the question is as open as all outdoors.

Can Ask Challenges help with problems and low performance issues?

It's basically what this third Play is about. Ask Challenges uses OEQs instead of scolding, hectoring, criticizing, and reprimanding as the opening move when we see something that's deviated from standard in life, work, and relationships.

Ask Challenges follow these steps.

1. You practice being a good observer with reliable and calm situational awareness.

2. You see someone who's out of sorts, or something that is out of the ordinary.

3. You discern the Tier 4/Highest Moral Action: Do I courageously communicate or not?

4. Using UPR, and being open and nonjudgmental, you Ask a Challenge:

    a. Open-ended—not closed, leading, negative, or suggestive of an "answer."

    b. Aimed at the general area of the "challenge."

    c. Follow-on Ask Challenges OEQs are on point with the specific challenge.

    d. The purpose is not to correct before we know the facts, but to first understand how the person is or to understand the situation.

    e. Listen keenly to catch the gist, emotions, details, and situation.

    f. Understanding lets you discern if you can help in a principled way.

In most cases, the other person is troubled or a situation is going south because of anxiety, worry, and a deficiency of available courage; challenges require your attentive sensitivity so you can help rather than make things more difficult.

Ask Challenges Tip Sheet

- Courageously practice encouraging people who struggle.
- When you're a leader, regularly seek out others and ask how they're doing.
- When appropriate, offer encouragement that is *actionable* instead of theoretical.
- Practice asking Ask Challenges OEQs, open-ended questions, using selfless curiosity.
- Use Ask Challenges to actually understand the other person, not to "change" them.
- Use Ask Challenges to learn about the other person and to appreciate their values.
- Use Ask Challenges without quitting or despair, even with performance issues.
- Ask "How can I help you?" only after the relational connection warrants it.
- Stop Ask Challenges when the other person wants direction.
- Use Ask Challenges to bring relationship improvements at work.
- Practice Ask Challenges to improve personal relationships.

Let me use an example from our friend Bella Cruz to show what Ask Challenges looks like. You might remember that she directs an addiction cessation program that's strapped by budget cuts, system stress, burnout, staff turnover, and a bad boss. She also has a new employee who enthusiastically competed for the job and now struggles with his caseload.

"I've used the basic CourCom Plays," said Bella. "'Butch' has trouble writing up client treatment plans and is way behind other new staff. I keep catching him playing *Solitaire* and *Minecraft*."

"What have you said to him?"

"I keep telling him that I haven't gotten his plans. He sort of just avoids me."

"That's frustrating. Do you want to give the Ask Challenges Play a try? Can you act like the avoidant Butch?"

Bella nodded.

"Hi, Butch," I said warmly (UPR, WOW), playing Bella's role. "Thanks for meeting with me. Last week I asked you to think about what part of writing client treatment plans you'd like to discuss today. Can you share them with me? (Ask Challenges to the area of concern.)

"Actually," said Bella, playing Butch, "I have trouble with every part—from problem statements and severity scales, to writing goals and interventions." She sounded sincere—perhaps this was an early breakthrough.

"It can be overwhelming, I said. "Butch, what part's the easiest?" (OEQ, focused, intent.)

"Talking to clients. The hardest are the interventions," she said seriously.

"Can you tell me what's hard about them?" (OEQ: I really want to know "Butch's" answer. Here, Courageous Communication becomes real, whatever the result. This is because you have the unselfish intent to help "Butch" and understand how he thinks.)

"There are too many options." Bella might've been channeling Butch.

"How could I help you with that?" (The Ask Challenges Final Help Question.) If I give in to anxiety, I'll ask it too early. If I'm patient, I'll be able to up my humility, give courage to the other person, and understand their position. In this way I earn the right to ask the Help Query, since asking too early could bring distrustful, sarcastic, or even manipulative responses. Here, I used it because it homes in on a specific issue rather than offering universal assistance, which is usually painfully counterproductive.

"Huh," said Bella. "I dunno." Butch is now backing away. (Did I ask too soon?)

"Butch," I said, "say I'm a brand-new counselor and I'm totally lost in choosing intervention options. So I'm now asking your advice. Can you help me?" (Ask Challenge at his issue now makes him a Subject Matter Expert for a colleague who needs his help.)

Bella paused to reflect. "That's a very interesting question. I guess you have to believe your clients, who lie to you way too often. But these interventions, man, they have this massive impact on people. What if I screw up? I could end up killing one of them."

By walking around in Butch's shoes, she might've found what he faced and felt.

"That's great, Butch," I said. "You're really helping me. So can you tell me how you end up deciding?" (Ask Challenge to understand his decision-making process.)

"You know what?" asked Bella. "I want to know what you think." (Ask Challenges Breakthrough: I connected, however thinly, with "Butch"; he now wants to team together.)

"Great role play, Bella," I said. "Did this CourCom help in any way?"

"Gustavo, I can't wait to do this with 'Butch.' You know what's crazy?"

"Please tell me."

"You trained us in empathy, with the 'E' in CLEAR? Well, I think I have all this empathy, I mean, I'm a single mom. When I'm with my babies, I tell you I'm there with them, completely. But I shut off my empathy for this Butch, who plays video games at work and doesn't do his intervention plans and makes my life harder—and I was like, you know, taking it personally.

"In our role plays," she continued, "I've seen you do UPR and WOW what, 10 times, 20 times? And I just now see the UPR and the WOW in Ask Challenges. It really got to me! Playing Butch, I got this empathy for him. I listened as I role-played Butch and I got this sinking feeling that he's told me these things but I didn't listen because I thought they were excuses. I guess this is another Tier 4 Mindfulness pivot, am I right?"

I said she was right and I thanked Bella for her courageous work.

As a courageous leader, Bella practiced asking challenges, which, as all behaviors and plays of courageous behavior, are for everyone who comes into contact with human beings; it's not only for supervisors.

Here are sample challenges. The first set is from a peer to a peer. The second set is from a leader to a team member.

Each situation first shows (a) a conventional, usually unplanned, spontaneous and often unhelpful comment. It's followed by (b) a thought-out, CourCom Ask Challenge example in italics. After the other person responds to your Ask Challenge, you can ask (c) follow-on Ask Challenge OEQs to further understand. Some examples show illustrative sequential Ask Challenges.

Examples.

Peer-to-peer Ask Challenges

- A peer seems unhappy, depressed, uncertain, withdrawn or confused.
  - (a) Hey, you don't look so hot. Are you okay?
  - (b) *Hi, Adam, do you have a minute? Can you tell me how you're doing?*
  - (c) *Did you know that you can always talk to me?*
- A friend appears to have trouble in a relationship.
  - (a) I hear things aren't cool with Bianca. What's going on?
  - (b) *Hey, Adam, thanks for this time. Can I ask how things are going with you and Bianca?*
  - (c) *Did you know that I'm always here for you?*
- A peer looks to be having difficulty with someone or something.
  - (a) What's happening?
  - (b) *Adam, this is a tough one. How are you doing with this thing?*
- A person appears tense or irritable around you.
  - (a) What's going on with you?
  - (b) *Adam, can I ask, how are we doing?*

Leaders use Ask Challenges about performance

- **The tough assignment.** Using good situational awareness, the leader knows a team member might find a particular assignment to be difficult, so the leader poses a series of Ask Challenges before problems can surface.

(a) Hey, are these things a problem for you?

(b) *Adam, these assignments aren't easy.* Now, a series of Ask Challenges:

Looking at it, what are your thoughts? (Listen openly; his answer can change your next OEQ.)

What might be good about this task? What might be not so good? (Getting a big picture.)

At first impression, what parts look familiar to you? What parts don't? (He has skills.)

Are there parts of this that you could help others with? (He has mastery and agency.)

Are there parts where you could possibly use help, as well? (You've made it clear that you're not trying to make things difficult. Ask Challenges should have established a safe space for both of you. Now you can usually offer to share your skills.)

If you get into a bottleneck, what are some steps you might think about? (Encouraging him to find his own solutions.)

- Subpar performance on a task.

  (a) Hey, I have to tell you, like, again, you're way behind. Get it done, this time, all right?

  (b) *What's going well for you with this task? Can you tell me more about that?*

  What parts of it present the biggest challenges?

  Do you have any thoughts about possible next steps? Can you say more about that?

  Who might be the best person to help here?

  Might I be able to help? (This is usually the last Ask Challenge query; in some situations, it will be the first.)

- A team member struggles with an unhappy customer and might need help.

  (a) Let me step in here. What can I do for you?

  (b) *(Quietly standing by in eyesight of Adam, so he can see you if he needs help.)*

  (b option—said quietly if he needs help): *Adam, let me know if you need anything.*

- A member struggles to work with the team.
  (a) What's the problem? I wish I could help, but I think this is really your problem.
  (b) *What's the most positive thing about this team that you can think of? What's the most negative thing? Can you tell me more about that? If you could, what would you change about your team? If you could, what would you change about your role on the team?* (What's the issue?)

    What would you change in me? Could you tell me more about that? (Give me advice—advice I'm morally obligated to consider seriously. Here's a strong opportunity to team with Adam to make positive changes.)

    What, if anything, might you want to change in yourself? (In coaching, this is the dynamite question—we must first change ourselves before trying to change others and the world.)

- A team member is often late to work or late submitting completed deliverables.
  (a) I know we talked about this. I pay you to get here on time and do work by deadlines.
  (b) *Thanks for meeting with me because you were late to work.* (No judgment.)

    What are your thoughts about this? Other says, "It's not really a big deal."

    Can you tell me more about that? Other: "I usually do it on time."

    Yes, that's true. (UPR and reflecting back.) Why do you think I'm taking your time to explore this?

    Other: "I don't know. . . .Well, maybe because it sometimes affects other people?" (Bingo!)

    In what ways? Other: "I guess sometimes, I hold them up." (Closer to ownership.)

    I appreciate your saying that. What are your thoughts about that? (Invitation to own it.)

    "I don't know." (He's backed off and is afraid to own being chronically late.)

    Can I give you my advice? (This is a non-OEQ Ask Challenges Final Help Question.)

Adam, I need you on our team. We need your skills. (Affirmation of the individual rather than of his work product.) *I think if you come to work and do things on time from today forward, you'll help us and our duty to do things right* (Tier 4 real purpose). *It'll save you money. You can earn more time off* (Tiers 2 and 3 self-interest), *and most importantly, we can continue to work and improve together* (Tier 4 relationship). *And, I won't feel like an idiot because I can't help in this situation.* (Appropriate humor can help.)

As you start a new week's behaviors, practice the skills of the preceding weeks (Figure 4.3).

You've practiced CLEAR, the Swiss Army knife of effective communication; Encourage Others, which we all need to be our best; and Ask Challenges to navigate problems.

You're now prepared to practice Plays to address the overexaggerated, overblown, not-so-scary bogeyman in our closet—conflicts.

√	WEEKS	
	1	I practice using Open-ended Questions instead of telling or correcting.
	2	I Ask Challenges out of curiosity and empathy to understand the other person.
	3	I Ask Challenges to connect at a real level and form a positive relationship.
	4	I Ask Challenges to the people in my personal life.

Figure 4.3   Ask Challenges Behavioral Practice

5

Step Five: Playsets for CourCom Conflicts

"Anger is an acid that does more harm to the vessel in which it is stored than to anything on which it is poured."

—Mark Twain[1]

WE KNOW ABOUT external conflicts and protracted interpersonal and emotional clashes. Like boxing, this painful form of social failure usually requires the consent and complicity of the parties—what the Arbinger Institute aptly calls *collusion*.[2] Each mysteriously commits to doing what we hate, decry, and condemn—making war on each other. It's amusing, observed historians Will and Ariel Durant, that we passionately demand world peace and just as passionately fight with our partners and can't live with our relatives, neighbors, and coworkers. Like monkeys that grab a fistful of walnuts in a hole but then can't withdraw the prize, we're familiar with conflicts but know very little about how to solve them.

Hence, our second group of CourCom Conflict Plays.

Over the years, when speaking about conflict, I've been asked about assertive and critical communication. Bella Cruz faced a toxic boss and had taken an assertive communication class to establish the

147

validity of her voice. She employed it with that manager, whose treatment of her then worsened. She wondered why. Bella and I found two big differences between assertive and Courageous Communication.

- Assertive communication offered us groundbreaking tools to confirm the legitimacy of each person's voice and their right to be heard. This was a logical response for women, minorities, and introverts who frequently found themselves overlooked if not bulldozed. It's speaking for the sake of the self and resists practices that induce unfair silence.
- CourCom is the practiced ability to speak rightly and respectfully to all persons in every circumstance. It exercises our basic human right to speak courageously in support of doing the right thing. It's speaking the HMA to model courage for everyone, to advocate for the common good without sweating personal kudos. It demonstrates UPR, seeks truth, and when appropriate, uses assertiveness.

More recently, Bella and others took a critical communication course to speak effectively when the risks of failure are crucial and great. It too offered excellent tools in listening, sensing, and communicating when much could be lost to unfocused dialogue.

By contrast, CourCom focuses on HMA-based listening and speech in *every* instance and willingly faces the risk of pushback. It advocates the daily practice of courageous Plays in routine conversations so we're equally prepared when the moral stakes—risks to people, principles, and high core values—are low or high or present in any form.

From here, we look at our three CourCom Conflict Plays:

The AeR: CourCom meets Emotional Intelligence
Fix the Fire: Reflect-back, the Situation-Check and the No-Thank-You
    Declaration
CBS: We get serious about reconciliation

I once tripped badly on my pride; the resulting face flop introduced me to our first CourCom Conflict Play. As you'll see, I call it Action-emotional Reaction, AeR.

I'd previously acted as a whistleblower and written books, unaware that I'd end up doing the former more times than I wished. This caused some to see me as an ethicist, leading to giving commencement addresses on character and appearing on CNN and CBS *This Morning* to comment on the state of ethics in America. I began to think I was a subject matter expert on how to act rightly. In reality, it meant I was begging for a harsh lesson in humility.

Clifton Sutcliffe[3] was board vice chair in a corporation in which I was a senior exec. One day, he asked me to lunch. In a crowded L.A. restaurant, he passed me a note. It asked me to secretly hire one of his relatives. To keep it hush-hush, he suggested that I use an unrestricted funds account. It was wrong; no, I thought, *he* was wrong, way wrong.

Nothing was so bad in those days that I couldn't make worse. Feeling superior to Clifton (per my exalted status and superior self-esteem), I dishonored Coach Tony's decade of hard self-governance training, Norm Schwarzkopf's dictate to lead by example, Edgar Bodenheimer's UPR imperative, and West Point's self-sacrificing principles to instead act arrogantly and to exhibit a prideful indignity.

I didn't pause to discern. "You can't be serious," I said, my subtext tone full of unspoken profanities. "You can't ask me to be unethical. This is flat-out impossible." I didn't add, "How dare you ask me, the great and perfect Grand Poo-Bah of ethics, to do something wrong?!"

My conscience stirred and Clifton recoiled. I couldn't miss my inner warning alarm: *Danger Gus Lee! Danger! You're wrong. You dissed a person. Fix it now. . . .*

But unchecked fear begets more fear as surely as ducks make ducklings, and, now afraid to admit my mistake, I neither apologized nor retracted my disrespectful words. My conscience was pinging. I'd probably stopped breathing, which tends to make the mind draw a blank.

Hell hath no fury like a board officer wrongly spurned. Clifton threw down his napkin and left. He then began questioning my hires and budgetary, operational, and project decisions in board committee meetings. He wanted an investigative body to prove his suspicions. The innuendos proved false but the absence of my courage was evident; I could manage my division for years without a hiccup in hires, complex initiatives, far-flung projects, and fiscal audits but, by pridefully disrespecting a person, I risked the hard work and deliverables of our employees and contractors. Yes, I was correct about not illegally employing his person, but I was very wrong in how I treated the other person.

Clifton then approached other execs to hire his relative, and some of them in turn pressured me either to cave in to the request to hire the relative or to report him to the bar association, or worse:

- "You were a D.A. His requests are in writing. He blackmailed you. Prosecute him!"
- "Threaten to show it to our board president. He'll probably remove Clifton from the board, and he'll probably then lose his job. Why are you delaying? He's coming after us now!"
- "You have a big budget. Just hire his relative. No one will care."
- "You know how to box. You were in the Army, a tough, cadence-calling US Army drill sergeant, for Pete's sake! Tell him to back off or you'll ask him to step outside."

My conscience said, *You did wrong. Apologize. Without self-interest. Not to get what you want, but to be who you are supposed to be. Do it now, not later.* My mistake cannot cost someone's job or reputation. I flushed the note and called Clifton; his secretary sent me to voicemail, on which I stated a full apology, adding that I'd destroyed the note he'd given me at our fateful lunch. He didn't call. His office refused requests for an appointment.

I waited in his company lobby. He left for the noon hour and I invited him to lunch. He declined. I repeated the process a few times a week and he relented. At lunch, he loudly mocked me for disrespecting him, his family, his relative, and his reputation. I apologized, facing my wrongs and his verbal assaults. I took them personally, not in anger, but in humility. Clifton chose packed restaurants frequented by peers; if my staff were nearby, he raised his voice. Tempted to defend myself, I took his attacks on the chin without bobbing, weaving, ducking, slipping punches, parrying, or sidestepping. I resisted the impulse to counterpunch and instead honored him as a human being, as one whom I'd hurt. Our lunches bore the logic of the ring; dropping your left meant a right cross to the chops; lifting the chin brought uppercuts; dishonoring a person brought consequences. It was pugilistically sound and morally logical.

I once had the honor of meeting the heavyweight champion of the world, who cheerfully and generously signed a pair of red pro gloves:

"To Gus, Yo pal, George Foreman." In 1974, Mr. Foreman, then the undefeated heavyweight champ, had lost to Muhammad Ali in Kinshasa, in today's Republic of the Congo, in "The Rumble in the Jungle." Mr. Foreman had worn himself out by pounding on Mr. Ali with his formidable strength, who'd leaned against the ropes to take the blows. Mr. Foreman had punched himself out.

Clifton renewed his familiar attack. "You were a total jerk! Inconsiderate, unthinking, a flaming %*@#! So full of yourself all you could do is lecture me!" He fell silent—I worried that he'd taken ill. He looked up. He had run out of words; like Mr. Foreman, he'd punched himself out. I, who had boxed for 13 years, thought Clifton Sutcliffe's beating would last forever and didn't see this coming. Like the flooding monsoon rains on the Korean DMZ, it simply stopped, like turning off a spigot.

He gathered himself. "When you disrespected me," said Clifton, "I felt very angry."

The words echoed. "Thank you, Clifton. I acted wrongly, without courage. I regret the pain that I caused you, very much."

"It was stupid," he said, "to put my request in writing and then pass it to a former prosecutor. Any chance you'll do me the favor of destroying it or giving it back?"

I said that it was gone; I'd mentioned its destruction in my first voicemail message.

He'd erased my voicemail without playing it. "I should've listened to it. I would've slept better." He sighed. "I really wanted to get a job for my relative. I'm not feeling very well. Please stay at the table for about fifteen minutes. Let me leave by myself."

Mr. Sutcliffe made peace with me. I want to share this as a cautionary tale. I didn't respect him and he accurately accused me of not acting decently to another human being. I believed it was right for me to accept his anger. He stopped blaming me and instead described what my action had done to him, and he did it without accusing or demeaning.

He said, *"When you disrespected me, I felt very angry."* In the totality of his attacks it was the single, most powerful thing he said. What really came through was that he said it calmly and honestly. Through his hurt and anger, he reached out, person to person, to say something that was truthful and hugely human instead of using accusatory, hostile, get-even, I'm-going-to-mess-you-up language.

Let's review the main points:

- He stated a truth without calling me names.
- It's a very clean way to point out a mistake without a slap to the face.
- By using UPR, he made a bigger impact than with his angry words.
- He actually sounded stronger and wiser.
- It stopped his escalation of the conflict.

And he accomplished all of that with eight little words.

As noted, his brief statement was what we'll call an AeR.

The First CourCom Conflict Play: Action-emotional Reaction—The AeR

"I call myself a Peaceful Warrior. . . because the battles we fight are on the inside."

—*Socrates*[4]

Action-emotional Reaction is a useful conflict Play that lets us respectfully and accurately address disrespectful conduct by someone else. I first referenced this type of action in Chapter 8 of *Courage: The Backbone of Leadership*.

It resembles the classic I-Message, which was designed by Thomas Gordon in the 1970s for two primary purposes: to assert the self and to de-escalate conflict, especially in parenting.[5]

The Action-emotional Reaction (AeR), by requiring courage, UPR, and humility, also addresses our internal angst about conflicts and in these respects advances the I-Message[6]:

- **Purpose.** The AeR speaks a clarifying truth into conflict. It respectfully honors the relationship by assuming responsibility for my emotional reaction to someone else's behavior. Using a short, stark truth about the self can also quickly reduce the intensity of a disagreement.
- **What it does.** The AeR lets us address conflict rightly instead of fearfully reacting in these ways: mischaracterizations and

self-deceptions ("it's okay that you disrespected me, it's no big deal"); denial ("we have no issues"); avoidance ("no need to do anything, it was just a simple failure to communicate"); cover-ups ("there was no disagreement"); or outright fabrications ("we're all in total agreement with each other").

■ **What's not the purpose.** De-escalation in the I-statement is usually something we desire but it isn't the aim of AeR. It's a principled statement, respectfully delivered, to let another person know that their words or actions had a specific consequence. De-escalation, which can provide momentary relief from anxiety, can also delay what needs to be fixed.

How to Do the AeR

The AeR has the underlying purpose of all CourCom Plays—change ourselves so we listen, understand, and communicate courageously. It has three moving parts:

1. BICBOF.

    Dealing with your escalating feelings is a first step because you're in the hotseat. BICBOF stands for "Breathe In Courage, Blow Out Fear." This prevents us from the common habit of allowing anxiety to stop our breathing and shut down our cognitive functions and draw mental blanks. Instead, we consciously, slowly, deeply, and diaphragmatically breathe in "our courage"—our ability to remain stable and centered despite negative feelings. When we slowly exhale, we're aware that we're blowing out our fears and tensions, and our tendency to close up.

2. What the other person did or said.

    The AeR names the other person's specific action that escalated your feelings. It's very different from saying, "When you were mean to me, I felt angry," or, "For years you've been doing this and I'm really ticked." A correct AeR describes a specific behavior in a specified moment instead of naming a general trait or habit and is delivered as close in time as possible to the event. Here are examples with the other person's action in italics:

- o "When you *yelled at me* in the parking lot, I felt angry."
- o "When *you argued with me before I finished*, I felt disrespected."
- o Period. Stop. Don't harangue human beings; it doesn't work.

3. My emotional reaction to the other person's actions or words.

By focusing on the emotions and feelings, we own the feeling. Thus we don't say, "You made me angry when you disrespected me," which is parallel to, "You made me cuss," "You made me throw that plate," or "You made me rob that bank"— three blaming expressions that we gave up for good in Step Two. I must know and understand my anxious feelings and that I can handle them with self-governance; someone else can trigger my angry feelings, but no one can make me angry and give in to my anger and express it—except me. That's a deep and genuine accountability for the self. In this second moving part, courage meets emotional intelligence. Here are the same examples from earlier, with the emotional reactions italicized:

- o "When you yelled at me in the parking lot, *I felt angry.*"
- o "When you argued with me before I finished, *I felt disrespected.*"

Tips for Doing the AeR

- **Use BICBOF: Breathe in Courage, Blow Out Fear**
- **Appropriate self-governance.** Even if your feelings are aroused, deliver the AeRs calmly. You can show an intensity that reflects feelings of anger and hurt—but without giving in to anger or impulses to get even. Eyes and facial expressions alone can convey this in a self-governed way. AeRs do not include large body movements.
- **UPR.** This usually comes first, but while always being an open, welcoming, spellbound listener, when delivering an AeR regarding a negative behavior, please stay neutral

in affect. UPR's warmth element in these instances is seldom honest or appropriate.

- **Singleton event.** AeRs refer to a single behavior. (Not: "When you cut me off in the meeting, and ignored me in the Q&A, and then didn't talk to me, I felt dishonored.") A correct AeR: "When you cut me off in the meeting, I felt dishonored."

- **Short & Sweet.** AeRs are brief. Keep the message clear. (A long tirade is not an AeR: "When I was talking about process costing, you interrupted about the contribution margin and about the upcoming audits and new bonuses and new acquisition risks so I felt totally disregarded.") An AeR would be: "When you interrupted my presentation, I felt totally disregarded."

- **Positive AeRs.** AeRs express a special appreciation. "Diane, when you edited those tiff files, I was incredibly grateful." (Positive feeling words include: *appreciated, certain, cheerful, confident, elated, energized, excited, freed, fulfilled, happy, honored, inspired, peaceful, pleased, proud, glad, reassured, recognized, safe, secure, satisfied, uplifted*).

- **Timing.** AeRs are given close in time to the other person's action. (Not: "When you said that thing about my report last summer, I felt offended.")

- **Prepare to quietly listen.** After giving the AeR, be respectfully attentive. If there's neither acknowledgment nor pushback, that's okay. You clearly and respectfully stated that the other person's action had an impact on you and you have touched their conscience.

- **Don't pile on and honor the period by stopping.** If you get a positive or a negative answer, don't add more. ("That reminds me, you also disrespected me when we were. . .")

(continued)

> *(continued)*
>
> - **Close on the relationship.** At the end of the dialogue, it's normally appropriate to say, "Thank you for listening. I appreciate you for doing so."
> - **Using AeRs when you see another person disrespected.** In these instances, you may want to start with a UPR, Ask Challenges, one-to-one dialogue with the person who did the disrespecting ("I'm wondering, what do you think about your interaction with Ms. Z?") You could later use an AeR: "When I saw you call X a name, I felt bad for both of you."

When you disrespected me, I felt very angry was Clifton Sutcliffe's classic and instructive AeR to me. It replaced calling me names and labeling me because I had dishonored him.

Caleb Novak could say to Danielle, "When you said, '*I eat too much,*' *I felt hurt.*" (Danielle could use Ask Challenge: "Caleb, how could I help you to eat more healthfully?")

Caleb didn't want to talk about his feelings, much less use them as a pivot point to connect at a real level with Danielle.

"Caleb, what's worse? Admitting what she already knows—every woman has the capacity to hurt a man's feelings—or retreating to your man cave, storing up your resentment and sullenly avoiding her until your anger and hurt subside, and then pretending that nothing happened?"

"But it doesn't feel right, that AeR."

"Yup, it's totally counterintuitive. Like keeping your eye on the ball as it approaches the plate. Courage is a shared community resource—you practice courage so you can do it for Danielle and your daughter. I don't think you want to teach her that men hide out when they feel hurt."

"Man, that's punching below the belt!"

"Yeah, as a recovering coward, I know that yikes-falling-elevator sensation. Too well. Truth hits me where it hurts, too."

Aiden Bellevue could say to Gary Persons, "When you criticize how I treat people, I feel threatened," rather than, "You're sarcastic and critical and you tick me off all the time!"

Gary could say to Aiden, "When you sandblasted Bob, I felt alarmed."

Bella Cruz, instead of complaining to her best friends about her terrible *jefe*, could say to her toxic boss, "When you threaten to fire me, I feel very afraid."

Here's a helpful list of negative feeling states:

Abandoned	Ambivalent	Angry	Annoyed	Anxious
Betrayed	Bitter	Cheated	Confused	Controlled
Crushed	Defeated	Diminished	Distracted	Distraught
Divided	Empty	Envious	Fatigued	Fearful
Flustered	Foolish	Frightened	Frustrated	Guilty
Harassed	Humiliated	Intimidated	Isolated	Jealous
Left out	Lonely	Low	Mad	Miserable
Nervous	Overwhelmed	Pained	Persecuted	Pressured
Rejected	Remorseful	Sad	Shocked	Skeptical
Stunned	Tense	Threatened	Tired	Trapped
Troubled	Unable	Uncertain	Uneasy	Unhappy
Unsettled	Vexed	Vulnerable	Weary	Worried

In my earlier book, I gave the example of how a nurse dealt with a physician's abusive tone by courageously repeating the same AeR:

"Doctor, I value the opportunity to have a professional and collegial relationship with you. But when you called me a name during surgery, I felt humiliated."

The physician replied, "You confuse me with someone who cares what you feel."

"I'm sorry you felt that way," she said. "This wasn't easy for me to say, and I appreciate your listening to me." In a later surgery, he again swore at her, and she repeated her AeR, only to be rebuffed a second time. In a third operation, the physician followed his pattern. So did the nurse. "Okay, okay, I'm sorry," he apologized, and stopped the insults.

As a courageous leader, Caleb said, with a wince and a lot of gut-twitching doubt and skepticism, "Danielle, when you said that all I do is eat junk food, I felt really bad."

Danielle paused. Caleb stopped breathing.

"Thanks, Caleb. That's clear. Tell me more about this coaching you're getting."

He breathed again. He smiled. *I'm still alive*, he thought. "I'm basically using the GOs in communication, mostly to honor you and my daughter. But I'm also using it in my new job."

Reader, when you start a new week's behaviors, keep practicing the skills from the preceding weeks (Figure 5.1).

√	WEEKS	
	1	I use positive feeling AeRs to give even stronger encouragement.
	2	I use negative feeling AeRs instead of stewing and storing resentment.
	3	I repeat negative feeling AeRs for repeat negative events.
	4	I explain AeRs and the practice using AeRs in my personal life.

Figure 5.1   Action-emotional Reaction Behavioral Practice

The Second CourCom Conflict Play: Fix the Fire with Reflect-Back | Situation-Check | No-Thank-You Declaration

"Listening is a magnetic and strange thing, a creative force. The friends who listen to us are the ones we move toward. When we are listened to, it creates us, makes us unfold and expand."

—Karl A. Menninger, MD, *leading psychiatrist*[7]

In a common joke, we meet an order of monks that lived under a vow of silence that could be broken once a year, at Christmas, when a single monk was permitted to utter one sentence. At the Christmas meal, Brother Thomas said, "I love the mashed potatoes."

A year later, Brother David replied, "The mashed potatoes were far too lumpy."

Another year passed. Brother Andrew said, "I can't stand all this bickering!"

We saw in Step Two that Buddy Checks are a gentle way to speak up. It's like an NFL veterans' training camp where NOs are banned, everyone's a teammate, simple pass patterns are based on the 3 GOs, the cafeteria serves healthy food, and no one hits you and none of your buddies gets cut.

But in the larger world, tackles hurt, comfort food is lethal, the other team is not your friend, and conflict is the name of the game. On this unfair gridiron, we need stronger Plays.

FIX THE FIRE equips us to speak up for right, keeps problems from worsening, and advances our courage and character. Here's a personal example.

On educational leave from the Army for grad school, I took a cross-country road trip from California with my buddy Dan Nishio to attend a cousin's wedding and tour the East Coast.

"We should buckle seatbelts each time before starting the engine," said Dan.

"Seriously?" I asked. "We don't even have seatbelts before we make night jumps out of those shaky, unpressurized, vibrating military aircraft."

"Man," said Dan, who would later become a top, prudent investment adviser, "car accidents are no joke. Seriously, it's not safe for you without a seatbelt."

Having an affection for self-destructive impulsivity, I snapped, "Dan, it's my life. You think I'm going to wreck my brand-new sports car? I'll be as careful as a Soldier in a minefield."

"That's hardly a reassuring simile," he said. "Well, the bags are packed and we're ready to go. But I'm not going anywhere until you buckle up." He meant it. He'd used a No-Thank-You Declaration on me. We'll later see more of that Play.

Courageous communication is spoken for the right thing; I reluctantly buckled up. Four thousand miles later, exiting Quebec, I fell asleep at the wheel so my convertible could execute a flawless triple aerial cartwheel at an uncontrollably high speed. We bounced across a boulder field to perform an elegant, endlessly long, twisting, topsy-turvy crashing dismount, transmogrifying the sparkly vehicle into a convincing copy of a crushed garbanzo can. Dan's buckle-up correction let us emerge with minor injuries; had I not been buckled up, my free-flying, seesawing body would have hit him like George Foreman thumping a punching bag. He'd given me a lifesaving Buddy Check and a Fix the Fire.

Fix the Fire is a courageous conflict Play with three options:

- *The Reflect-Back*, for when someone criticizes or attacks you
- *The Situation-Check*, when someone takes a clearly wrong action
- *The No-Thank-You Declaration*, when someone suggests that you do a wrong thing

We all witness wrongs between people and wish we could do something about them.

I don't mean the environment, violence, poverty, discrimination, education, health care, war, and foreign affairs. I'm talking about effectively working out hard issues with the people you love and with whom you live, work, argue, fight, and struggle; those you can hurt and turn to anger and tears; and those who can make you ache and cry. This is the arena in which there are great stakes, for which we badly need to be skilled and in which we're so ill-equipped.

Lacking courage leaves us disoriented in dangerous territory.

Fix the Fire lets us be more proactive and hence stronger and mentally and emotionally more coherent. Fix the Fire Plays may not produce full and immediate repairs, but taking right action is almost always better than passivity.

I've asked leaders across many fields why they didn't intervene in conflicts that obviously hurt people, affected their ability to lead, and prevented team building. These discords also damaged morale, results, and financial bottom lines. Here are some of their answers (with conscience and I-thought-of-this-idea-later ideas in parentheses).

You'll find many will hearken back to Step Two when you stopped the 3 NOs.

- I didn't know what to do (later I realized that doing something would've been a lot better).

- I don't like conflict and I'm not good at it (this sounds like a cop-out, doesn't it?).
- I told myself it wasn't my business (but I later, painfully, regretted that decision).
- I was afraid I'd get into trouble (damn, that makes me sound like a little kid).
- I was afraid I'd make things worse (okay, that's not a reason, it's an excuse).
- I didn't see anyone else doing anything, so I said, why should I? (cop-out, redux).
- I didn't want to butt into other people's business (so I allowed bad things to happen).
- I could lose my next promotion or even get fired (but I didn't do the right thing and I keep thinking about that when I should be sleeping).
- I was afraid (I confess that I don't like the sound of that).

What answers would you add to this list?

Here's the first Fix the Fire option.

The Reflect-Back: When Someone Criticizes or Attacks You

"Is it true? Is it kind? Is it necessary?"

—Amy Carmichael[8]

Sixteen-year-old Jeru, hurt by not getting what he desires, yells at his dad, "You'd better %*@! wake up to real life! Everyone else gets to do it but me!"

Instantly vexed, to protect his power and to recover pride, the dad could roar back like an angry bear, "DON'T YOU DARE RAISE YOUR VOICE AT YOUR FATHER!" to trigger tears, slammed doors, thrown objects, self-destructive thoughts, and a bad month in which both feel unheard, unloved, and helpless while the dad feels disoriented and unappreciated.

Okay, we can accept *that* doesn't work. So as a courageous dad, he sees his teen's incoherence and internal disorganization—as Gracie's mother might say—this poor child's hair is on fire. To model courageous coping with his incipient anger and accumulating frustration, he gathers himself to face his internal turbulence in the same fashion as a Soldier about to confront the enemy; he takes two (or ten) deep, diaphragmatic breaths, does BICBOF, punches in his ever-ready UPR app and, in a practiced way, calmly says, *"I'm not treating you fairly."*

That was a radically respectful and sacrificial parent/leader Reflect-Back.

It bursts with humility, compassion, healing, and promise. Notice that it comes from courage, strength, and compassion and not from fear, weakness, and appeasement.

Courage has now suited up and is on the field. Like magic or some wondrous alien technology, the son's and the father's internal and external conflict levels immediately abate. Jeru's outward hostility is disarmed; aided by parental affirmation, he begins to internally reorganize. Relief replaces rage.

Dad might be the fairest of the fair, but he shouldn't hold his breath because Jeru probably won't see that until he's in his 30s. At a meeting of the Academy of Medical Sciences at Oxford, researchers explained "managing adult responsibilities only became somewhat bearable in your 30s" for both men and women.[9] If Jeru has more than a decade to go, why would a dad cave in to the emotional outbursts of an anxious, immature, and hormonal teen?

But as we will see, the parent neither caved nor agreed.

Agreeing would mean bursting into song and yodeling a Disney ditty while declaring, "I've been both despicable and unfair. Please permit me to compensate by buying you a new Zeus bronze metallic 3T Stingray Corvette and let me fly you to Paris with all your friends."

Instead, the parent courageously *acknowledged* the fearful words from a teen whose hair is so violently aflame that it can be seen by weather satellites. Parents must be more skilled than their children in love, respect, humility, patience, and self-governance—particularly because it's a tough world out there and it's their duty to prepare their children for its harsh realities in which they'll increasingly not be able to always get their way.

There's a big delta between "I agree with you and I must be an unfair jerk," and *I see your anxiety and suffering so I'll acknowledge your reality by reflecting-back your statement.*

But does it work between adults?

My staff is discussing an emerging issue and we're seated at my office's small conference table. A loud crash makes some lurch and spill coffee on laptops.

Alphonse, a manager from a satellite office, has angrily banged the door open and charges into the room. He glares at me. "Do you know what the %*@! you're doing!?" he screams. He's fearful, angry-hot, incoherent, internally disorganized, and ready to rumble because of something he thinks I've done.

My Tier 1 option whispers, *Destroy this creep for insulting you and your power. Get in his face and scream back, "You freak! You're %*@ ! fired and kiss your pension good-bye! Now get the %*@! out of here before I get violent!"* But conscience whispers: *No, come on now, that would be wrong.*

Having grown up with adults who practiced revenge as a hobby, a Tier 2 option says: *Bruise him for disrespecting you. Yell, "Shut up! You're demoted! Do this again and you'll regret it. Now un-ass my office!"* Conscience says, *Well, Bunkie, that's wrong, too.*

A Tier 3 option suggests: *Punish Alphonse for embarrassing you. Say, "You can't interrupt us! This is totally unacceptable! Make an appointment. We'll discuss the consequences later."*

But conscience and training remind me to follow the Confucian tenet: *Subdue the self and act rightly,*[10] which we call doing the Highest Moral Action.

Tier 4 adds, *always model principled conduct in the face of stress.* So I stand and face Alphonse at a respectful distance, breathing BICBOF to use UPR, to govern myself, to demonstrate the courage of compassionate humility instead of the fragility of my cheap arrogance. Now I can see that Alphonse is full of fear, given to anger, incoherent and on fire. *Discern and do the HMA.*

Being the Socratic warrior means mastering myself so I can speak with the practiced voice of philosopher kings and forgotten prophets.

"I've done something wrong," I said to Alphonse, taking responsibility in the moment. Ignorant of facts, I acknowledge his suffering and his need to be heard, and for me to recognize that he's burning up in emotional incoherence.

What do you think happened?

First, here's what some trainees said at this point in the story.

"But, Gus, you didn't do anything wrong and didn't even know what he was talking about."

Yet, I didn't know that I *hadn't* messed up. If I speak to protect my pride, I'm not a courageous Tier 4 leader. I lose UPR, humility, and self-governance, the ability to listen, ask OEQs to understand, or do the right thing. *I thus feed the fire.* My moral imperative? Show UPR.

"You have to put this guy in his place. He was asking for it."

That's our instinctive Tier 1, 2 and 3 default options. My job isn't to punish those who refuse to recognize me as an exceptionally wonderful person; I'm just a recovering coward who was scooped off the street when I was a kid by some YMCA boxing instructors who saw I needed to get some guts. I'm to help a person who's lost his sense of self, be it an adolescent badly infected by peer pressure or an adult whose feelings have been hurt.

"But if you use those words to agree, he could hold it against you in court! How can you admit to doing something when you don't even know if you did it?"

There's a lot of fear in our litigious society. I'd be cautious about using a Reflect-Back if Alphonse were prone to suing people. But he wasn't. As a recovering lawyer, it's my experience that the Reflect-Back actually reduces the chance of a conflict becoming litigation, which is what happens when humanity fails and payback anger prevails.

"But, Gus, this guy's obviously a real pain and I can't see giving in to him."

That's the real question for all of us, isn't it? Our own pride wants to call the plays, hog the ball that never gets passed, and lose the game. Which side wins in my internal conflict between the HMA and getting even? Between using courage or obeying impulses? Protect my emotional comfort or help someone who's on fire? Of course, "emotional comfort" is a misnomer; in conflict, that's already gone. But I can exercise moral competence and act courageously and confidently in a highly integrated way.

How did Alphonse respond to the Reflect-Back?

Like magic, he calmed down. His familiar facial features returned, his shoulders dropped, muscles untensed, and he recovered his O_2 after losing his air to anger and shallow chest breathing. This is the power of UPR and the quiet authority of honoring all persons.

The Reflect-Back rained cooling waters on Alphonse's fires of fear, anger, and vengeance. Tensions dissipated; his sense of internal organization reasserted itself and both of our pulses slowed to normal.

He took a deep, shuddering breath and said that a decision I'd made without consulting him had bumped a key person from a legislative committee, and that its chair had just screamed at him, hurting his pride, embarrassing him, and making him look unimportant.

"I'm very sorry I did that, Alphonse," I said. "I shouldn't have done anything without asking your opinion. I won't repeat that mistake. Is there any way I can help?"

He told me. I said I'd take those actions before lunch and would make an appointment to see him in his office. With napkins from the coffee station, he mopped up the spilled coffee. I helped him. He apologized to the participants. "I've made quite a mess," he said.

"I started it," I said. "This story has my fingerprints all over it."

Tips on Doing a Reflect-Back

A Reflect-Back can also be appropriate when the other person says something very important.

- Reflect-Backs can capture another person's positive statements. During merger talks, a Swedish high-tech firm's CEO told my boss that she'd crossed the ocean to meet him because our American company's core values spoke to her. My boss gave a memorable Reflect-Back: "Values," he said, "can speak louder than words."[11]
- UPR's spellbound listening lets you catch the words and the meaning, the gist, so you can reflect them back. "Your depreciation rate is way off" can be reflected back as, "I made a miscalculation." (Then ask an OEQ, "Can you tell me more about that?")

(continued)

(*continued*)

- Reflect-Backs aren't echo-backs that parrot the other person's words. That's thoughtlessly mechanical and smacks of mocking: "You relied too heavily on the résumé and you hired the wrong candidate" is not reflected back by saying, "I relied too heavily on the résumé and I hired the wrong candidate." That's how kids torment each other on long car trips.
- Reflect-Backs are short.
- After giving a Reflect-Back, remain still and quiet to allow the other person to process it.
- Reflect-Backs honor the other person's level of emotional depth. If they're fearful, upset, or angry, you wouldn't want to exhibit a deep calmness that could come across as an arrogant superiority to their stronger emotions. Your Reflect-Back would respect the other person's emotional state by a tone that recognizes the seriousness of their feelings and of the situation without mimicking or scorning their fear or anger or, of course, without losing your own self-governance.
- Then continue the dialogue with CLEAR.

I've used Reflect-Backs that didn't produce magical moments but allowed parties to stop worsening hurt feelings and to honor and respect each other by acknowledging the fire. We act courageously not because we think we'll get results, look good, win fans and produce ticker-tape parades. It may in fact invite the opposite. We do it because it's the right thing, regardless of outcome in the immediate frame. This isn't pixie-dust we're sprinkling—we're modeling Courageous Communication.

As you practice each of Reflect-Back's behaviors (see Figure 5.2), remember to keep practicing the skills of the preceding weeks.

√	WEEKS	
	1	I practice positive Reflect-Backs with UPR with the gist of the other person's words.
	2	I practice good short, negative Reflect-Backs and then am respectfully quiet.
	3	I practice closing Reflect-Back dialogues with CLEAR.
	4	I practice Reflect-Backs in my personal life.

Figure 5.2   Reflect-Back Behavioral Practice

The Situation-Check: When Someone Takes a Clearly Wrong Action

"We have come to rely upon a comfortable time-lag of fifty years or a century intervening between the perception that something ought to be done and a serious attempt to do it."

—H. G. Wells[12]

Our second Fix the Fire Play is the Situation-Check, or Sit-Check.

We know what this is; we'd instinctively yell out a verbal Sit-Check if a child wandered into a busy street.

But some would hesitate if they saw a pet being abused, a person being bullied, or a wrong action being taken by an adult. Too often, we see trouble brewing at work or in a school and slip slowly into indecision. More would hesitate if the person were a stranger, but face it—we also struggle to be constructively honest when people we know are in the middle of making a mistake. To obey our overemphasized fears, we don't offer respectful Sit-Checks to spouses, significant others, family members, friends, or acquaintances so we can suffer the consequences for years if not lifetimes.

Let's ride the Way-Back Historical Machine for our next story. It's set in the dawn of human time: the 1970s. The war in Vietnam had become endless, and had split the United States into two profoundly angry political halves with a generation gap; unrest triggered arson and troop interventions on college campuses, resulting in student deaths. The war would take the lives of 58,000 Americans and almost four million people in total.[13] Redford, Streisand, Lucas, Spielberg and movies about distant galaxies and great white sharks commanded Hollywood; vinyl, radio, disco, Stevie Wonder, Led Zeppelin, and the Rolling Stones ruled the Earth; we went to the Moon; computers were the size of small houses and were served by priest-like engineers in white coats and shoe covers who spoke in hushed tones. President John F. Kennedy, Dr. Martin Luther King Jr., and Senator Bobby Kennedy had been assassinated; race riots burned inner cities; Soldiers were despised, discriminated against, and spat upon; cops were hated; firefighters were shot while responding to fires; Charlie Manson's groupies did murder while sex, drugs, and rock 'n' roll became the new generational motto. Double-digit inflation, unemployment, a stagnant economy, and a gas shortage crisis loomed as the country, like a giant, helpless amoeba, repeatedly divided itself into countless angry and confrontational factions.

It was just after Christmas in 1978. United Airlines Flight 173 was being piloted by a notoriously controlling autocrat known to be a bad listener. He predictably ignored his flight engineer's warnings of low fuel. The pilot continuously circled Portland International Airport in Portland, Oregon, while trying to individually solve a dashboard light problem—a tech issue that was the flight engineer's job. The pilot was so distracted that he expended his fuel, causing his airliner to fall from the sky with 189 souls on board to crash in a suburban neighborhood. The flight engineer who tried to tell his arrogant captain that they were near fuel starvation was among the crew and passengers who died in the crash.[14]

Notably, the National Transportation Safety Board accident report did not state that the pilot *had a reputation for silencing coworkers and creating a culture of fear among the ranks*.[15] That's the guiding issue that overcame a dashboard light or an intimidated crew member. The leader lacked the moral courage to give up getting his own way so he could do the right thing.

I imagine an AeR from the flight engineer: "*Captain, I'm afraid if you keep focusing on the dashboard light instead of flying the plane, we'll run out of fuel and crash.*" If the pilot continued to be distracted, the engineer, to save the lives of others, could have delivered an emphatic, unmistakable verbal Situation-Check:

"Captain, we're about to flame out! You must land us **right now***!"*
But he didn't say it.

Do we have less dramatic examples than Flight 173? More than can be counted.

As you scan the list below, do you find yourself wishing that someone would *do something*?

That's why we have CourCom's Sit-Check, which appears after each example in italics. Each Sit-Check begins with a collegial greeting, a "CG." A sample CG appears in the first example and would be appropriately different in each situation.

- A parent learns that someone else's child is being badly bullied at school.

   Thank you for your time. You probably know, but my daughter just told me that your child is being badly bullied at school. Or, to the principal or vice principal: CG. I think you ought to know this; I've learned that the Jones child is being badly bullied at school.

- A person circulates rumors about X in the break room.

   (In a private conversation with that person): CG. I heard your concerns about X in the break room. I'm wondering if you've raised those issues with X?

- A sales VP takes personal credit for a contract that you secured.

   CG. Can you help me with something? I'd like to understand how you assign credit for contracts.

- A peer tries to sell a firm's intellectual property to a rival.

   CG. Biff, I overheard your phone call. Can you talk to me about your thinking?

- A person cheats on a certification test.

   CG. Let's say you saw me cheating. How would you try to help me?

- A person skips safety checks and takes risks in work settings.

   CG. If you saw me skip a safety check, how would you help me out?

- A health care worker doesn't wash hands or follow septic procedures.

   CG. You know, I often slip up. Did you just forget to do something?

- A would-be driver is obviously impaired or reckless.

   CG. Hey, buddy, let me help you. I'll get you a ride.

> ### Tips on Doing a Verbal Sit-Check
>
> - Be aware of your surroundings; situational awareness is always important even if lions, tigers, and bears aren't in your area.
> - We live with humans who err; don't waste time being surprised by wrongs and then focusing on how shocked you are that humans act in predictably selfish and thus unprincipled ways. ("I can't believe he did that!") Not being confounded or dismayed allows you to go directly to discerning the HMA.
> - First, with BICBOF and UPR: don't give in to anger, outrage, or accusation. If there's time: Ask Challenges. Give an AeR.
> - If there's no time, the wrong action continues, or it represents a very present hazard: Directly state your concern, be brief, respectfully wait for a response, be prepared to use a Reflect-Back and repeat your concern. We can help others by not reflexively drifting off stage.

What happens if a verbal Sit-Check requires more than words? Sometimes it does.

The Physical Situation-Check

I'd given what I'd hoped was a stirring talk on moral courage to the 3,000-plus student body of a Bay Area inner city high school. It was either pretty good, or people were relieved it was over, resulting in a standing ovation. I then heard the sad denouement—the ruckus of a major-league fistfight that drew hundreds of students as adults quickly exited. It was a bad sign, so I joined the kids.

A huge, oversized student was hitting a small fellow in temples and jaw, the traditional targets for KOs, concussions, and brain damage. Bad things happen in tussles, but when Person B doesn't keep his chin down and cover up, and Person A knows how and where to punch, death leaves the cheap seats and steadily edges to ringside.

I swam through the crowd—the smaller kid was already out on his feet and was being horribly suspended by brain-jarring punches—and sweet reason had lost its opportunity. I bear-hugged the big guy from the rear and carried him off. The deafening roar whiffed away as if a recording of a screaming mob scene had been switched off; we're often shocked into silence by moral action. It wasn't about a native son author who'd returned to his hometown to give a talk about moral courage, or a Chinese guy in his 60s who had carried off the school bully, or about any individual. It was about witnessing the very uncommon verb of courage in a very common space.

The fellow in my arms was well north of 200 pounds and uncounted hamburgers and milk shakes above my weight class. He struggled halfheartedly, no doubt worn down by his relentless punching. Unable to break my grip and probably curious about his fate, he let me cart him away. His victim had to be less than 125 pounds dripping wet—a thin, bony featherweight with quick-bleeding thin skin. For years, I'd been that smaller kid.

I turned into an empty corridor. "You are not a problem," I said clearly. "I'm Gus. We're buddies going way back. What's your name?" He was calm. I lowered his feet to the ground and slowly released him, my arms swollen with blood and meth-like adrenaline and cortisol. (Fear drains blood from the brain to infuse the major muscle groups to fight lions and bears.) I breathed slowly to blow out adrenaline and return some blood to my frontal lobes. Just like after a bout, my hands shook a little in the fading jet wash of stress hormones.

"Deke," he said. (Not his real name).

"Deke," I said. "Look at you. Already a man. You could've killed that little guy. You're way too big to be mean. Your job now is to watch out for the little ones. Can you do that?"

Deke pondered. "@#% you!" he suggested and left. I've always had a way with words.

The physical Sit-Check had averted the victim's further brain damage and might've prevented a youth homicide. I then shared an uncomfortable lunch with the faculty in the school library. I asked if they'd called 911 for the injured kid. No one knew, so someone left to check. I asked why no one had intervened to save the victim or call the police.

"We're not strong enough," said one. "We don't work out like you."

"I could lose my job." "I'm terrified by conflict."

"The smaller kid is a wise-ass troublemaker with a smart mouth. He baited the bully. It's his fault."

"We could get sued," said another.

These statements aren't limited to public school teachers, who face neglected and often unfed children, many of whom, as in my childhood, are not strangers to poverty, instability, and quickly sparked, bloodletting violence. The uncomfortable answers I heard that day are increasingly becoming a shared national response to our multiplying problems.

We want to do the right thing. If we're sincere about this, we'll need to practice courage.

At a pool on a hot 100° afternoon in Davis, California, a mother of two had expertly observed that the lifeguard had been goofing off, ignoring the children in the crowded pool to flirt with boys, and constantly applying sunscreen. A hubbub drew everyone's attention; an inert four-year old had been pulled from the water by a stranger and appeared lifeless. The lifeguard saw this and left her chair to kneel by the boy. But she clearly did not know how to save the child, who had turned a translucent blue.

The mom instantly left her kids in the care of the dad and did the essential Sit-Check:

"Is he breathing?" she asked. The lifeguard didn't know and had not checked to see. The mom respectfully but forcefully took over, and after not seeing or hearing a breath, opened the boy's airway to begin the steady breath of life while the onlookers stopped breathing. Why? Because they were witnessing a rare act of moral courage.

The mom's efforts seemed fruitless. But she was encouraged by his faint pulse.

She later said that she had prayed and willed the boy to breathe, for his chest to show even the tiniest movement. Hopes flagging, she sustained her failed effort while some turned away, unable to watch any longer.

But then, just as she heard the emergency vehicle's siren in the distance, the little boy's chest moved and he spastically jerked, ejecting an enormous mass of water onto the pool deck. Arriving EMTs found the boy recovering and ambulanced him to the hospital. The mom didn't know if the child had suffered brain damage. But he'd certainly been administered several ghastly doses of mistrust of the adults in his family, of lifeguards in general, and perhaps of water in any form. It's possible that he has only the vaguest impression of the woman who used a physical Sit-Check to save his life while most others did little else but watch in agonized paralysis.

Giving a verbal or physical Sit-Check means solving problems. But we often miss how to do it effectively. When we crack the code and find the root cause of a problem, lights come on and we know where to make repairs.

An African proverb guides us: "The answer lives inside the problem."[16]

The mom followed up her physical Sit-Check with verbal ones. She gave respectfully courageous and direct feedback to the family member who was on his screen and hadn't noticed his nephew lying face-down in the bottom of the pool; to the lifeguard who chatted with boys and missed the child's drowning; to the pool manager who'd hired a lifeguard that didn't know her job, safety procedures, or CPR, and who had failed to monitor her work and coach her in her duties. The rescuing mom addressed the people at the top for what had happened to a kid who ended up at the bottom.

Was the root cause the hiring, the training, the inattention? I'm not so sure. Let's look at some other deadly examples.

Are car accidents caused by traffic, mechanical issues, or human error? In 20 years, the Afghanistan war took the lives of 2,448 US Soldiers.[17] In the same time span, car accidents killed 691,045 Americans,[18] which translates into 34,552 Americans dead and two million injured per year.[19] In those 20 years, the Afghan war killed 122 Americans a year, creating a ratio of car accident deaths to combat fatalities of 282 to one.[20] Again, in the same time span, more than 700,000 Americans died from drug overdoses.[21]

What's considered to be the leading cause of our terrible car fatalities? The records say it's "human error," led by distraction, drunk driving, speeding, reckless driving, running red lights, fatigue, and youth.[22] In most cases, the causes aren't mechanical. They're the result of bad choices from losing our internal conflict between driving safely or driving while texting and buzzed; driving wisely or speeding; driving while rested or while tired; and driving with everyone buckled up, or not.

Is human error really the root cause? Or is it something else?

Smoking kills 480,000 of us a year; 34,000,000 continue the habit.[23] We spend nearly $2 billion a year on alcohol,[24] which sickens millions and kills 95,000 of us a year. Smoking and alcohol deaths are "painful and agonizing," offering us all graphic evidence of what happens when habits aren't altered.[25] Thirty-two million Americans, 12 percent of us, abuse drugs.[26] When things fail, human error is the usual suspect; it also causes most airline accidents.[27]

But pinning crashes and avoidable deaths on human error misses the point, for using the label of *human error* suggests to us that there's no real solution; humans were involved, so sue somebody for wrongful death, move on, and it's business as usual and let's keep doing what we feel like doing.

I submit that if we track the beast to its lair, we'll find that the actual culprit is *moral* error. Unlike the umbrella term of "human error" that invites no remediation (it is what it is), moral error can be effectively addressed by practice-based training.

I recognize that knowing you should act is not the same thing as actually doing it.

Intervening with a Sit-Check can be hazardous to life, limb, others, and employment. I was trained to help and save others; many lack, haven't received, or sought that training. Employ care, discernment, logic and discretion before using Sit-Checks and always employ courageous UPR.

As you practice Sit-Check behaviors (see Figure 5.3), remember to keep practicing the skills of the preceding weeks.

√	WEEKS	
	1	I practice UPR, humility, and self-governance when I see a wrong take place.
	2	I mentally rehearse speaking up when a wrong occurs.
	3	I verbally practice using a Sit-Check to speak to a predictable wrong.
	4	I reflect on using the Sit-Check and becoming the person I'm supposed to be.

Figure 5.3   Situation-Check Behavioral Practice

The No-Thank-You Declaration: When You Are Asked to Do Something Wrong

"When my daughter was born, I couldn't even spell 'no,' much less say it to her."

—*Stephen A. Brown, writer*[28]

Our third Fix the Fire option is the No-Thank-You Declaration, the NTD.

Do you find it easier to say yes than no? Many do.

There are many reasons. We don't like to disappoint people or hurt their feelings. We fear the uncertainty of declining a request and can feel guilty when we do.

Those who haven't admitted and stopped the 3 NOs will continue to fear conflict and discomfort and will expend a great deal of stress and energy to avoid both—and then will experience the pleasure of a long-troubled conscience. How does this happen?

By agreeing to things that conscience and logic say should be politely bypassed.

Those who haven't practiced the GO of self-governance will continue to fear missing out on attractive personal habits that they know are self-destructive. Not being able to say no to yourself is poor preparation for declining undesirable offers from others.

I Feel Guilty When I Say No, a former best-selling book by Manuel J. Smith, expresses the feelings of many, even though it recommends declining a wrong action to "get your own way" rather than to do the right thing.[29] A psychologist once told me that one should say no when the opportunity doesn't add value to your life and your desires. Again, that viewpoint is framed in taking care of Number One at the cost of others and principles greater than the self.

On a stronger note, Warren Buffett, an expert at consenting to opportunities that make great profits, said, "We need to learn the slow 'yes' and the quick 'no.'"

Steve Jobs added, "Focusing is about saying 'no.'"[30]

I can sigh aloud when I think of how more admirable my life would've been for those around me had I said no to things that my conscience had jumped up and down, waving its arms, and sounding warning alarms to warn me against doing. But in those days, I told myself, "I'm not good at saying no," and to ensure I was right, proceeded to act the fool.

It's my experience with thousands of people that we can all use a simple CourCom Play to practice declining "opportunities" that are really just bear traps.

What might a courageous NO THANK-YOU DECLARATION, an NTD, look like?

In basic training, Stephen A. Brown, a Phi Beta Kappa conscientious objector draftee en route to becoming an Army medic and future writer, had just received a drill sergeant's booming, ear-shattering and inappropriate direct order.

"Drill Sergeant," said Private Brown, "you are far too kind. I must respectfully refuse."

This creative response was a literary echo of Major General John Burgoyne's line in the G. B. Shaw play, *The Devil's Disciple*. That aristocratic British general had just been asked to preside over a kangaroo court.

"No, sir," replied Burgoyne. "I feel my own deficiencies too keenly to presume so far."[31]

That line elegantly captures saying *no* in a nutshell.

Tips for Doing the No Thank-You Declaration

- When saying no, use UPR, as always.
- Act with humility (even if you're not an aristocratic British major general).
- Clearly and politely say, "No," with a short phrase of your reasoning.
- Continue UPR and civility and CLEAR (and close on the relationship).

Here are possible responses to being asked to do something wrong, using the NTD:

- On a workday, your best friend urges you to binge all night on video games.
    "It'd be fun, but no thanks. I really need my sleep."
- A friend in need asks you to help him cheat on a test to avoid getting an F.
    "Aren't there better options? I care for you too much to help you cheat."
- Your tipsy pal angrily demands in a loud voice that you give him his car keys.
    "I won't do that. Let's go. I'll drive you home so you can catch some z's."

  o Your boss tells you to submit a software program's bug list before it's ready.
    "I'll have to label it, 'Incomplete.'"
- A friend invites you to watch porn.
    "No thank you. It rots my brain, robs me of sleep and isn't good for either of us."
- You're in a committed relationship; someone wants you to meet an unattached person.
    "No thanks. I'm in a relationship."
- You're offered a job that pays more but you doubt the integrity of the firm.
    "No, thank you. I don't think I'd be a good fit."
- A peer wants you to give a lower score to a job applicant, perhaps for biased reasons.
    "That'd be wrong. Can you tell me why you asked?"
- At work in the hospital, a buddy steals drugs and tells you to keep quiet.
    "I'm disappointed in you, buddy. Please put them back, now."
- A coworker texts while driving and ignores your, "When you text, I feel really afraid."
    "Please stop right now and let me out. I mean it."

As you undertake each No-Thank-You Declaration behavior (see Figure 5.4), remember to keep practicing the skills of the preceding weeks.

√	WEEKS	
	1	I rehearse using UPR, humility, and being quietly resolute and saying no.
	2	Seeing there's little "risk," I practice NTDs with easier, low-intensity situations.
	3	Seeing there's little "risk," I practice NTDs with harder, higher-intensity situations.
	4	Having success with NTDs, I add the Play to my regular CourCom Playbook.

Figure 5.4   No-Thank-You Declaration Behavioral Practice

The third conflict Play, CBS, goes directly into the heart of discord—a negative and tense situation that has been prepared and softened by the preceding five CourCom Plays.

The Third CourCom Conflict Play: The CBS—We Get Serious About Reconciliation

"Before Nelson Mandela was arrested in 1962, he was an angry young man. He founded the ANC's military wing. When he was released, he surprised everyone because he was talking about reconciliation and forgiveness and not about revenge."

—Archbishop Desmond Tutu, Anglican cleric and theologian[32]

Reconciliation is a big, rare, and special word. Science director Gary Persons had adopted his Tier 4 Pivot: *fix myself first* (my challenge isn't Aiden, it's my own stubborn nature and lack of consideration for others) before we discussed the next Play.

Gary's abrasiveness wasn't limited to Aiden. He'd courageously accepted that CLEAR would equip him to communicate more effectively with everyone else. CLEAR would also serve as the groundwork for using CourCom Conflict Plays that would lead to the radical idea of reconciling a relationship instead of erasing an employee.

We began by Gary practicing CLEAR; I played the role of the difficult Aiden Bellevue. Gary upped his warm, open, and welcoming behaviors, sensed he'd gone too far into a fictional familiarity and dialed it back. When he felt prepared, he set a meeting with Aiden. Accustomed to summoning people to his upper floor executive suite, Gary radically offered to instead meet in Aiden's office.

Gary and I touched base after the meeting,

"My heart pounded like, you know, a big bass drum," he said. "I breathed slowly and stopped saying to myself, *I hate conflict and this is going to go badly. So I did what I could control: start and stick with UPR.*"

This is how the rest of the meeting went.

Gary said, "Hi, Aiden." Gary was warm without being goofy and open without being false. It was his meeting in Aiden's space, but he still acted in a welcoming and modest way. His voice began in a squeak to recover its depth and pitch. (Victory!) "Thank you for meeting with me."

Aiden snorted in an off-putting way. "How will you hound me today, Dr. Persons?"

Sustaining UPR and collegiality under pressure, he remembered to inhale slowly and deeply through his nose. He said, "Aiden, I'm not going to do that. You have a big project. I haven't checked in to see how you're doing with it." Gary focused on Listening with Empathy.

"B.S.," snapped Aiden, kicking back and loudly dropping his feet on his desk.

Earlier, I'd played a scornful and mocking Aiden; Gary knew it was coming and was neither surprised nor put off. *Empathy.* "I get why you think that. We've been in a bad place. Can I sit?" Aiden shrugged. Gary sat.

"I value our professional relationship," said Gary, "and I haven't done a good job in supporting you. I'm changing things in myself to improve how we work together. I invite your thoughts about that."

"Fine," snapped Aiden. Silence.

Ask another OEQ. "Good. How are you doing under our latest budget cuts?"

Aiden sat up. "I don't get any of this. What the hell are you doing, Gary?"

Gary was prepared. "I'm trying to be a better boss. To see if I can be of any real help."

"Frankly, you astonish me," said Aiden. "Okay, I'll play. I could use four more analysts."

"I wish I could do that. I might be able to get you one. Would that be better than none?"

Four analysts were impossible; Gary had restrained his scorn and well-practiced sarcastic response to preposterous requests. He stayed with his unnatural but practiced UPR, listened carefully with his newfound empathy, and asked open-ended questions. Gary was as self-governed as gentle St. Francis tending to birds and he listened to Aiden as avidly as if his antagonistic colleague were the world-renowned inventor Nikola Tesla.

"Fine. We done here?" replied Aiden.

"Yes," said Gary, standing. *Close on relationship*: "Aiden, thank you for your time. I really appreciate it. I'll get back to you by the close of business Friday to see if I can get you an analyst. I really hope you have a good day." He half-smiled, said good-bye and left.

"It was the best meeting I ever had with him." Gary said to me. "CLEAR kept me from messing up and helped me do it right. I didn't react to his rudeness. I didn't disrespect or criticize him. He had nothing to attack me for. I also got him a good analyst. I keep using CLEAR with that guy?"

"Yes, but only for the rest of your life," I smiled. "Any thoughts about how you just referred to Aiden?"

He paused. "I just called him, 'that guy.' No UPR. I wish he'd call me 'Gary' instead of 'Dr. Persons,' which he manages to turn into a slur. Can we now do CBS?"

"Absolutely. CBS is a duo relationship Play. It's facilitated by a coach. It works best if I train you and Aiden at the same time. Would that work for you?"

Gary was quiet. "Okay. Tell me what 'CBS' stands for."

"Yes, the mystery of those letters. So Aiden doesn't feel like he's behind the curve, I recommend that you and Aiden discover that together." Gary nodded.

"I'd like each of you," I said, "to complete a CBS pre-work form that could take 10–30 minutes to do. That form will reveal what 'CBS' stands for.

"When I get the pre-work back, I'll email you times for a one-hour meeting.

"The two of you agree on a time and we'll do the CBS. What do you think?"

"How well does CBS work?" asked Gary.

I grinned. "That's the beauty of it. It's what you and Aiden are going to decide."

The CBS Pre-work Assignment

Complete, sign, and email it to Gus by _____. Have a copy during the meeting.

1. AGREEMENT: I agree that I own part of the conflict with _____ and that I alone can end my part. I commit to fully participate in good faith in the CBS.

2. ACCEPTANCE: I accept that the CBS seeks a functional reconciliation between _____ and me so that we can share a professional, principled, and admirable relationship. It need not be a friendship and is not a capitulation. It is a new accord based on Unconditional Positive Respect, humility, self-governance, and maintaining a practical and effective relationship without disrespect, anger, or accusations by either party.

3. THE CBS ASSIGNMENT: Please reflect on the observable behaviors you choose in each of the three categories. Please write down observable behaviors such as "not listening" and "raising your voice," and not personality traits such as "rude" or "inconsiderate."

- 3 observable behaviors you wish _____ to **Cease** doing with you.

_____

_____

_____

(continued)

(*continued*)

■ 3 observable behaviors you wish _____ to **Begin**
demonstrating with you.

_____
_____
_____

■ 3 observable behaviors you wish _____ to **Sustain**
doing with you.

_____
_____
_____

　　Read your 9 CBS behaviors, in an alternating fashion, with
_____ who will record your CBS behaviors verbatim. He
will read his 9 CBS behaviors to you; you record them verbatim:

Cease: _____
_____
_____

Begin:_____
_____
_____

Sustain: _____
_____
_____
_____

SIGNATURE _____   DATE _____

I'd earlier met Aiden in training and welcomed both men as they faced each other across a small table. Each had signed the CBS Form and had brought his list of 9 CBS behaviors.

"Thank you both for participating, it's good to see you together. Let me read what you've agreed to do." Both were quiet as I read aloud their signed commitments to the CBS reconciliation process.

Aiden's deep-set eyes were guarded and observant, ready for the next blow that life was going to deliver to his psychically bruised chin. He was of medium height with broad shoulders, suggesting a history of hard physical labor. Dressed casually in a well-worn sport coat, he was a contrast to the tall, slender, diplomat-like Gary, who was more formally presented and given to wearing bow ties.

"I want you both to consider," I said, "that your conflict is centered in the disappointments from a broken relationship and the resulting negative feelings. Your obvious points of argument are a natural result. Any thoughts about those possibilities?"

Aiden nodded, followed by Gary's sigh.

"The pre-work you did represents the heart of the CBS process. I'll go through it and then answer your questions. After that I'll state the ground rules. I'm inviting you to do the CBS together and I'll facilitate. Then, we'll close by agreeing about how to go forward with some accountability to each other.

"CBS, as you know from the pre-work, stands for three behaviors:

- **Cease.** You'll ask the other to *stop* three negative behaviors so the two of you can form a professional, principled and admirable relationship.
- **Begin.** You'll ask the other to *start* three new, positive behaviors to create a professional, principled and admirable relationship.
- **Sustain.** You'll ask each the other to *continue* three positive behaviors to create not a friendship and lifelong buddies, but a professional, principled, and admirable relationship.[33]

"Aiden and Gary, most duos, or dyads, that get caught in mutual discord suspect in the beginning that they won't agree to each other's behavioral asks, or requests, and later are surprised when they find agreement.

"CBS suggests that antagonists can actually cooperate. I've been asked if CBS is a 'conflict resolution' tool. I don't think so.

"For decades, I've seen my leadership guild try to 'resolve conflicts.' In my experience, it mostly fails. Part of it is that we misstate the issue, so our remedies are going to miss the target.

"Say the two of you commit to stop acting negatively. That wouldn't produce positive behaviors, effective operating conditions or a fresh, forgiving relationship. Because the relationship remains broken, you'd remember your injuries. Agreeing merely to stop verbally punching each other is a start but not a solution. At this point, many withdraw into sullenly ignoring each other. Eventually, a sneaky passive-aggressiveness leads to a rekindling of old disagreements. Most conflict work only produces temporary and uneasy truces between renewed warring.

"As you read earlier in the pre-work, the purpose of CBS is to reconcile two people so they can form and create a professional, principled and admirable relationship. That means it's:

- **Free of negative behaviors:** No disrespect, scorn, not listening, criticizing. It's stopping bad acting.
- **Professional:** Professionals are held to a higher standard of conduct to match your responsibilities and your duty to not give in to baser instincts. A professional must serve others at the cost of self-advancement. It's acting rightly above the level of your feelings.
- **Admirable:** You interact with each other every day in a praiseworthy manner. You model doing the right thing with each other in a way that draws the admiration of others. You act rightly to inspire others to act rightly. You act like the person you're supposed to be.

"Any questions?" I asked.

"Did you make up that definition of 'professional'?" asked Aiden.

"No, and a good question. It's the classical definition of noble professions,[34] and modern professional conduct codes. What do you think?"

"I like it," said Aiden.

"Could we," said Gary, "use that definition in our organization?"

"Yes, and another good question. I think it's accurate. I've seen it help people get their courage. Courage is the goal of CourCom Plays. It's the goal of CBS. Remember playing catch?"

They nodded. "CBS is two people playing catch. Aiden throws three times; Gary catches them. Then Gary throws three; Aiden catches them. In CBS, the throws, or 'passes,' are your requests to the other for specific behaviors. Each of you will later decide which passes you liked.

"We'll do this in three stages: *Share Behaviors*; *Agree to Behaviors*; and *Battle Buddy Accountability*. We start with Share Behaviors and go through each of your nine behaviors of ceasing, beginning, and sustaining.

"You'll read your requested behaviors to each other and alternate. Good?

"Then here are the ground rules:

- Please listen to the behaviors without criticism or complaints. You'll get to push back in the second stage, Agree to Behaviors.
- Ask questions to the other person, not to the facilitator.
- Read your behaviors aloud, slowly and clearly, so the other person can record them.
- When listening to the behaviors, record them verbatim. When finished, say 'Got them.'
- You can ask the other person to repeat the behavior or behaviors.
- Unless there's an objection, please call each other by your first names."

"Why first names?" asked Aiden, frowning.

"I'd like to hear your thoughts on that," I said.

"Yeah, I get it. I've used 'Dr. Persons' as a way to put him down. Okay."

"Thank you," I said. "Aiden, you will read aloud, slowly and carefully, the three observable behaviors you want Gary to *cease*, to stop doing, if you two are to have a professional, principled, and admirable relationship.

"Gary, without giving corrections or criticism, record, verbatim, and listen spellbound to Aiden's three requested behaviors. If you miss a word, respectfully ask Aiden to repeat that part. When you've captured Aiden's words say, 'Aiden, I got it. May I read your words back?'

"If Aiden agrees, Gary, you'll read the requests aloud back to Aiden.

"If Aiden hears a variance, he respectfully points out the correct wording. Gary notes it and reads it back. We do this until Aiden says, 'Gary, you got it.'

"Then you switch. Gary, you read your three requested *cease* behaviors; Aiden, you record them verbatim and say, 'Gary, I got it' and read them back and Gary offers corrections until the copied words match the originals. Why do you think this might be important?"

"It puts my words into Gary's mouth," said Aiden. "And his, into mine."

"Yeah," said Gary. "Talk about humility on steroids."

"Gentlemen, that was perfectly said by both of you. We then repeat the process for the *begin* and *sustain* requested behaviors. That concludes the first stage. I'll explain the second and third elements later. Questions? Gary, prepare to listen and copy. Aiden, please lead off."

CBS Share Behaviors

"Dr. Persons," said Aiden, "I mean, uh, Gary. The three behaviors I want you to cease, stop doing, in our professional relationship are: first, don't criticize my statements with your words and facial expressions."

"Isn't that two behaviors?" asked Gary of me.

I opened my hand in Aiden's direction. "Gary," he said, "please treat it as one."

"Second," said Aiden, "stop using staff meetings to criticize me, however obliquely. . .and third, stop talking about me behind my back."

Gary said, "Aiden, I got them," and read them back. For the third requested behavior, he said, "stop gossiping."

"See what I mean?" said Aiden to me. "He does what he wants!"

I opened my hand toward Gary. Aiden reread the third behavior to Gary and asked Gary to record it verbatim, which he did. He then read it back accurately.

"I don't gossip," muttered Gary. "Aiden wasted a behavior. He should've listed something real."

I pointed toward Aiden, who seemed to be more engaged.

Gary collected himself. "Aiden, the observable behaviors I want you to cease doing for us to have a principled relationship are, stop fighting my attempts to give you advice. . ."

"Gary, that's bull! You don't give advice. You criticize!"

I waited. Gary got it. "Yes, Aiden," he said slowly. I've noted that your three *ceases* are about my criticisms."

Aiden nodded. "Okay. Sorry for reacting," he said to me, "that I got hot."

I pointed toward Gary. Aiden apologized to Gary. I waited.

Gary accepted it.

They're interacting. "You two are doing very well. We good? Gary, please proceed."

"Second," said Gary, "stop spending work time to form a coalition against me. Third, please stop sending all-hands complaint emails that should only come to me, alone."

Aiden got it, said, "Gary, I got it," and read it back verbatim.

"Easier than I thought," said Gary.

"Guys," said Aiden, "I got to tell you, this is very hard for me."

They both looked at me. I waited. Aiden hunched his big shoulders, looked away and inched back from the table. Ten seconds went by. In America, a lifetime.

"Why is that, Aiden?" asked Gary finally.

"We're sitting here like everything's cool and we're rational," said Aiden, "but we walk out that door, it's going to be back to business as usual. It'll be back to being the pure %?!@#."

I waited. I thought: *Reflect-Back, Gary.*

"This all seems fake. . . and out that door, I'm going to be a jerk," said Gary.

Yes!

"You keep surprising me, Dr. Persons, uh, Gary," said Aiden. "Let's keep going."

CBS Agree to Behaviors

In the Agree to Behaviors stage, Gary began by commenting on Aiden's *cease* requests.

"I don't gossip," he said.

"Then," said Aiden, "my request will be easy for you to accept."

Gary thought for a second. "Yes, Aiden. You're right."

In the end, each demurred to only one request. They were able to negotiate each one to an agreed behavior.

Most CBS Plays follow that pattern.

Battle Buddy Accountability

In the Battle Buddy Accountability, they signed to own their new nine requested CBS behaviors to build and support a professional, principled, and admirable relationship.

Each agreed to hold to his commitments for his own integrity and path to courage for the sake of their personal professionalism and the organizational mission of serving others, even if the other person failed.

We act courageously for its own sake. Our courage isn't a barometer that goes up and down depending on the constantly changing behaviors of others in our closely packed atmosphere.

Our Basic CourCom Plays in Step Four helped us to understand others in a deeper way before we react by speaking in a more superficial and self-defending manner. They modeled respectful and effective communication and strengthened relationships and trust. These are essential Plays in leadership, team building, and problem solving. CLEAR, Encourage Others, and Ask Challenges reduce both the likelihood and the acuity of conflicts.

CourCom Conflict Plays in Step Five have equipped us to speak into discord. The AeR, Fix the Fire, and CBS strategies will serve us well during those particularly anxious interactions with others who, in conflict, often inflict a lack of self-governance and reason on us and others.

Bravo! You've completed Part II.

Now we move to Part III. Ready for some personal life-strategic planning? You've planned for school selection, internships, trips, jobs, relationships, housing, family, entertainment, and perhaps bingeing on games. You now know how to do all of those things, and more, without letting anxieties interfere.

Read on to boldly go where few have traveled.

Let's put a plan together so you can become the person you're supposed to be.

PART

III

You Decide:
Choosing Your Core

"The only person you are destined to become is the person you decide to be."
—Janet Champ and Charlotte Moore[1]

IN MY PREVIOUS book on courage, I referenced the use of core values by corporations. Some firms selected their values as part of strategic planning in which they consulted with the entire organization. A few of them deployed core values as actual operating principles to build teams and train everyone to lead at their level. But many were fabricated by a few top people behind closed doors, led by the marketing department, who selected "values" as consumer-friendly flytraps for unwary customers and unsuspecting job applicants. Most companies picked core values that became quickly theoretical because they didn't train people to live up to them.

Readers of the first book, knowing that companies had named their core values said, "Tell me about how to get my own personal ones."

So now we're not talking about institutional core values, but about *you* and *your core identity* in a lifelong process of being.

Few of us purposefully choose personal core values or do individual strategic life planning. As a result, we can unintentionally end up referring to *artificial core values*. (Who among us doesn't want to claim "transparency," "meaning" and "justice"?) But if they aren't intentionally applied in day-by-day behaviors and habits, we accidentally produce negative and harmful gaps between what we sincerely believe and advocate and what we actually do and how we behave. These gaps, or deltas, reduce our credibility to ourselves and to others.

I've witnessed in myself and others an evolution of *personal core values*.

1. We become what we experience and our initial set of values tend to come from our family of origin.[2] Mine practiced and modeled the 3 NO's.

2. As a child, I saw the terrible harm caused by these behaviors and hoped and promised to never repeat them, unaware that I had already absorbed them. With that hope, I'd begun experimenting with *aspirational core values*.

3. As a teen and adult, I recognized my negative behaviors under stress—my actual core values. I'd defaulted to what I'd practiced rather than to what I had wished. To think better of myself, I drifted into claiming *theoretical core values* such as "career, family, integrity."

4. I was seeing that folks who did the right thing inspired love and admiration. They consciously respected all persons, consistently did the right thing for others, and were an oasis of peace in a troubled world. In San Francisco's Tenderloin, where I spent 10 years of my youth, addictions were normal and catastrophes were inevitable. But some individuals, like Coach Tony, turned aspirational and theoretical *into actual core values* by using recovery programs and Battle Buddies to quit their bad habits.

5. I saw people do the Three GOs and recognized it as moral courage. They'd all come from fear or failure and got tired of it.

6. I later grouped the admirable behaviors into core values. I saw *courage* as the core value of respecting all people, controlling emotional impulses, and owning the integrity to consistently do the right thing with others regardless of risk. *Leadership* is the core value of courageously inspiring and developing others to be their best selves for admirable and even noble purposes. Of course, we can also adopt self-destructive core values as our operating principles.

True core values are consciously applied to how we purposefully live in dynamic accountability to self-discerned behavioral standards. True core values operate in the center of our identity. They are what we are aiming for. They inform, guide, surround, and permeate mindsets, thought, speech, action, decisions and how we treat principles, the self, others, and the world. They invite kindness or harshness and resemble the Force in a mythic galaxy far, far away.[3]

6

Your Identity: Naming, Claiming, and Aiming

WHEN BOARD MEMBER Clifton Sutcliffe asked me to unethically hire his relative, I revealed my true core values—my negative and defensive operating principles.

What did I defend first? Was it something essential, grand, and beautiful, true, necessary, and kind, something from stunning post-Homeric Greek literature or Du Fu and Li Bai's Golden Age poetry, an eternal value of great consequence that would inspire others, serve our marriage and family, raise principled children of courage, heal the nation, and usher in world peace?

Not quite. I had instead instantly protected my *pride* and *ego*, the discounted values on the clearance shelves of every failed ethics store that can't win friends and influence people, the stuff in the aisle of unwanted habits, and the exact opposite of the heart of heroes. Worse, my ego quickly donned the off-putting cloak and elevated chin of arrogance, a low form of Tier 2 sporting a vanity mirror.

My core values hadn't gone missing. I had them. I just didn't know what they were. Nor did I know how low they could go.

But Clifton and nearby diners recoiled as my values made their entrance with the subtlety of a 30-ton humpback whale breaching in a placid sea. It was as if I'd unwittingly recorded my true and uninspiring core values on a placard and pinned them to my back so all could know who I really was. In the grip of my inferior functions, I was blind to my actions and couldn't read my own writing.

Most of us haven't named the values to which we hold ourselves. As you've seen in my cautionary tale, under stress, those values surface, like hives. But not knowing our present core values gives us a wide-open field—a fine open buffet—from which to choose the best ones.

Choosing well takes courageous discernment. Living out those values requires the practice of courage.

As your coach, I've been challenging you to intentionally jettison your habituated reactions to fear and anxiety. I've invited you to accept at a deep level that when we respond to fear, it damages those around you. I've suggested that you try on new and courageous ways of facing predictable, everyday stressful situations.

Each step you've taken has achieved meaningful goals, reduced old weaknesses, and strengthened and freshened your ability to move upward.

In a bold and deeper manner, it's about who you are and who you intend to be.

The Tier 4 GPS tool set a direction for us. It revealed the gap between the unreflective baselines of Tiers 1, 2, and 3 behaviors and an intentionally courageous Tier 4 identity. Tier 4 reminds us that we're more accurately defined by what we do rather than by what we think, know, want, or lack.

Looking through the window of my study, I can't help but smile at the beauty of Longs Peak, where the Arapaho once braved ice and wind to collect eagle feathers. Eleven kilometers southeast of Longs looms Mount Meeker; together, they form the Twin Peaks Massif. Longs tops 14,000 feet but Meeker, at 343 feet lower, is harder to climb technically on certain routes. To the Arapaho, they were *Neniis-otoyou'u*, which translates to "the mountain guides."[1]

Courage has guided you to the heights. The deep, slow, calming breath you take here differs from the one you took at the start of the trek. In smoggy Los Angeles, residents quip that air isn't real unless you can see it. Here, you've climbed five steps to where the mountain air is clean and crisp. It's no joke that you can see farther into the beyond and deeper into the self.

I think courage merits at least an 11-volume, 13,549-page, five-billion-word epic.[2] Yet, in *The Playbook*'s couple hundred pages and less than two hours of listening or reading, we've discovered that practicing courage empowers you not to best others or take advantage of them, but to steadily become who you are supposed to be so you can even help those you dislike.

Here, you recall the ultimate goal of the journey: to live your story in courage to become your best self. Why? Because others need your modeling of a strong and courageous character and because everyone has the right to practice a selfless integrity and to not live in fear.

"Courage" is derived from Old English and French *corage*, the Latin *coraticum* and *cor*.[3] In current French, Spanish, and pinyin, "heart" is *coeur, corazón* and *xīn*. In any tongue it means your innermost core that defines your comprehensive self, the embracing entity that some call the soul. Each describes the central self—your identity in a nutshell.

This is the fascinating intersection of all that you are: the past and present; emotions and intellect; love and fear; personality and character; wonderful and not wonderful relationships; work and meaning; body, spirit, and. . . soul. Through all that is you, courage can shine as a central practice. Its significance is universal. It has always played a central role in the life and survival of every global culture.

You build your physical core by walking, doing crunches, planks, bird-dogs, pull-ups, and alpine climbing techniques and moves. You build the vital center of identity and integrate your internal coherence by practicing the 3 GOs and CourCom Plays based on the solid ground of intentionally selected guiding standards.

Your climb through Five Steps has exercised your core, your coeur, and your enduring heart, the vital foundational center of the innermost you. The language of the heart is courage. It's also the vocabulary of this higher elevation, this Deeper Country, this part of the world that stands apart from our gnawing fears, where our highest values intersect with the elusive identity that you have always wanted.

Your Personal Core Principles

In Question #18 from the Bio Form in Step One, you were asked to select *one* answer to describe your Core Primary Identity. While having to choose only one option runs counter to our natural desire to not be limited to a single, central theme, #18 invited you to venture into the exercise of truly defining yourself. This question gave you Option L, where you could write in your own choice.

A traumatic childhood shook hands with my innate human fears to produce less than admirable original core principles. These emerged as: "Guard against emotional pain and punch out people who threaten me." Other than proving to be ineffective (emotional hardship is a natural admission price of life) and semi-catastrophic (I had to convince Yolo County Sheriff's deputies to not arrest me for battery),

I can now offer a truer Option L self-concept:

"My core identity, despite life's inevitable difficulties, is practicing courageous behaviors to do the highest right and to endeavor to bring the most good to others." In this, research reminds us that courageously doing the right thing generates positive impacts on everything in our lives and is clearly more helpful to others than constantly spreading my personal fears.

We all can change artificial, aspirational principles into true ones, and true principles into courageous ones. (If you don't adopt new principles now, when will you?) How might you answer Question #18 now?

You can use your experience, discernment, conscience, and insights from the Biography to list the behaviors you'd most like to own.

Whatever behaviors you choose, I suggest that one of your values, to protect and guarantee the others, should be courage—to live courageously.

If you decide to choose Courage, I remind you that *aiming* for a courageous identity requires intentionality, a plan, and accountability.

Aristotle identified intentionality, *proairesis*, as a requirement to sustain excellence.[4] Intentionality is a singular mindset to achieve a needed outcome.

One planning method is the Individual Courage Advancement Plan, the ICAP, a tool you can routinely use to assess your progress.

In all of this, accountability is, of course, our new best friend.

Together, they can be a form of your own *Neniis-otoyou'u*, your soaring, cloud-catching mountain guides. They encourage us to climb higher, above the common level of life, and that because others have done it for the sake of others, we can do so, as well.

7

The Individual Courage Advancement Plan: ICAP

CORPORATIONS, GOVERNMENT AGENCIES, nonprofits, and key executives pay organizational consultants to help them escape the entanglements of the day-to-day so they can do serious strategic planning. This allows them to focus on the essentials, not get caught in the weeds, and steadily thrive on the path forward.

The ICAP is your strategic assessment and a plan of action to overcome your fears, gain courage competence, and become your best self in the long game.

Like *The Playbook*, it asks you to deeply reflect on questions we seldom ask and even less frequently answer from our inner core. Like the Bio Form in Step One, it's a self-appraisal that lets you gauge the great progress you began in Parts I and II.

The following questions are a courage refresher and warm-up for using your ICAP as an assessment, planning, and navigation tool to continue your journey.

- *Who are you really?* In terms of doing the right thing in treating self and others?
- *Who are you supposed to be?* In terms of courage, clarity, and core identity?

- *What's the gap between the two?*
- *What's your plan to close the gap?* (You need a plan, a map, and milestones.)
- *What are the roadblocks that could stop you?* (You know them very well.)
- *What steps will you courageously take to overcome the roadblocks?*
- *How will you sustain progress toward your identity in courage?*

The ICAP Overview with Five Parts

1. Baseline Insights and Takeaways
2. My Progress in Overcoming Fears and Becoming Courageous
3. Practicing CourCom Plays
4. My ICAP Goals
5. My Core Identity

Before you begin filling in your ICAP answers, please review the entire Bio Form and the instructions for each part to understand how the parts fit together in the whole plan.

We begin with Baseline Insights and finish with identifying your Core Identity.

Answering the first four parts helps you discern your answers in the fifth and sixth parts.

1. Baseline Insights and Takeaways

Each of your 53 Bio Form Step One responses gives you rare insights into how you treat values, yourself, others, and your life. On the anniversaries of reading *The Playbook*, I suggest that you review your 53 answers.

It's also highly recommended that you retake the Bio Form every three years to see how and where you've changed.

Eleven Bio items have a direct impact on overcoming fear, strengthening courage, and becoming your best self. These 11 items are listed by Bio question number in Figure 7.1. You can chart your movement from original Bio Answers to the (suggested Courage Final Answers in parentheses).

Now let's look at your Milestones.

BIO Q #	BEHAVIOR	POINT A: JOT DOWN YOUR BIO ANSWERS	POINT B: COURAGEOUS DESTINATIONS
3	Hardest carry-over impacts from teens/ childhood		(Resolved)
4	My worst feature from the list		(Changed 100%)
5–13	Most important behavior for me to improve		(Completed 100%)
16	My 3 worst behaviors		(Stopped 100%)
19	My one essential thing yet to do		(Not: travel, foreign language, or a thing, i.e. *Be morally courageous*)
21	3 behavior changes spouse/SO wants		(Completed 100%)
23	Thing I dislike most in myself		(Changed 100%)
25	My biggest fear		(Overcome 100%)
26–37	The one I most need to change/ improve		(Changed/Improved 100%)
38–53	The thing I most need to change/ improve		(Changed/Improved 100%)

Figure 7.1   Courageous Destinations

2. **My progress in overcoming fears and becoming courageous: Milestones**

   3 NOs: Disrespect | Gives in to Anger | Hideouts: Avoid, Denial, Excuses, Blame

   3 GOs: UPR | Self-governance/Humility | Discern, Do, Train in the HMA

   Our common fears are in 3 NOs. The 3 GOs summarize our foundational behaviors of courage. (See Figure 7.2.)

COURAGEOUS ISSUES	WHAT I WILL CHANGE	MY BATTLE BUDDIES
The NOs I've stopped:	(Train others?)	
My NOs that persist:		
The GOs that are my habits:	(Train others?)	
GOs that aren't yet my habits:		

Figure 7.2   What Will I Change?

3. **Practicing CourCom: From Novice to Expert**

   Track your progress from Novice to Expert. Get out of Novice as quickly as you can.

   Our basic stance in courage from which we begin all behaviors and plays is UPR.

	BASIC PLAYS	Novice	Learning	Expert
1	CLEAR: UPR, WOW, Spellbound listener			
2	Encourage Others: UPR, Do the HMA			
3	Ask Challenges: The Open-ended Question			

Figure 7.3   Basic Plays

	CONFLICT PLAYS	Novice	Learning	Expert
1	Action-emotional Reaction			
2	Fix the Fire: Reflect-back | Sit-Check | No-Thank-You			
3	CBS: UPR			

Figure 7.4   Conflict Plays

We've learned and practiced that we can reconcile difficult and painful relationships.

Courage and CourCom are always in season.

Keep practicing!

4.   My ICAP Goal & Objectives

Please review your answers to the five ICAP Overview parts before reflecting, discerning and completing the ICAP Goal section.

A courageous life goal is a strategic and extraordinary outcome of intentional identity. It goes beyond fleeting and pedestrian desires such as wealth, status, recognition, celebrity and owning your own sports team. It is more tightly defined than our common and hazy hopes for happiness.

A goal is a long-range, over-the horizon achievement. A *courageous life goal* meets the definition of grandeur and is worthy of your continued focus. With a high purpose, you, like a magnetic needle, will aim ever upward and outward instead of downward and inward.

But we humans tend to choose too many goals. When we do this, we split our attention, waste motion, dissipate our vital energy, and invite the inability to achieve any of them.

In decades of doing organizational strategic planning, I've seen brilliant executives repeatedly self-inflict Planning Sins One and Two: they choose selfish, results-hungry goals, and, like unfed hikers, choose more than three goals for a five-to-seven year strategic cycle.

Unlike most, courageous leaders and individuals, recognizing the centrality of courage, intentionally opt for a *courageous life goal*.

To increase your likelihood of achieving it, the ICAP suggests that you initially choose only one goal. After achieving it, you can select another.

What might Courageous Goals look like? Here are examples:

Quit my previous identity of fear and anxiety, and my life of stress
Live every day with active UPR to do the Highest Moral Action
Build a courageous identity based on the 3 GO's
Love principles, my family and others more, and love career and work less
Become a courageous leader of self and others, who discerns, does and trains
    others in the Highest Moral Action
Become a Courage Trainer to train others
Incorporate courageous behaviors into an organization

A. What is your primary, courageous, life goal?

How might you do this? First, you could quickly write down the personal characteristics of the most principled people you know or know of. You could do this now. _____
_____ | _____ | _____ | _____
_____ | _____ | _____ | _____
With these inspiring features in your conscious thinking, and freed from our terrible NOs, you can then record on a piece of paper the words, "My Courageous Life Goal v. 0.0." Under it, write the essential characteristics of the person you know you were always supposed to be. Tape this document so it's daily in your routine field of vision.

Then, discern – morally reason with good conscience and wise friends – how to improve the Statement to capture the real you – the you that's liberated from falsehoods, fictions and fables of the past. This is your Goal Statement v 1.0. You can amend it to v 1.1 or 2.0, 3.0, etc.

> My Courageous Life Goal v 1.0:
>
> _____

B. Courageous Tactical Objectives (the Parts) to my Life Goal:

Achieving your goal becomes more practical when you break the goal into separate objectives. If you think of your Courageous Life

Goal as the meal that will sustain the inner you for the next few years, it easily breaks down into things such as beverages, salad, soup, a spot of comfort food, the main course, and a dessert. We can eat a meal in an hour; in our example, "making the salad" will take months.

A shorthand rule of time? A goal takes years and objectives require 6 to 12 months.

You describe your goal by accurately identifying your objectives. Objectives follow a logical sequence of execution; washing lettuce precedes drying it. After eating every course, you've finished the meal; accomplishing all the objectives realizes your Goal.

Here are SOME examples of Objectives: *Admit my glaring, primary fearful faults of character | Correct them with plans, encouragement, Battle Buddies and deadlines | Stop the 3 NOs | Practice and master the 3 GO's | Practice and master CourCom | Replace my negative Self-talk with reminders to be strong and courageous for the right reasons | Train Others in the NOs, GOs, and CourCom | Cherish and value my spouse or significant other | Show UPR to my children | Encourage each member of my family to overcome their worst faults | | Improve all my family relationships | Reconcile broken relationships | Form only principled, not transactional or use-based, relationships | Admit my glaring, primary faults in mental and physical health, diet, exercise, sleep, screens, distractions and stress | Correct them | Live my life without regarding anyone as an enemy or a rival | Correct my lesser faults | Consciously seek joy with others and work | Consciously do not give in to grudges, criticism, arrogance, despair, grumbling, criticism or a sense of helplessness | Always help others*

Objectives then break down into tasks; a task small enough to usually be accomplished in weeks. If a task requires months to complete, it may be an objective. You can always re-label objectives and tasks. Can you can break down your Courageous Life Goal into four Objectives?

My Courageous Tactical Objectives:

1. _____

2. _____

3. _____

4. _____

OBSTACLES →	COUNTERMEASURES
☐ I disrespect | Give in to anger	☐ I truly practice UPR
☐ I fear change	☐ Change can be okay for me
☐ I have no time	☐ I have the time to overcome fear
☐ I deny | Avoid | Make excuses	☐ I can accept the truth | face fear
☐ I fear giving up the familiar	☐ I will stop protecting my faults
☐ I procrastinate	☐ I'm getting up to do it now
☐ I fear embarrassment	☐ I can handle embarrassment!
☐ I blame others	☐ My best self takes responsibility
☐ I tried that & it didn't work	☐ Good. Now try again!
☐ I fear disapproval of others	☐ You're a lot stronger than that
☐ Things aren't bad enough yet	☐ Don't wait until they are
☐ I have a lot of resentment	☐ Don't waste your time on that
☐ I fear failure	☐ We all fail. Get over it!
☐ People won't let me	☐ Ask Challenges, OEQs w/UPR
☐ I feel hopeless or helpless	☐ Do something about it now
☐ I fear/worry & then worry about the fact that I'm worrying about that	☐ That's really a waste of your time
☐ I think it'll be too hard	☐ Try it. (About ten times)
☐ Quitting is easier	☐ Not on you, it's not
☐ I've never been good enough	☐ You are now!

Figure 7.5   Obstacles and Countermeasures

■ Accountability: my trustworthy Battle Buddies

Without authentic accountability, we can slip back into the 3 NOs and be distracted from reaching our goals. A trustworthy Battle Buddy isn't responsible for what you do but is accountable to catch you when you take detours or deviate from your best self. You owe the same UPR duty of care to your Buddies. Always thank them from the heart. List some of the greatest treasures in anyone's life: your trustworthy Battle Buddies. Two in each category is ideal and a reflection of your good fortune.

Life Goal Battle Buddies

1. _____

2. _____

Personal Battle Buddies

1. _____

2. _____

Work Battle Buddies

1. _____

2. _____

Bravo!

As your coach, I want to close the ICAP with the strong suggestion that you deeply commit to complete it and that you keep it in your daily consciousness.

It's a good idea to keep your strategic life goals visible so achieving your goals becomes part of your mindset.

I'd keep the ICAP physically close. You can then scan it before kicking off a new month. Every quarter, with your Battle Buddies, work team, or *Playbook* study group, at a fun lunch or dinner, you can tell stories and authentically encourage each other's progress toward your goals—becoming the people you are supposed to be.

If I was not good enough to be even a lousy football player, why do I keep using football analogies? It's because, like life, it has simultaneously moving parts, not all of which are particularly friendly, and being cowardly and bending the rules in this game wipe out results. So here we go. . .

Just before taking the field before Super Bowl XXXIX, 49er offensive coordinator Mike Shanahan, Bill Walsh's cerebral protege who developed 14 staffers to become head coaches, gave a daunting instruction to his quarterback, Steve Young. A brainy athlete who could throw the ball the length of the field and outrun defensive backs, Young was a Hall of Fame player and future lawyer who had yet to win a Super Bowl. The order? Recite the entire game plan and its 300 plays and options. He needed his QB to be clear about himself and about everything, so he could execute the plan.

"I went through every one," said Young. "Every formation, every motion, every read, I went *boom-boom-boom-boom*, like *Rain Man*. . . and then I did it again."[1] Shanahan, who became the second winningest NFL coach, said that he knew they'd win by a big margin, which they did because his key player knew his stuff. Steve Young set a Super Bowl record for touchdowns and was named game MVP. Of course, in this story, you're the key actor in your own life narrative.

In like fashion, you can quickly refer to your key, personal Memory Cards and reread them before an important conversation, a stressful meeting, or before you start a complex project or relationship. You want to be clear about your core identity, about who you are, to remember your game plan, your Goals, and basic Plays to model your best self to help others.

Don't let your ICAP join unused binders on your shelf or hide in a file cabinet. Let it remain fresh as an active tool as you map out and follow your unique path to your courageous self. The ICAP, with the cut-out memory aids in the Appendix, will be visual and practical reminders that you actually have a plan to sustain and grow your strong identity.

Completing the ICAP now will equip you for our final exercise together:

Crossing the River.

8

Crossing the River

READERS OF COURAGE: *The Backbone of Leadership* are familiar with the concept of the River of Fear. If you were in a Courageous Leadership Skills Intensives program, your final exercise would be a simulated crossing of that river. I remember learning to tie my shoes and speak English. Both involved intent, a certain degree of risk taking, and practice. Result? Necessary lifetime skills supported by muscle memory so I'd neither trip on the laces nor remain permanently tongue-tied. Likewise, physically stepping toward our courage on the far bank of a notional river impacts muscle-mind-heart-memory and installs a kinetic imprinting of the fact that you can defeat your anxieties.

The River of Fear (see Figure 8.1) represents a border between being a good (Honest, Honorable, and Ethical) individual and a courageous person with Courage, Integrity, and Character. It represents our final barrier between uncorrected reactions to our multiplying apprehensions and our practice of the behaviors of courage. It's what separates our former self from our evolving self.

It's also a symbolically dynamic way to depart from unworthy needs of the ego to adopt a bold new core identity that helps others and aids you. In Five Steps to Courage, it's the last exercise we'll do together.

Courageous Leadership
Crossing the River of Fear

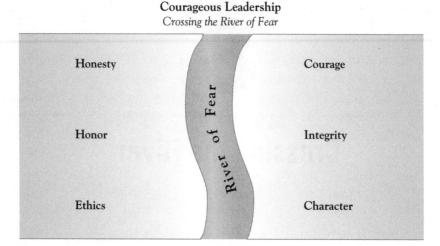

Figure 8.1   Crossing the River of Fear

Source: Lee, Gus; Elliott-Lee, Diane (2006). *Courage: The Backbone of Leadership* (1st ed.). Jossey-Bass.

Like fear itself, you can hear the roar of the river before you see its rushing gray waters. Facing it, the waters always look too wide, its rapid currents too turbulent, its depths too foreboding. And. . . it's cold.

On this side of the river, shiver the good people of Tier 3. They work but they incessantly fear failure, worry excessively, and often cut corners to get ahead; this allows disrespect, bias, and excuses to infect their world. Good people don't abuse or act the bully, but they're passive when they see it take place. The NOs are common; GOs are rare.

Hearing the truth makes good people uncomfortable.

Crowded behind you are Tier 1 and Tier 2 people, driven by fear to dominate others, demand their way, and discredit and harm those who disagree with them. They practice the religions of the Self and More despite the reality that more is never enough for our insatiable egos. Here, love is an unhappy hostage to ego.

In Tiers 1 and 2, hearing the truth doesn't set them free. It makes them angry.

But all three groups keep glancing across the river at the land on the distant shore. It's said that the Tier 4 country is endowed with fabled riches, but no one's ever seen it. The territory is small and never seems to have enough workers. Its people are warmly dedicated to behaving with courage and, in a bizarre way, always strive to do the right thing. They display a happy sociability, routinely help others, and forgive wrongs. In many ways, they simply don't act like people; perhaps it's the Shire without the Sackville-Bagginses, Smeagol, and Lotho. With the universal practice of UPR, discrimination has become rare. They welcome hard truths and invite candid feedback as sturdy aids to their self-improvement. By adopting courageous Tier 4 identities, this has become the Deeper Country of brave lions and courageous leaders that was referenced in the Introduction.

You now stand on the near bank of the River of Fear. You wonder: Can only those with a rare, Tier 4 core identity reach the far bank?

The answer is clearly, No. Anyone can make it across the water. For this courageous, backbone-strengthening act of committing to cross is in itself a major play to help create the identity we need. The vast span of the river to the Deeper Country appears wide. But it's truthfully as close as the route from your core—your heart of courage—to your head and its familiar childhood fears.

Tier 4 isn't real estate. It's an internal country, deep in your chest. Courage lets you access what's already within you to change your mindset, your habits, and your core identity.

The burning question is: Will you cross the river?

Crossing the River Exercise

Crossing the River is symbolic and movement based. Like a moral stage play, it has three acts, and like courage and a long-distance race, it depends on the finish. When we're stressed, the river's width seems uncrossable, the currents become deadly, the depths too frightening, and the coldness promises to be below our endurance.

For the London Marathon, long-distance runner Sara Hall, 38, of California, the second fastest American woman, trained smart, ate well, and didn't do things that would detract from her goal. She started well, ran the middle distance with discipline, and kicked so hard for the last 200 meters that it broke her terrible fatigue and fears. In the London race, she used her practiced finish to "surge past world champion Ruth Chepngetich in the last 150 meters to claim second place. . . and a personal best time." She said, "I kind of just, in faith, started throwing myself forward and willing everything in my body forward."[1]

You've practiced how to start the journey to courage in Step One; dropped bad habits that detracted from your goal in Step Two; and trained in courage in the final Steps. You are near the finish line and ready to cross the river.

We are told that Joshua bin Nun, the bravest and toughest desert warrior next to the great prophet Moses, endured 40 years of nomadic hardship and the death of his entire generation in the Sinai before he faced his river. Then, for the safety of others, he had to cross the Jordan into forbidding Canaan. The prospects of battling unbeaten armies on the far bank with a motley, undisciplined gaggle accustomed only to slavery, and leading this entire unlikely venture without Moses, who'd been his leader since before the exodus from Egypt, filled him with fear. For the book of Yehoshua (Joshua) in the Torah tells us that God then gave Joshua six encouragements and four commands to be strong and courageous and concluded his message with a fifth, final, and extremely personal exhortation to be "strong and very courageous."[2] Joshua, thus equipped with the resolve of a new internal identity, and understanding that he was in a long race, successfully crossed the Jordan.

Rivers are borders between what was and what is to be. On Christmas Day night, 1776, after half a year of crushing and shameful defeats, George Washington risked the entirety of the failing American Revolution by crossing the hazardous, ice floe–packed Delaware River to make a surprise nighttime attack. He attempted this desperate, eleventh-hour adventure with a barefoot, defeated army during a historic freezing Little Ice Age, and a hurricane-like ice blizzard that kept a third of his force from reaching the far bank. Landing late in daylight with frozen troops without the advantage of surprise, he nonetheless led the defeat of Hessians and British in three key battles that saved the Revolution.

Such is the nature of moral river crossings. Regardless of the weather or season, it seems too wide for our courage, too cold for comfort, and too intimidating for our frights. And each of those impressions is totally incorrect.

How to Do the Exercise

Equipment: Find a space, pick three markers, get a bath towel and a hot or cold drink.

This can be done outdoors or in. Doing this solo, as a couple, a family, a book or study group, or with a few friends, you only need a small area in which to take about twenty steps.

- A larger group, such as businesses, business teams, schools, social groups, or military units, will require a larger space.
- You'll need three markers such as chairs, tables, backpacks, sports gear, or bikes.
- I recommend getting a bath towel and a hot or cold drink— whatever you'd most enjoy after emerging from a (virtually) cold river.

For you and a small group, place your three objects in a straight row about five paces apart; these are your "milestones." On top or near the third marker, place your towel and drinks.

Then position yourself several paces back of the first marker.

Larger groups, depending on size, will place markers with greater separations. Now that you're set up:

Welcome to your capstone event: Crossing the River of Fear.

This is the exercise you've heard about. It's our version of a commencement, a new beginning following significant, change-based learning and transformational decisions based on newly acquired abilities in courage.

The exercise has three stations marked by the objects you placed in front of you.

The area between you and your third marker? That's our virtual River of Fear. Its currents are fast, its color is gray slate, and its low temperature brings a quick chill to the bones.

Earlier, you were asked to stand to admit your reactions to fear. Now, you're invited to advance from your former stomping grounds into the Deeper Country of your new, best self.

In this rare moment you can commit to making significant, life-changing private decisions, cross an internal barrier, and carry the strength of revalidated commitments into the reality of your life and the private interior space of your core identity.

The start   To the front are three phase lines denoted by the three markers. To move from the start to the three phase lines merely requires a personal recommitment to three mindsets with which you're gaining an increased intimacy.

To begin your crossing, you make an initial affirmation of a mindset of UPR, Unconditional Positive Respect, that you will exercise for all persons, in every situation despite foes, fatigue, or foul feelings.

If you're now willing to make that commitment to UPR, *take a single step from dry land into the water.*

Good. You are now virtually in the River of Fear. You can feel the cold water cover your feet. With UPR, you've entered the field, you're in the river, and in the game.

Move to the first phase line and marker   To move forward to the first marker, I ask you now to reaffirm your resolve to give up all three NOs (Disrespect; Gives in to Anger; Hideouts: Avoids, Denies, Excuses, Blame). If you're willing to make this life decision, *please decisively take five or six steps (twenty or more for large groups) into deeper water.*

Very good. Without the destructive NOs, you've reached the first phase line. The cold water is now above your waist. Feel the sharp current? Take a good, shoulder-width stance and try not to lock your knees. Do not let the current move you from your straight path. Everyone here is now a loyal Battle Buddy. If someone loses their footing, you can help steady them.

Move to the second phase line and marker   To reach the second phase line, I am asking you to please reaffirm your commitment to practice the 3 GOs (UPR; Self-govern with Humility; DAT: Discern, Act, Train in doing the HMA) and to focus on the one that's toughest for you. Have that hard-to-do Go in your mind? Ready?

If you're willing to recommit to the GOs, *and to work at mastering the one that seems right now to elude you, walk all the way, in deeper water, to the second phase line and marker.*

Excellent! You're in mid-river, armed with your behaviors of courage, halfway between the Lower-Tier lands behind you and the Tier 4 Deeper Country ahead of you. The current is stronger, the water is chest-high and colder, but your stance is firm. This is just a passing moment that shivers the body but cannot touch your inner core. You're almost to the warm, dry land of the Deeper Country.

It's weird. Why? I'll tell you why: because you're confidently standing in a place that most humans avoid at any cost and will perform bizarre and fearful antics to avoid standing in this space that you now so calmly occupy.

Enjoy the reality that you can stand and face your fears. Inhale and absorb the present confidence of courage in the middle of what your doubts had once made both unlikely and undoable. Take it from one who feared everything—this is what it feels like when the shivers pass and you've overcome your fears.

Move to the third and final phase line, marker, and the Deeper Country   To complete your crossing, I'm asking you to commit to use CourCom plays so your UPR, quitting NOs, and deploying GOs become real in your interactions with human beings.

If you're willing to commit to use CourCom, *walk into the increasingly shallow water and steadily stride to the last marker on dry land.*

Fantastic! By reaffirming to use CourCom and two other mindsets of courage, on the reliable and steady platform of UPR, you've crossed the River of Fear! I hope you thoroughly enjoy drying off with your towel and sipping your beverage as you celebrate completing your capstone on your journey to courage.

You are presently in the Deeper Country of your own inner identity.

Reader, I toast the good courage that you will henceforth model for others.

Courage was always your strength to claim. You have now done so. To your courage!

The ancient texts of our human heritage found that courage is superior to fear and indifference. You have found that it already strengthens the self and acts rightly to help others.

In a somewhat more recent text, the Cowardly Lion in *The Wizard of Oz* sings an ode to courage.[3] I have added to his ditty the names of some people you now know.

What makes a King out of a slave?
What makes the flag on the mast to wave?
What makes the elephant charge his tusk in the misty mist or the dusky dusk?
What makes the muskrat guard his musk?
What makes Coach Tony train a Chicken Little?
What makes Skywalker find his deep mettle?
What makes a firefighter go into a fire?
What makes a Soldier cross over the wire?
What makes a Hobbit find strength in a fix?
What makes Bella no longer say nix?
What makes Fitz jump to admit his bad NO?
What makes Gary honor a terrible foe?
What makes an exec stay the course by herself?
What makes MacDonald save NASA's good health?
What makes a mom save a drowned little boy?
What makes Aiden improve, to give his boss joy?
What makes Christie face discord that others do flee?
What makes Caleb attentive, giving Danielle great glee?
What makes Gracie ignore scorn to lead in the fray?
What makes Anita give blame a forever holiday?
What makes you read this book without distraction?
What makes a coward do the Highest Moral Action?
What makes the Hottentot so hot?
What puts the ape in apricot?
Whatta they got that I now got?

"Courage!" say his companions.

You can say that again!

So they do.

Epilogue

THE PLAYBOOK HAS offered you Five Steps and the basic plays to replace fears with courageous behaviors so that you can become your best self. As habits, they equip you to be the strong and bold Tier 4 individual you were supposed to be.

While many will do almost anything to avoid knowing important truths about themselves, you've used the Character Mirror to take a hard and dramatic look at yourself. In a culture of denial and excuses, you bravely admitted your habitual NOs not only to yourself, but to others who are important to you. You've enlisted trusted people to be your loyal Battle Buddies on your journey to become your best self.

In an era of disrespect, you have learned about our essential and abiding need for UPR, and you have practiced it despite the nature of the times.

When doing the right thing seems to become harder for others, you now own a process to discern the Highest Moral Action and to practice the plays to aid you in leading your life, helping others, and writing your story, with rare and remarkable courage.

Unlike most, you no longer think of courage as an abstract concept or distant theory. For now you know that it's not only an active verb, but a personal one over which you are claiming a personal ownership.

Many default by unconscious habit to uncertainty, disrespect, and avoidance when facing discomfort, conflicts, and the River of Fear. You now possess an action-based playbook and memory cards to deal rightly and confidently with them. You have crossed that barrier and have played in that once-unfamiliar Deeper Country.

Knowing that courage is personal but not private property, you have already exercised moral generosity by teaching and encouraging others to cross their own rivers.

Riding the adventurous life arc of courage and character, people of all backgrounds have found more significance and meaning in their relationships and work. Replacing anxiety and worry with courage may equip you to find contentment and a sense of quiet, inner joy.

More remarkably, courage, by helping us to overcome our fear of disrespect, of not being loved, and of not having enough, frees us to give more selflessly and love more grandly from the radiating strength of a new core identity. When change becomes real and visible, it uplifts those around you and brings everyone close to the possibility of transformation.

As we end our time together, I would like to offer a final guidance to commission you in courage. It will be familiar to Courage Training participants and to those who helped me overcome my fears.

May it have lasting meaning for you as your core identity comes closer to the heroic moral ideal:

Go into the world with good courage
Hold fast to that which is right
Respect all persons
Do not be surprised by slings and arrows
Do not return evil for evil
Face your fears, cross your rivers
Always model courage for others
Help them while boldly animating your birthright
Striving to live out principles that are greater than self.

Appendix: Cut-out Memory Cards

The 3 NOs	
DISRESPECTS OTHERS	Is inattentive, ignores, shuns, scorns, dishonors, shows bias, sexually harasses.
GIVES IN TO ANGER	Yells, intimidates, curses, threatens, coerces, attacks, hits objects, harms others.
HIDEOUTS: Avoids Conflict, Denial, Excuses, Blames	Avoids conflicts by looking the other way, flees, fails to help others. Denies the truth, "I have no problems, *you* do." Makes excuses by rationalizing, covering up, and arguing. Blames others by gossiping, backstabbing, making accusations, or lying.

The 3 GOs	
UNCONDITIONAL POSITIVE RESPECT (UPR)	Respects all people, listens carefully, fully attentive, unbiased, fair, even with difficult and challenging people, gives Buddy Checks.
SELF-GOVERN with HUMILITY	Stops self-absorption, treats others as at least as important as myself, is other oriented, improves own faults, stops the 3 NOs.
DAT: DISCERN, ACT, TRAIN	Discerns Highest Moral Action (HMA). Acts/Does the HMA despite risks to self-interest. Trains Others to Do the HMA.

COURCOM BASIC PLAYS		
CLEAR UPR	ENCOURAGE UPR	ASK CHALLENGES UPR
Collegial opening Listens spellbound Empathy Asks OEQs closes on the Relationship	Encourages the GOs Notices the good Validates selflessness Does these routinely	OEQ's Open-Ended Questions Asks to understand Focuses on challenge Tries to understand the person, not just "change" them Asks more OEQs

CLEAR Tip Sheet

Be Calm: BICBOF (Breathe In Courage Blow Out Fear)

Be WOW (Warm Open Welcoming)

Use CLEAR (open on Collegiality, Listen, Empathy, Ask, close on the Relationship)

Intentionally open conversations with UPR and truly prepare to listen.

Practice active, spellbound listening to catch the gist and details.

Practice using empathy to emotionally receive where the other person is.

Use CLEAR in everyday work and personal communications.

Welcome feedback from others on your effectiveness.

Be WOW, particularly when you don't feel WOW.

Strive to improve your overall listening in all situations.

Strive to improve your memory of what others say to you. (Take notes.)

COURCOM CONFLICT PLAYS

AeR UPR	FIX the FIRE UPR	CBS UPR
State other's Action State your e-Reaction (Short and calm)	Reflect-Back Situation-Check No-Thank-You Declaration	Cease Begin Sustain (Agree)

BASIC SELF-GOVERNANCE TO LIVE WELL

Practice a mindset of courageous transformation instead of willpower or wishpower.

Recruit reliable Battle Buddies into a daily accountability network.

Be on a healthier, nutrient-dense diet of low sugar, saturated fat, and salt.

Exercise safely at least 30 minutes every other day.

Get up from sitting and move every 30–60 minutes.

Practice a healthy sleep hygiene routine.

Stop negative self-talk, complaining, and self-pity.

Reduce stress, use slow diaphragmatic (belly) breathing, count to 10.

Spend time with positive and healthy people.

Notes

Introduction

1. Gus Lee and Diane Elliott-Lee, *Courage: The Backbone of Leadership* (Jossey-Bass, 2006).
2. Habits for Well-Being. https://www.habitsforwellbeing.com/20-inspiring-quotes-on-courage/#:~:text=20%20Inspiring%20Quotes%20on%20Courage%201%20"%20Courage, run%20it%20is%20easier.%20...%20 20More%20items...%20. Accessed November 11, 2021.
3. Mike Myatt, "The #1 Reason Leadership Development Fails," *Forbes* (December 19, 2012), http://www.forbes.com/sites/mikemyatt/2012/ 12/19/the-1-reason-leadership-development-fails/. Accessed July 12, 2021.
4. John P. Kotter *John P. Kotter on What Leaders Really Do* (Harvard Business Press, 1999), p. 1. Professor Emeritus Kotter is Harvard Business School's iconic leadership expert.
5. Dr. Paul Brand, *The Gift of Pain* (Zondervan, 2020). Brand was a medical missionary in West Asia who was born in India and did pioneering medical research on leprosy. I've heard many similar perceptions of Americans in Asia and Africa.
6. "How Many Football Fans Are There?" *Reference*, April 14, 2020, https:// www.reference.com/world-view/many-nfl-fans-ad650cc48 aba3841. Accessed December 6, 2021.

7. David Harris, *The Genius: How Bill Walsh Reinvented Football and Created an NFL Dynasty* (Random, 2008), p. 131.

8. "Green RT Slot Z Opp Fake 98 Toss Z," "Lightning Flash Stop Plays," *1985 49ers Playbook Bill Walsh*, https://www.scribd.com/document/29248523/1985-San-Francisco-49ers-Offense-Bill-Walsh. Accessed October 24, 2021. Montana and Young set passing records; were league MVPs; won five Super Bowls; were Super Bowl MVPs four times, first-ballot inductees to the NFL Hall of Fame and left the game without serious injury.

9. Harris, *The Genius*, p. 79.

10. "Bill Walsh," A Football Life, Season 4, Episode 16, NFL Films, 2015.kotter.

11. J.M. Barrie, "Courage: The Rectorial Address Delivered at St. Andrews University," May 3, 1922 (Hodder and Stoughton, 1923) p. 37.

12. Steven Corbett and Brian Fikkert, *When Helping Hurts: How to Alleviate Poverty without Hurting the Poor. . . and Yourself* (Moody, 2014), p. 59.

13. "Martin Luther King Jr. "Quotes: Strength to Love," *Goodreads*, https://www.goodreads.com/ quotes/137136. See also, "Martin Luther King, Jr. Quotes: Quotable Quotes," *Goodreads*, https://www.goodreads.com/quotes/186960-courage-is-an-inner-resolution-to-go-forward-despite-obstacles#:~:text=Martin%20Luther%20King%20Jr.%20>%20Quotes%20>%20Quotable,Cowardice%20represses%20fear%20and%20is%20mastered%20by%20it. Accessed June 10, 2021.

14. Possibly attributed to cultural commentator David Brooks, author of *The Road to Character*.

15. We *use* apps and *apply* sunscreen; we *deploy*—commit—parachutes and boots on the ground in essential endeavors of the heart and in selfless missions.

16. The ratio of my courage to my fears.

Part I

1. Non-historical names are pseudonyms unless otherwise indicated.

Chapter 1

1. "Courage Quotes," Goodreads, https://www.goodreads.com/quotes/tag/courage?page=6/. Accessed November 11, 2021.
2. "Reduce Screen Time," National Heart, Lung, and Blood Institute, NIH, https://www.nhlbi.nih.gov/health/educational/wecan/reduce-screen-time/index.htm. Accessed August 21, 2021.
3. Edward R. Laskowski, M.D, "What Are the Risks of Sitting Too Much?" *Mayo Clinic*, August 21, 2020, https://www.mayoclinic.org/healthy-lifestyle/adult-health/expert-answers/sitting/faq-20058005. Accessed June 7, 2021.
4. Aryana Chitnis, "The Science Behind: Your Conscience," Thesciencebehind.net (Oct. 9, 2020), https://www.thesciencebehind.net/post/the-science-behind-your-conscience. Accessed July 5, 2021.
5. A liberal reinterpretation of a quote by author Robert Gilbreath, author of *Escape from Management Hell* (Penguin, 1993).
6. Daniel H. *Pink, Drive: The Surprising Truth About What Motivates Us*, (Riverhead, 2009), p. 59.
7. "Does Fear Motivate Workers—Or Make Things Worse?" *Wharton Management*, upenn.edu, December 4, 2018, https://knowledge.wharton.upenn.edu/article/fear-motivate-workers-make-things-worse/. Accessed June 7, 2021.
8. Gavin de Becker, *The Gift of Fear: Survival Signals That Protect Us from Violence* (Little, Brown, 1997).
9. "Moral," *Lexico, the Oxford English Dictionary*, https://www.lexico.com/en/definition/moral. Accessed October 24, 2021. See also, "Moral," *Merriam-Webster Dictionary*, https://www.merriam-webster.com/dictionary/moral. Accessed October 24, 2021.
10. James Nestor, *Breath: The New Science of a Lost Art* (Riverhead, 2020).
11. Dr. Seth J. Gillihan, "Why Every One of Your Fears Is a Lie," *Psychology Today* (January 1, 2020), https://www.psychologytoday.com/us/blog/think-act-be/202001/why-every-one-your-fears-is-lie. Accessed June 7, 2021.

Chapter 2

1. J.R.R. Tolkien, *The Lord of the Rings* (Houghton Mifflin Harcourt, 2004), p. 934.

2. In the Greek, *thárros* means courage so one can *entharrýno*, give courage, encourage, to counsel, to help and support. *Kourágio*, another Greek word for courage, interestingly also means "comfort."
3. John Lennon, Paul McCartney, "Nowhere Man," *Rubber Soul* album, EMI, 1965. McCartney, in a September 1984 interview, said of Lennon, "He was. . . wondering where he was going, and to be truthful so was I. I was starting to worry about him."
4. The original phrase is, *Do the harder right instead of the easier wrong*, from West Point's *The Cadet Prayer* by COL Clayton E. Wheat, Chaplain, US Military Academy, 1918–1926. For courage to be a real verb for us, we focus on the *hardest right*. We'll see this later as *the Highest Moral Action*.
5. Robert K. Weiss, *The Blues Brothers*, Universal Pictures, 1980.
6. "It is curious that physical courage should be so common in the world, and moral courage so rare." Mark Twain, *Eruption* (Harper, 1940).
7. Brand, *The Gift of Pain*.
8. Rob Reiner, David Brown. *A Few Good Men*, Castle Rock Entertainment, 1992. Nicholson portrayed a Colonel N. Jessup.
9. "Fitz" is a composite of firefighters from Boston to San Francisco and a few Army officers.
10. Susan Scutti, "Yes, Sitting Too Long Can Kill You, Even If You Exercise," CNN Health (September 12, 2017), https://www.cnn.com/2017/09/11/health/sitting-increases-risk-of-death-study/index.html. Accessed June 23, 2021. "So if you have a job or lifestyle where you have to sit for prolonged periods, the best suggestion I can make is to take a movement break every half hour," said Diaz. "Our findings suggest this one behavior change could reduce your risk of death." Keith Diaz, Columbia School of Medicine.
11. Herman Pontzer, David A. Raichlen, Brian M. Wood, Melissa Emergy Thompson, Susan B. Racette, Audax Z.P. Mabulla, Frank W. Marlow, "Energy Expenditure and Activity Among Hadza Hunter-Gatherers," *American Journal of Human Biology*, *27*: 628–637, 2015.
12. Tim Keller, Keynote address, "How to Change Deeply," New Canaan Society (July 14, 2015), https://www.pinterest.com/pin/57702438952874210/. Accessed December 1, 2021.
13. Chapter 1, "Cuentos," César Chávez Middle School Biography, https:// chavez.cde.ca.gov/ModelCurriculum/Teachers/Lessons/Resources/Biographies/Middle_Level_Biography.aspx. Accessed December 1, 2021.

14. Emma Pattee, "Anxiety Is in Your Body, Not Your Mind." *Elemental*, medium.com (April 4, 2021). Accessed June 30, 2021, citing ADAA research.
15. M.S. Staicu and M. Cutov, "Anger and Health Risk Behaviors," *Journal of Medical Life 3*(4): 372–375. Published online 2010 Nov 25. PMCID: PMC3019061; PMID: 21254733. https://www.ncbi.nlm.nih.gov/pmc/articles/PMC3019061/. Accessed October 10, 2019.
16. Jack H. Jakes, *If Not Now, When? Duty and Sacrifice in America's Time of Need* (Berkley, 2008). Col. (Ret) Jacobs and I taught at West Point at the same time.
17. "Does Fear Motivate Workers—Or Make Things Worse? *Knowledge@Wharton*, December 4, 2018, https://knowledge.wharton.upenn.edu/article/fear-motivate-workers-make-things-worse/. Accessed March 11, 2021. See also, Robert Evans Wilson Jr., "Fear vs. Power," *Psychology Today* (March 11, 2013), https://www.psychologytoday.com/us/blog/the-main-ingredient/201303/fear-vs-power. Accessed March 11, 2021.
18. Staicu and Cutov, "Anger and Health Risk Behaviors."
19. "Unfortunately, the aftermath [of expressing anger] reinforces negative consequences that hurt you in the eyes of others and continues the cycle of insecurity. . . that ultimately hurt the angry individual." Jean Kim, MD, "Anger's Allure: Are You Addicted to Anger?" *Psychology Today* (August 25, 2015), https://www.psychologytoday.com/us/blog/culture-shrink/201508/angers-allure-are-you-addicted-anger. Accessed December 2, 2019.
20. "Hide Quotes," *Brainy Quotes*, https://www.brainyquote.com/topics/hide-quotes_4. Accessed September 24, 2021.
21. Joseph Grenny, "Avoiding Conflict Is Killing Your Bottom Line," *Vital Smarts* (April 16, 2010), https://www.vitalsmarts.com/crucialskills/2010/04/avoiding-conflict-is-killing-your-bottom-line/. Accessed June 30, 2021.
22. "R.D. Laing Quotes," *AZ Quotes*, https://www.azquotes.com/author/8410-R_D_Laing. Accessed October 27, 2021.
23. I now train others to find new courage and renewed hope from past moral failures and regrets.
24. As noted, pseudonyms are used to represent actual people or composites of actual people as well as for actual organizations.
25. Robyn Ward, "The Cost of Conflict in the Workplace: $359 Billion Lost Every Year to Workplace Conflict," *ADR Resources* (February 16,

2016), https://robynshort.com/2016/02/16/the-cost-of-conflict-in-the-workplace/. Accessed March 10, 2021.

26. William Shakespeare, *Henry IV*, Part I, Act 5, Scene 4, 120–121.

27. "Frank Herbert Quotes," *Brainy Quote*, https://www.brainyquote .com/quotes/frank_herbert_109952. Accessed October 27, 2021.

28. Adam Grant, *Think Again: The Power of Knowing What You Don't Know* (Viking, 2021).

29. "Challenger Loss: $3.2 Billion," *Los Angeles Times* (March 11, 1986), https:// www.latimes.com/archives/la-xpm-1986-03-11-mn-3099-story.html#:~:text=The%20Challenger%20disaster%20cost%20 the%20nation%20%243.2%20billion,of%20blame%2C%20the%20 head%20of%20NASA%20said%20today. Accessed December 1, 2021. The Shuttle loss cost $3.2 billion; that is $8.06 billion in 2021 dollars.

30. Richard P. Feynman, "The Presidential Commission on the Space Shuttle *Challenger* Accident Report," Appendix F, *Rogers Commission*, 1986, https://science.ksc.nasa.gov/shuttle/missions/51-l/docs /rogers-commission/Appendix-F.txt. Accessed March 14, 2021. They reduced it by a factor of one thousand.

31. Howard Berkes, "Remembering Allan McDonald: He Refused to Approve Challenger Launch, Exposed Cover-Up," *NPR* (March 7, 2021), https://www.npr.org/2021/03/07/974534021/remembering-allan-mcdonald-he-refused-to-approve-challenger-launch-exposed-cover. Accessed June 23, 2021. McDonald passed away in 2021 at the age of 83.

32. Joel Spark, "Roger Boisjoly, Challenger Disaster Whistleblower, Dies at 73," *Space Safety Magazine* (February 6, 2012), http://www .spacesafetymagazine.com/space-disasters/challenger-disaster/roger-boisjoly-challenger-disaster-whistleblower-dies-73/. Accessed July 4, 2021.

33. "Study Suggests Medical Errors Now Third Leading Cause of Death in the U.S," *Johns Hopkins Medicine News and Publications* (May 3, 2016), https://www.hopkinsmedicine.org/news/media /releases/study suggests_medical_errors_now_third_leading_cause_of_death_in_ the_us. Accessed March 11, 2021.

34. In March 2019, before cancer surgery, I told the MD that the operation would be complicated because of masses of abdominal scar tissue from earlier surgical errors beginning at age two. The MD ignored me, perforated the bowel, and made more errors which caused infections, pneumonia, an ileus, other complications, requiring a long

hospitalization and massive IV antibiotics. Dying, I said good-bye to our children. Diane, Dr. Ronald Quenzer, and Providence saved me but I couldn't stand, eat, sleep, or read. I lost a year of work, 40 pounds, and all my muscle. I told the MD I wouldn't sue him for medical malpractice and requested that he listen to me for the first time. I asked him to not repeat the errors he had inflicted on me. The MD didn't acknowledge my statements. I wrote a negative review of his care. Many professions lack effective accountability systems in which denial of the truth often rules.

35. "Ben Franklin Quotes," *Brainy Quote*, https://www.brainyquote.com/quotes/benjamin_franklin_ 383794. Accessed October 27, 2021.

36. "Recognizing Flashover Conditions Can Save Your Life," *U.S. Fire Administration* (May 5, 2020), https://www.usfa.fema.gov/blog/cb-050520.html. Accessed December 15, 2021.

37. *Quote Finder*, https://www.quotefindr.com/2021/ 08/02/if-at-first-you-dont-succeed-blame-your-parents/. Accessed October 27, 2021.

38. Stephen R. Covey, *Seven Habits of Highly Successful People* (Free Press, 1990).

Chapter 3

1. "Courage," *Quote Investigator*, https://quoteinvestigator.com/2019/07/14/courage/. Accessed October 28, 2021.

2. Ancient Chinese and Greek philosophers theorized that only "superior men"—an inborn elite—can gain virtue and did not recognize that all humans are equally capable of gaining courage by practice.

3. Aristotle, *The Nicomachean Ethics, Book Three*, VI.1, translated with Notes by Harris Rackham (Wordsworth Classics, 1996), p. 65.

4. C.S. Lewis, *The Screwtape Letters* (Centenary Press, 1942).

5. "Clare Booth Luce Quotes," *AZ Quotes*, https://www.azquotes.com/author/9110-Clare_Boothe_Luce. Accessed December 3, 2021.

6. Amy Tan, *The Joy Luck Club* (Putnam, 1989), p. 11.

7. A pseudonym.

8. "Dr. Seuss Quotes," *Goodreads*, https://www.goodreads.com/quotes/22613-a-person-s-a-person-no-matter-how-small#:~:text=Quote%20by%20Dr.%20Seuss%3A%20"A%20person%27s%20a%20person%2C,thought%20of%20this%20quote%2C%20please%20sign%20up%21%20Hanem.Abdelwahab. Accessed October 28, 2021.

9. Professor James Franck, administering the oral exam, said "I'm glad it's over. He was on the point of questioning me." "The Eternal Apprentice," *Time*, Vol LII, No. 19 (November 8, 1948), Content.time.com/content/time/0,9263,7601481108,00.html. Accessed August 3, 2021.
10. Malcolm Gladwell, *Outliers: The Story of Success* (Little Brown, 2008), p. 99.
11. David Halberstam, *The Fifties* (Ballantine, 1993), p. 31.
12. Steven Shapin, "Inside the Centre: The Life of J Robert Oppenheimer by Ray Monk," *The Guardian* (November 16, 2012), https://www.theguardian.com/books/2012/nov/16/inside-centre-robert-oppenheimer-ray-monk-review. Accessed August 2, 2021. Oppenheimer directed the scientific operations of the Manhattan Project that created the atomic bomb, giving him global recognition and deeper depression.
13. "Gracie" is a combination of three executives with whom I worked in health care and government.
14. According to the UN and UNICEF, 250 million people face discrimination. "10 Facts About Discrimination," *Fact File* (September 15, 2016), https://factfile.org/10-facts-about-discrimination. Accessed August 2, 2021. According to the World Bank, women suffer discrimination in 187 countries (out of 193). Kate Whiting, "7 Surprising and Outrageous Stats About Gender Inequality," *The World Economic Forum*, March 8, 2019, https://www.weforum/agenda/2019/03/surprising-stats-about-gender-inequality/. Accessed August 2, 2021.
15. *Quote Investigator*, https://quote.investigator.com/2019/04/18/staircase/. Accessed August 3, 2021.
16. The Book of Matthew, chapter 7, verse 12, *New King James Bible* (Thomas Nelson, 1991); *The Analects, Lún Yǔ*, 5.12, Simon Leys, translator, *The Analects of Confucius* (Norton, 1997), p. 21.
17. David A. Sousa, *How the Brain Learns*, 4th ed. (Corwin, 2011).
18. "Discipline," Inspiring Quotes, https://www.inspiringquotes.us/topic/8343-discipline/page:7. Accessed October 28, 2021.
19. "Mahatma Gandhi Quotes," *Brainy Quotes*, https://www.brainyquote.com/quotes/mahatma_gandhi_150732. Accessed October 28, 2021.
20. Guatemala, Ecuador, Panama, Venezuela, Colombia. The other leading nations in individualism are Australia, the United Kingdom, the Netherlands, and New Zealand. Geert Hofstede, *Clearly Cultural: Making Sense of Cross-cultural Communication*, ClearlyCultural.com/geert-hofstede-cultural-dimensions/individualism/. Accessed July 30, 2021.

21. Tia Ghose, "Everyone Thinks They Are Above Average," LiveScience .com, *CBS News* (February 7, 2013), https://www.cbsnews.com/news/ everyone-thinks-they-are-above-average/. Accessed August 15, 2021.

22. Eric Jaffe, "The World Sees Americans as Disorder-Level Narcissists: Actually, Many Americans See Themselves That Way, Too," *Bloomberg CityLab* (December 11, 2015), https://www.bloomberg .com/news/articles/2015-12-11/study-the-world-sees-americans-as-disorder-level-narcissists. Accessed August 15, 2021.

23. They were all men. Darwin Smith, Joe Cullman; Colman Mockler; Ken Iverson, Fred Allen, Charles Walgreen, George Cain, Alan Wurtzel, Stanley Gault, David Maxwell, Carl Reichardt, Lyle Everingham. As of this writing, Sheila Barr chairs Fannie Mae, Rosalind Brown is CEO of Walgreens, and Michael Hsu is Kimberly-Clark's CEO.

24. *Good to Great: Why Some Companies Make the Leap and Others Don't* (HarperCollins, 2001), pp. 17–40. It is the sequel to the previously referenced, James C. Collins, Jerry I. Porras, *Built to Last: Successful Habits of Visionary Companies* (HarperCollins, 1994).

25. A reference to Peter Clemenza's line, "Leave the gun, keep the cannoli," from *The Godfather*, directed by Francis Ford Coppola, Columbia Pictures, 1972.

26. Don Emerson Davis Jr., and Joshua N. Hook, "Measuring Humility and Its Positive Effects," *Association for Psychological Science* (September 30, 2013), https://www.psychologicalscience.org/observer/ measuring-humility-and-its-positive-effects. Accessed July 29, 2021.

27. Anna Katharina Schaffner, Ph.D., "What Is Humility? The Power of Humility with 5 Practical Exercises," *Positive Psychology* (April 15, 2021). The exercises: gratitude; awareness of complaining; count three good things that happen every day; be aware of small gratitudes; and appreciate nature, https://positivepsychology.com/humility/#:~: text=While%20other-orientedness%20is%20a%20core%20 interpersonal%20feature%20of,An%20appreciation%20of%20 the%20value%20of%20all%20things. Accessed August 13, 2021.

28. J. D. Aten; "How Humble Leaders Foster Resilience: An Interview with Dr. Bradley Owens on the Value of Humility," *Psychology Today* (February 26, 2019), https://www.psychologytoday.com/us/blog/hope-resilience/201902/how-humble-leaders-foster-resilience, as cited in Schaffner, "What Is Humility?"

29. Ted Turner Quotes, http:/www.BrainyQuote.com/authors/ted-turner-quotes. Accessed July 29, 2021.

30. Joshua N. Hook, Don E. Davis, Jesse Owen, Everett L. Worthington, Shawn O. Utsey, "Cultural humility: Measuring openness to culturally diverse clients," *NIH National Medical Library* (July 2013), https://pubmed.ncbi.nlm.nih.gov/23647387/. Accessed August 15, 2021. See also, Joshua N. Hook, Don E. Davis, Jesse Owen, and Cirleen DeBlaere, *Cultural Humility: Engaging Diverse Identities in Therapy* (American Psychological Association, 2017). See also, Everett L. Worthington Jr. (Ed.), Don E. Davis (Ed.), and Joshua N. Hook, *Handbook of Humility: Theory, Research, and Applications* (Routledge, 2016).

31. Inspired by Uriah Heep's fawning and unctuous statement ("I'm well aware I'm the 'umblest person going") from Charles Dickens, *The Personal History, Adventures, Experience and Observation of David Copperfield the Younger of Blunderstone Rookery (Which He Never Meant to Publish on Any Account)*, commonly known as *David Copperfield* (Bradbury and Evans, 1850).

32. Benjamin Isaac, *The Invention of Racism in Classical Antiquity* (Princeton University Press, 2006).

33. P. M. Gollwitzer, "Implementation Intentions: Strong Effects of Simple Plans," *American Psychologist 54* (1999), pp. 493–503, as cited in Rick Melnyck, "Implementation Intentions: How to Make Good on Your Goals!" Entertaining and Actionable Self-improvement, *Prime Your Pump*, April 2019, https://primeyourpump.com/2019/04/09/implementation-intentions/#:~:text=There%20are%20several%20steps%20you%20need%20to%20take,3%20%283%29%20Create%20implementation%20intentions%20or%20'if-then'%20plans. Accessed August 4, 2021.

34. Benjamin Gardner and Amanda L. Rebar, "Habit Formation and Behavior Change," Psychology, *Oxford Research Encyclopedias* (April 26, 2019), https://doi.org/10.1093/acrefore/9780190236557.013.129. Accessed August 4, 2021.

35. Proverbs 7:17, *The NIV Study Bible*, Kenneth Barker, ed. (Zondervan, 1995); Confucius, *The Analects of Confucius*, Chapter 7, 7.31.

36. David Hume, Treatise on Human Nature, *An Enquiry Concerning Human Understanding* (2nd ed.) (Hackett Classics, 1993). Originally published 1739.

37. Salynn Boyles, "Why Willpower Often Fails: Power of Temptation Stronger Than We Think, Study Says," *WebMD*, medically reviewed

by Louise Chang, MD (August 7, 2009), https://www.balance/news/20090807/why-willpower-often-fails. Accessed August 2, 2021.

38. Cancers; coronary heart disease; Type 2 diabetes; hypertension; sleep apnea; depression and other mental disorders; chronic pain; impaired body functions; and increased risk of death. "The Health Effects of Overweight and Obesity," *Healthy Weight: CDC* (September 17, 2020), https://www.cdc.gov/healthyweight/effects/index.html. Accessed August 13, 2021.

39. "The $72 Billion Weight Loss & Diet Control Market in the United States, 2019-2023—Why Meal Replacements Are Still Booming but not OTC Diet Pills," *Business Wire* (February 25, 2019), https://www.businesswire.comnews/home/20190225005455/en/The-72-Billion-Weight-Loss-Diet-Control-Market-in-the-United-States-2019-2023---Why-Meal-Replacements-are-Still-Booming-but-Not-OTC-Diet-Pills---ResearchAndMarkets.com. Accessed August 6, 2021.

40. Crescent B. Martin, M.P.H., M.A., Kirsten A. Herrick, Ph.D., M.Sc., Neda Sarafrazi, Ph.D., and Cynthia L. Ogden, Ph.D., M.R.P., "Attempts to Lose Weight Among Adults in the United States, 2013–2016," NCHS Data Brief No. 313 (July 2018), *National Centers for Health Statistics*, Centers for Disease Control and Prevention, https://cdc.gov/nchs/products/databriefs/db313.htm. Accessed August 5, 2021.

41. Robert Kegan, Lisa Laskow Lahey, *Immunity to Change: How to Overcome It and Unlock Your Potential in Yourself and Your Organization* (Harvard Business Press, 2009).

42. A pseudonym.

43. Mike Emlet, MD, *Overeating: When Enough Isn't Enough* (New Growth Press, 2019).

44. Based on "Risk Factors for Death and Disability, 2019," data for the United States, *The Institute for Health Metrics and Evaluation*, www.healthdata.org/united-states. Accessed August 17, 2021.

45. It's recommended to have more than one Battle Buddy who act in your true best interests. They would never make light of you or your efforts to strengthen your courage and self-governance.

46. The Mayo Clinic Staff, "Healthy Diets," *Nutrition and Healthy Eating*, Mayo Clinic website, https://www.mayoclinic.org/healthy-lifestyle/nutrition-and-healthy-eating/basics/healthy-diets/hlv-20049477. Accessed August 17, 2021.

47. "How Much Exercise Do Adults Need?" *Centers for Disease Control and Prevention*. https://www.cdc.gov/physicalactivity/basics/adults/index.htm. Accessed August 17, 2021. Also see, Honor Whiteman,

"Moving Every 30 Minutes May Help You Live Longer," *Medical News* (September 12, 2017), https://www.medicalnewstoday.com/ articles/319355. Accessed August 18, 2021.

48. "In Brief: Your Guide to Healthy Sleep," *The National Heart, Lung, and Blood Institute* (NHLBI), https://www.nhlbi.nih.gov/files/docs/ public/sleep/healthysleepfs.pdf. Accessed August 17, 2021.

49. In a study, 92% of nurses suffered from stress. Slow, belly breathing, counting to ten and changing your physical space proved effective. Amanda Hurlburt, "Stress management for nurses," *Post-Acute Advisor* (October 31, 2017), https://postacuteadvisor.blr.com/2017/10/31/ stress-management-for-nurses/. Accessed August 17, 2021.

50. The Mayo Clinic Staff, "Alcohol Use; Weighing Risks and Benefits," *Nutrition and Healthy Eating,* Mayo Clinic website, https://www .mayoclinic.org/healthy-lifestyle/nutrition-and-healthy-eating/in-depth/alcohol/art-20044551. Accessed August 17, 2021.

51. *Gospel in Life,* "Talking to Yourself, Not Listening to Yourself—Psalm 42 Meditation," by Tim Keller, YouTube, May 6, 2020, 8:36, https:// www.youtube.com/watch?v=RZQQwAActog. Accessed August 15, 2021.

52. Viktor Frankl, *Man's Search for Meaning* (Beacon Press, 1959).

53. Experience teaches that Courage Training fails with persons demonstrating strong narcissistic tendencies, i.e. exaggerated feelings of self-importance; an excessive need for admiration; a lack of empathy and conscience; exploiting and manipulating; splitting staffs between those that are pro and con about the individual; spending time thinking about achieving power or success; a deep concern about their appearance; and a refusal to see their own faults, or to accept training. These individuals can be better served by therapy. *DSM-5,* https:/narcopath.info/about-npd/overview/dsm-5/. Accessed July 30, 2021. *New York Times* columnist and author David Brooks observed that our society is experiencing a dramatic rise in this type of personality, making "intellectual humility. . . accurate self-awareness at a distance" and courage even more vital. David Brooks, *The Road to Character* (Random House, 2015), pp. 6–9.

54. Ken Blanchard, *Catch People Doing Something Right: Ken Blanchard on Empowerment* (Executive Excellence, 1999).

55. Marian Wright Edelman, "The Time Is Always Right to Do Right," *Huffington Post* (April 2, 2017), https://www.huffpost.com/entry/the-time-is-always-right_b_9592976. Accessed September 8, 2021.

56. Edgar taught me to use *UPR* before I gave it a name. He advanced it as the essential way to act rightly in the world. UPR applies with greater force for those in government, as our ability to harm is so quickly multiplied. Ergo, I couldn't dishonor the law or the defendant. Did UPR help me be a better advocate? Certainly, for UPR freed me from turbulent feelings to meet the high professional standards to which I had taken an oath, whether the defendant was convicted or released from custody. (It is incidental to UPR, but the defendant later fatally impeached himself by contradicting his alibis. He also alienated jurors by blaming his 13-year-old victim. The jury convicted him of all charges; he received maximum, upper-term sentences. His victim recovered, as did my family.)

57. "Ethics Unwrapped," Moral Relativism, McCombs School of Business (2021), https://ethicsunwrapped.utexas.edu/glossary/moral-relativism. Accessed August 25, 2021.

58. "Judgment," *Zero-to-Three*, https://www.zerotothree.org/resources/series/judgment. Accessed August 25, 2021.

59. Danielle Pergament, "Exactly How Much Appearance Matters, According to Our National Judgment Survey," *Allure* (February 10, 2016), https://www.allure.com/story/national-judgement-survey-statistics. Accessed August 25, 2021.

60. Chris Melore, "2 in 5 Grocery Shoppers Use Self-checkout—To Avoid People Judging Their Purchases!" *Society and Culture, Study Finds* (September 5, 2021), https://www.studyfinds.org/grocery-shoppers-self-checkout-embarrassment/. Accessed September 8, 2021.

61. Erin Duffin, "Do You Approve of How Congress Is Doing Its Job?" *Economy & Politics; Politics and Government, Statista*, 2021 (August 10, 2021), https://www.statista.com/statistics/207579/public-approval-rating-of-the-us-congress/. Accessed August 26, 2021.

62. G. Hofstede and G. J. Hofstede, "Archives," *Geert Hofstede, Hofstede's Globe*, http://www.geert-hofstede.com/. Accessed August 26, 2021.

63. Project GLOBE 2020, Global Leadership and Organizational Behavior Effectiveness, Robert J. House, PhD, Wharton School, founder and principle investigator, https://globeproject.com. Accessed December 15, 2021.

64. Robert J. House, Paul J. Hanges, Mansour Javidan, Peter W. Dorfman, Vipin Gupta. *Culture, Leadership, and Organizations: The GLOBE Study of 62 Societies* (Sage, 2004).

65. Words are from the study, except for those in quotes.

66. Sadly, the casual observer can see that many of the cited "visionary" and "Good to Great" firms subsequently changed leaders, and core values, and have fallen from prominence.

67. J. R. Rest, D. Narvaez, M. J. Bebeau, and S. J. Thoma, *Postconventional Moral Thinking: A Neo-Kohlbergian Approach* (Psychology Press, 1999).

68. A longitudinal and internal study of character development in West Point Cadets, who are educated to do the harder right instead of the easier wrong, found that the majority of West Point seniors had not even achieved Rest's Stage 3 of moral development of self-regulation. Paul T. Bartone, Scott A. Snook, George B. Forsythe, Philip Lewis, and Richard C. Bullis, "Psychosocial Development and Leader Performance of Military Officer Cadets," *The Leadership Quarterly 18*, (2007): 501. Academic cheating persists in the nation's service academies. As of this writing, West Point's leadership is considering approaches to strengthen its character education programs.

69. "Discernment Quotes," *AZ Quotes*, https://www.azquotes.com/quotes/topics/discernment.html. Accessed September 2, 2021. See also "Problem Solving Quotes," https://www.goodreads.com/quotes/tag/problem-solving. Accessed September 2, 2021.

70. Derived from Middle English *discernen*, the Latin *certus* and the Greek *krīnein*. "Discern," *Merriam-Webster Dictionary*, https://www.merriam-webster.com/dictionary/discern#:~:text=History%20and%20Etymology%20for%20discern%20Middle%20English%20discernen,decide%2C%20determine"%20—%20more%20at%20certain%20entry%201. Accessed August 26, 2021.

71. "Conscience," *Wise Sayings*, https://www.wisesayings.com/conscience-quotes/. Accessed September 8, 2021.

72. "Conscience," *Lexico, Oxford Dictionary*, English and American versions, https://www.lexico.com/definition/conscience/. Accessed August 29, 2021.

73. "Conscience," *Merriam-Webster Dictionary*, https://www.merriam-webster.com/dictionary/science#etymology. Accessed August 29, 2021.

74. Paul Bloom, "Do Babies Know Right from Wrong?" *Opinion, CNN* (February 14, 2014), ttps://www.cnn.com/2014/02/12/opinion/bloom-babies-right-wrong/index.html. Accessed August 31, 2021. Bloom is the author of *Just Babies: The Origins of Good and Evil* (Crown, 2014). Bloom concludes that babies are born with consciences that can tell right from wrong and good from evil.

75. "Prof. Dan Ariely—Two Reasons Why the MBA Oath Club Works," *INCA MBA Oath Club,* www.incaembaoathclub.org/wp-content/ uploads/2015/09/Dan-Ariely-Two-Crucial-Effects-INCAE-MBA-Oath-Club.pdf. Accessed August 29, 2021. See also Daniel Ariely, *The (Honest) Truth About Dishonesty: Why We Lie to Everyone, Especially Ourselves* (Harper Perennial, 2013).

76. "Prejudice," Topics, *Brainy Quote,* https://www.brainyquote.com/ topics/prejudice-quotes. Accessed September 8, 2021.

77. Many frauds are logically and "brilliantly conceived," e.g. 1920 Ponzi, 1929 stock market crash; 1980s insider training; 1990s Dot-Com and Savings and Loan, Enron, WorldCom, et al.; Madoff, subprime frauds of the 2000s, et al. Logic is applied in premeditated murder, crimes against women and children, and reason was used to justify genocide, imperialism, slavery, racism, lynching, relocation, and torture.

78. Daniel Lattier, "Nazi Germany Was Well Educated," *Charlemagne Institute, Intellectual Takeout* (October 21, 2015), quoting Stanford Professor Steven Zipperstein, https://www.intellectualtakeout.org/ blog/nazi-germany-was-highly-educated/. Accessed August 29, 2021.

79. Tyler Cowen, "Why Did So Many Germans Support Hitler?" *Political Science: Marginal Revolution* (March 30, 2005), https://www.marginal revolution.com/marginalrevolution/2005/03/why_did_so_many. html/. Accessed August 29, 2021. Popular support for Hitler and the Nazis was initially moderate but skyrocketed to high national enthusiasm after German forces took over Austria and Czechoslovakia and then invaded and conquered Poland, France, Denmark, Norway, Belgium, and the Netherlands.

80. Srikanth Mahankali, "68 Always Do The Right Thing Quotes," *DP Sayings* (July 5, 2021), www.dpsayings.com/do-the-right-thing-quotes/. Accessed August 29, 2021.

81. A pseudonym.

82. Ann Blake-Tracy, "Editor of Lancet: Medical Research Is Unreliable at Best or Completely Fraudulent," International Coalition for Drug Awareness website (June 22, 2015), https://www.drugawareness.org/ editor-of-lancet-medical-research-is-unreliable-at-best-or-completely-fraudulent/#:~:text=Richard%20Horton%2C%20Editor%20of%20Lancet%20A%20shocking%20admission,is%20UNRELIABLE%20AT%20BEST%20IF%20NOT%20COMPLETELY%20BOGUS%21. Accessed September 2, 2021.

83. "Lolly Daskal Quotes," *Goodreads*, https:// www.goodreads.com/ author/quotes/7406515.Lolly_Daskal. Accessed December 2, 2021.

84. Joseph Grenny, "Avoiding Conflict Is Killing Your Bottom Line," *Vital Smarts* (April 16, 2010), https://www.vitalsmarts.com/crucial skills/2010/04/avoiding-conflict-is-killing-your-bottom-line/. Accessed June 30, 2021.

85. Ibid, Collins. Jim Collins, *Good to Great and the Social Sector: Why Business Thinking Is Not the Answer, a Monograph to Accompany Good to Great* (HarperCollins, 2005).

86. The iconic wise wrangler and mountaineer of Cheley Colorado Camps, founded in 1921. The "Trigger Bill" character represents the building of high character and sustained resilience. He was based on horseman, philosopher, and storyteller Everett May, the deputy sheriff of Estes Park, 1953–1958. A Stanley Park arena is named for him; he died in 1968.

87. "A Stitch in Time Saves Nine," *The Phrase Finder*, https://www .phrases.org.uk/meanings/a-stitch-in-time.html#:~:text=%27A% 20stitch%20in%20time%20saves%20nine%27%20originated% 20in,1732%3A%20"A%20Stitch%20in%20Time%20May%20 save%20nine. Accessed October 28, 2021.

88. I teach students and trainees that the starts of World War II, Korean and Vietnam Wars, and the two Gulf Wars, were predictable.

89. "The Pack Rat," Cheley Colorado Camps, https://www.cheley.com/ news/pack-rat-newsletter#:~:text=Frank%20Cheley%20said %20in%201921%2C%20"Cheley%20aims%20to,definitely %20to%20the%20creation%20of%20a%20better%20world. Accessed October 28, 2021.

90. "91 Quotes for Training Employees," Vantage Circle, https:// blog.vantagecircle.com/quotes-for-training-employees/. Accessed December 15, 2021.

91. Sousa, *How the Brain Learns*.

92. https://execuprov.com.

Part II

1. "Einstein," Problem-solving Quotes, https://www.goodreads.com/ quotes/tag/problem-solving. Accessed September 2, 2021.

2. Thanks to Ben Bain, who helped me think of conflicts in the frame of *pre-during-post* à la the Haddon Matrix, a paradigm used in injury prevention.

Chapter 4

1. Dick Lee and Delmar Hatesohl, "Listening: Our Most Used Communication Skill," *Find Your Interest, University of Missouri Extension,* https://mospace.umsystem.edu/xmlui/bitstream/handle/10355/50293/cm0150-1993.pdf?sequence=1&isAllowed=y. Accessed December 15, 2021.

2. "Training the Trainers Seminar," Office of Personnel Management, Denver, CO (2002), re: "Supervisory Leadership. Module 2: Effective Communication," *Food and Drug Administration,* Rockville, MD. "Poor Communication Is the #1 Reason Couples Split Up: Survey," *Huffington Post* (November 20, 2013), https://www.huffpost.com/entry/divorce-causes-_n_4304466. Accessed September 22, 2021.

3. "*Communication Quotes,* AZ Quote, https://www.azquotes.com/quotes/topics/communication.html. Accessed September 28, 2021.

4. CLEAR was first introduced in Chapter 7, *Courage: The Backbone of Leadership* (Jossey-Bass, 2006).

5. Illustrations by Libby Vanderploeg, Abrams Noterie, an imprint of Abrams, 2018.

6. Frankl, *Man's Search for Meaning.*

7. "Encouragement Quotes," Brainy Quotes, https://www.brainyquote.com/topics/encouragement-quotes. Accessed September 26, 2021.

8. "Catch People Doing Something Right," *Conversations with Ken Blanchard,* December 24, 2014, https://howwelead.org/2014/12/24/catch-people-doing-something-right/. Accessed September 27, 2021.

9. "State of the American Workplace," *Gallup,* 2017, https://www.gallup.com/workplace/238085/state-american-workplace-report-2017.aspx?thank-you-report-form=1. Accessed September 26, 2021.

10. James M. Kouzes, Barry Z. Posner, *Encouraging the Heart: A Leader's Guide to Rewarding and Recognizing Others* (Jossey-Bass, 1999), p. 4. The author added information about the ruck march.

11. Although prolactin is associated with lactation, both men and women produce prolactin under stress.

12. Kouzes and Posner, *Encouraging the Heart,* 55–58.

13. Daniel Pink, *Drive: The Surprising Truth About What Motivates Us* (Riverhead, 2009), 207–208. See also, Dan Ariely, Uri Gneezy, George Lowenstein, and Nina Mazar, "Large Stakes and Big Mistakes," *Review of Economic Studies,* 76 (2009), 451–469, https://rady.ucsd.edu/faculty/directory/gneezy/pub/docs/large-stakes.pdf. Accessed December 15, 2021.

14. Dan Pink, "This Is How Big Time Performers Get the Feedback They Need," *Pinkcast 4.13,* https://www.danpink.com/pinkcast/pinkcast-4-13-this-is-how-big-time-performers-get-the-feedback-they-need/?u tm_source=Dan+Pink%27s+Newsletter&utm_campaign= b839be2eeb-&utm_medium=email&utm_term=0_4d8277f97a-b839 be2eeb-312961525&goal=0_4d8277f97a-b839be2eeb-312961525. Accessed September 28, 2021.
15. A pseudonym.
16. "Asking Questions Quotes," AZ *Quotes,* https://www.azquotes.com/ quotes/topics/asking-questions.html. Accessed September 26, 2021.
17. *Kirby and the Forgotten Land,* Nintendo, 2022; *Minecraft,* Java ed. for Mac, 2017.

Chapter 5

1. "Conflict Resolution Quotes," AZ Quotes, https://www.azquotes. com/quote/298588?ref=conflict-resolution. Accessed September 28, 2021.
2. Arbinger Institute, *Leadership and Self-Deception* (The Arbinger Institute, 2000).
3. A pseudonym.
4. "Socrates Quotes," AZ Quotes, https://www.azquotes.com/author/ 37865-Socrates. Accessed September 27, 2021.
5. Ibid., Gordon. "'I' Statements not 'You' Statements," *International On-line Training on Intractable Conflicts, University of Colorado,* http:// www.colorado.edu/conflict/peace/treatment/istate.htm. Accessed October 4, 2021.
6. Another AeR description appears in Chapter 8 of *Courage: The Backbone of Leadership* (Jossey-Bass, 2006).
7. "Listening Quotes That Express the Importance of Listening," *Everyday Power,* https://everydaypower.com/listening-quotes/#:~:text =%20Listening%20Quotes%20That%20Express%20the%20 Importance%20of,could%20not%20now%20show%20greater%20 kindness...%20More%20. Accessed October 1, 2021.
8. Amy Carmichael, *Edges of His Ways* (CLC Publications, 2016); see also, https://fakebuddhaquotes.com/if-you-propose-to-speak-always-ask-yourself-is-it-true-is-it-necessary-is-it-kind/.
9. Melissa Matthews, "People's Brains Don't Reach Adulthood Until Age 30, Study Finds: Scientists explained our brains don't reach

adulthood until our 30s at a new meeting on brain development. Our brains are constantly developing over a span of three decades. This means that certain behaviors, like excessive alcohol consumption, can be particularly damaging when we're young," *Men's Health* (March 19, 2019), https://www.menshealth.com/health/a26868313/when-does-your-brain-fully-mature/. Accessed October 3, 2021.

10. The expression is, *Kê jifu li* from *Fei Xiaotong, Xiangtu Zhongguo*, translated by Gary G. Hamilton and Wang Zheng as *From the Soil: The Foundations of Chinese Society* (University of California Press, 1992), p. 25.

11. Christopher A. Kay, CEO, Integware.

12. "Intervening Quotes," Brainy Quote, https://www.brainyquote.com/topics/intervening-quotes. Accessed October 10, 2021.

13. Tom Valentine, "How Many People Died in the Vietnam War?" The Vietnam War website, April 11, 2014, https://thevietnamwar.info/how-many-people-died-in-the-vietnam-war/. Accessed October 7, 2021.

14. "Aircraft Accident Report, United Airlines, Inc., McDonnell-Douglas DC-8-61, N8082U, Portland, Oregon, December 28, 2978," *NTSB-AAR-79-7, United States Government*, https://www.ntsb.gov/investigations/AccidentReports/Reports/AAR7907.pdf. Accessed September 2, 2021.

15. "United Flight 173," *Pilot Friend*, www.pilotfriend.com/disasters/crash/united173.htm. Accessed September 7, 2021. "The Tragic Story of Malburn McBroom (or, How Fear Will Ruin Your Business)," *Smart Marketer* (September 23, 2020), https://smartmarketer.com/the-tragic-story-of-malburn-mcbroom-or-how-fear-will-ruin-your-business/. Accessed September 2, 2021.

16. Told to me by a graduate student from Uganda.

17. Samantha Lock, "How Many U.S. Soldiers Died in Afghanistan?" *Newsweek* (August 16, 2021), https://www.newsweek.com/number-us-soldiers-who-died-afghanistan-war-1619685. Accessed October 4, 2021.

18. "Fatal Crashes," *Summary, National Highway Traffic Safety Administration*, https://www-fars.nhtsa.dot.gov/Main/index.aspx. Accessed September 12, 2021.

19. "Motor Vehicle Crash Deaths: How Is the US Doing?" *Centers for Disease Control and Prevention*, https://www.cdc.gov/vitalsigns/motor-vehicle-safety/index.html/. Accessed September 12, 2021. The statistics are from the year 2019.

20. "Costs of War," *Watson Institute International and Public Affairs*, Brown University website, https://watson.brown.edu/costsofwar/figures/2019/direct-war-death-toll-2001-801000. Accessed September 12, 2021.

21. Drug Abuse Statistics, *NCAD, National Center for Drug Abuse Statistics*, https://drugabusestatistics.org. Accessed December 3, 2021.

22. Elizabeth Laiza King, "Top 15 Causes of Car Accidents and How You Can Prevent Them," *HuffPost* (December 6, 2017), https://www.huffpost.com/entry/top-15-causes-of-car-accidents_b_11722196. Accessed September 12, 2021. See also, Pine Solomon, "Top Causes of Car Accidents: The 25 Leading Causes of Accidents on the Road," *Serious Accidents*, https://seriousaccidents.com/legal-advice/top-causes-of-car-accidents/. Accessed September 12, 2021.

23. "Smoking and Tobacco Use," Centers for Disease Control and Prevention, https://www.cdc.govtobacco/data_statistics/fact_sheets/adult_data/cig_smoking/index.htm./. Accessed September 12, 2021.

24. More than what some states spend on public education.

25. "Excessive Alcohol Use in the U.S.," Public Health and Alcohol, *Centers for Disease and Control* (January 14, 2021), https://www.cdc.gov/alcohol/features/excessive-alcohol-deaths.html. Accessed October 8, 2021. See also, "How Much Money Is Spent on Alcohol Per Year," *Pathfinders* (November 23, 2018), www.pathfindersaz.com/how-much-money-is-spent-on-alcohol-per-year/. Accessed October 8, 2021. See also, "Is It Painful to Die from Liver Failure and Alcoholism?" Addiction Resources website, www.addictionresource.net/blog/is-liver-failure-painful/#:~:text=Dying%20as%20a%20result%20of%20alcoholism%20is%20painful,percent%20of%20cirrhosis%20deaths%20were%20alcohol-related%20in%202013. Accessed October 10, 2021.

26. Drug Abuse Statistics, *NCAD*.

27. "Maintenance Error Decision Aid Investigation Process," *Boeing* (Second Quarter, 2007), https://www.boeing.com/commercial/aeromagazine/articles/qtr_2_07/article_03_1.html. Accessed September 12, 2021.

28. Stephen Brown showed me, a minority guy just out of the Army and out of my element, how to do college in the turbulent Sixties. He later won a doctoral program, Ford Fellowship at the University of Chicago, and we've raised our families in parallel.

29. Manuel J. Smith, *I Feel Guilty When I Say No* (Bantam, 1975). It's described as providing "revolutionary new techniques for getting your own way."
30. F. Diane Barth, "Why Is It Hard to Say No and How Can You Get Better at It?" *Psychology Today* (January 15, 2016), https://www.psychologytoday.com/us/blog/the-couch/201601/why-is-it-hard-say-no-and-how-can-you-get-better-it. Accessed October 8, 2021.
31. Harold Hecht, Producer; Guy Hamilton, Director; *The Devil's Disciple* (1959). Hecht-Hill-Lancaster, USA, based on the George Bernard Shaw play, set during the American Revolutionary War.
32. "Reconciliation Quotes," *Brainy Quote*, https://www.brainyquote.com/topics/reconciliation-quotes. Accessed October 4, 2021.
33. *Stop, Start, Continue* is a useful tool in planning and teambuilding. I use CBS to help parties reconcile.
34. The classic noble professions existed to fight common enemies of humanity that were so terrible that they could never be defeated by human effort. Yet dedicated individuals were to selflessly and sacrificially hold those enemies at bay to prevent avoidable harm. Noble professionals would refuse pay and not seek wealth; they were to be supported by their grateful communities. Humanity's unbeatable foes were injustice, suffering, premature death, and evil. The noble professions were thus law, medicine and theology. I learned this at West Point's National Conference on Ethics in America—author.

Part III

1. Quote Investigator, https://quoteinvestigator.com/2020/12/08/destined/. Accessed October 6, 2021.
2. "We become what we practice," *Mary Martin, PhD*, March 20, 2020, https://www.marymartinphd.com/post/we-become-what-we-practice#:~:text=We%20become%20what%20we%20practice%20from%20moment%20to,with%20our%20experience.%20What%20have%20you%20been%20doing%3F. Accessed December 5, 2021.
3. Suggested by the opening title and words of Obi Wan Kenobi from George Lucas, Producer and Director, *Star Wars*, retroactively retitled, *Star Wars IV: The New Hope*, 1977.

Chapter 6

1. Center for the Study of Indigenous Languages of the West, College of Arts and Sciences, University of Colorado, https://www.colorado .edu/center/csilw/language-archives/arapaho-word-lists/place-names. Accessed October 12, 2021.
2. This describes Will and Ariel Durant's *Story of Civilization*, which took 40 years to write.
3. "Courage," *Merriam-Webster Dictionary*, https://www.merriam-webster.com/dictionary/courage. Accessed June 16, 2021.
4. G.E.M. Anscombe and P. T Geach, *Three Philosophers* (Oxford: Clarendon Press, 1961).

Chapter 7

1. NFL Films, Steve Sabol, "San Francisco Forty-Niners," Super Bowl XXIX, Episode 17, *America's Game* (NFL Films, 2006).

Chapter 8

1. Molly Elizabeth Seidel, 27, of Wisconsin, is the fastest. Seidel's marathon time: 2:24:42. Douglas, Scott, "How Albert Korir Decisively Won His First World Marathon Major in NYC," *Runner's World* (November 7, 2021), https:// www.runnersworld.com/news/a38067987/nyc-marathon-2021-mens-results/. Accessed December 5, 2021. Hall's time: 2:22:01. See also, Cindy Kuzma, "London Marathon Elites Prove Every Runner Needs a Strong Finishing Kick," *Runner's World* (October 9, 2020). https://www.runnersworld.com/training/a34318407/finishing-kick-in-races/. Accessed December 5, 2021.
2. Joshua 1:1–9, 2:24–42. *The New International Version Study Bible*, Kenneth Barker, ed. (Zondervan, 1995). In this, Joshua copied his mentor Moses who, fearing to return to Egypt to bring the Israelites out of bondage, fearfully protested going forward five times. Exodus 3:11, 13; 4:1, 10; 13.
3. "L. Frank Baum Quotes," Goodreads, https://www.goodreads.com/quotes/444053-courage-what-makes-the-flag-on-the-mast-to-wave. Accessed December 6, 2021.

Glossary of Acronyms

UPR   Unconditional Positive Respect, for all persons in all situations

HMA   Highest Moral Action: ID'd by discernment, done and taught with courage

3 NOs   Disrespect | Giving in to Anger | Hideouts: Avoid Deny Excuses Blame

3 GOs   UPR | Self-governance w/Humility | Discern, Act, Train the HMA

AeR   CourCom Play: Action-emotional Reaction: Your feelings impact me

BICBOF   Calm the Self: Breathe In Courage, Blow Out Fear/ Frustration

CBS   Conflict Play: Cease | Begin | Sustain specific behaviors

CLEAR   Basic CourCom: Open on Collegiality | Listen spellbound | Empathy with intent | Ask OEQs | Close on the Relationship

CQ   Courage Quotient: Ratio of stopped NOs to deployed GOs

CourCom   Courageous Communication: Not for voice but for the right

DAT   Part of 3rd GO: Discern, Act, Train others to do the HMA

ICAP   Assess/Planning Tool: Individual Courage Advancement Plan

OEQ   CourCom tool: Ask Open-ended Questions to understand the other

RPR　CourCom Play: Steady, frequent feedback: Routine Performance Returns

Tier 1　Core identity: Taking & exerting power; abusing, exploiting, harming others

Tier 2　Core identity: Controlling, intimidating, coercing and using others

Tier 3　Core identity: Getting ahead, getting results, not failing, avoiding conflict

Tier 4　Core identity: No NOs, 3 GOs, selflessly care for & help others

WOW　CourCom tool: Calm yourself: Be Warm, Open, and Welcoming

About the Author

Gus Lee is a best-selling author of eight books. He uses practice-based, character-centric Courageous Leadership Skills Intensives to help people overcome their fears to allow the adoption of practical behaviors of courage. He created the radical and kinetic *Five Steps to Courage*, *Unconditional Positive Respect* and *Courageous Communication* to train executives across 50 professions from Hewlett-Packard, Lockheed Martin, Microsoft, education, health care, business schools, and global NGOs and missions in Africa and Asia, to government agencies, public safety departments, and military combat units. He has been a thought leader for Development Dimensions International, Duke Fuqua School of Business, and a platform trainer for the Center for Creative Leadership. Gus has coached executives from every continent. He and his wife, Diane, wrote *Courage: The Backbone of Leadership* and five other best-sellers on a central theme of moral courage. He has written for *Time* and *Encyclopedia Britannica* and spoken on CBS *This Morning*, CNN, NPR, and Voice of America.

A member of a broken and abusive Chinese immigrant social group, Gus grew up in an African American neighborhood and was raised from age seven by three YMCA boxing coaches who stuck with him for 10 years despite his cowardice and terror about life. He got into West Point with multiple medical waivers and learned courageous leading from mentor H. Norman Schwarzkopf, later a renowned general; and Warren Bennis, founder of modern leader development. Gus has been a corporate COO; high-tech chief learning officer; EVP; SVP; government senior executive; US Senate ethics investigator; supervising deputy district attorney; acting deputy attorney general; trainer for California's then-140,000 attorneys and 5,000 prosecutors; FBI and POST trainer; Army officer, command judge advocate, Drill Sergeant, boxer, and paratrooper; was West Point's first Chair of Character Development and an Army-wide character instructor.

He and Diane, a retired faculty member and advanced practice nurse, enjoy their children and grandchildren, have mastered *Chutes and Ladders*, and volunteer in community. Gus's company is Leaders of Character, LLC, and he blogs at guslee.net.

Index

3 GOs (UPR, Comprehensively
    Self-govern and Humility,
    Discern, Do, Teach the
    Highest Moral Action) 73,
    75–77, 190–191
  acquisition of, 95
  Comprehensively Self-govern/
    Act with humility, 88–97
  Discern the HMA/Do the
    HMA/Train the HMA,
    118–119
  inventory, 118
  memory cut-out cards, 220
  overview, 75–77
  practice, 214–215
  Tier 4 GPS, 86
  Unconditional Positive Respect
    (UPR), 75, 76, 77–88
3 NOs (Disrespect, Gives into Anger,
    Hideouts: Avoids Conflict,
    Denial, Excuses, Blames)
    41–50, 92
  admitting/quitting/repairing, 49,
    50, 51–52, 70–72

anger, 46, 54–59
Avoids Conflict, (a Third NO
    Hideout), 48
Blames (a Third NO
    Hideout), 48
boomerang effect, 48f
cessation, 160–161, 175
Denial, opposite of courage, 16
Denies (a Third NO Hideout), 48
Disrespects Others (First NO),
    46, 50–53
examples, 45f
Excuses (a Third NO
    Hideout), 48
fuels racism, 46
give up, 214
Gives into Anger (Second NO),
    54–59
Hideouts (Third NO), 46, 59
impact, 74–75
memory cut-out cards, 219
overview, 41–50, 92
ranking, 48f
recording, 49

Accomplishments, 24
Action-emotional Reaction (AeR)
        (first CourCom Conflict Play,
        Courageous
        Communication),
        148, 152–158, 170, 188
    behavioral practice, 158f
    BICBOF, Breathe In Courage,
        Blow Out Fear,154
    examples, 156, 157
    function, 152–153
    how to do, 152–153
    main points, 152
    negative feeling states, 157
    positive AeRs, 155
    purpose, and what is not the
        purpose of,152, 153
    tips, 154–156
Active listening, 126, 128, 129
Actual core values, 190–191
Addiction, facing, 98
Admit, Quit and Repair (part of
    intentionally forming
    identity), 41 (45?)
Admitting, an act of courage, 70–72
Adult responsibilities,
    management, 162
AeR, Action-emotional Reaction,
    see Action-emotional
    Reaction
After Action Review, need for, 67
Alder, Shannon, face the questions
    we avoid, 21
Alphonse, expresses anger to the
    author, 163–165
Americans
    9% follow-through on New Years
        resolutions, 93
    33% actually work; 50%
        disengaged at work, 132

70% observed to cheat to
    college, 110
80% judge others on looks,
    106
85% dispirited by poor
    leadership, 132
95% avoid conflict, 114
98% would perform better with
    encouragement, 132
400% deficit in leaders across
    all levels, 5
250,000 are killed by accident
    annually in U.S.
    hospitals, 63
"kings and queens of
    over-estimation," 89
most individualistic, self-focused
    and ego-promoting, 92
self-centered to a degree of
    mental illness, 89
unable to cope with
    disappointment, 5
Angelou, Maya, on prejudice, 110
Anger, Gives In to (Second NO),
    46, 54–59, 84, 101, 151
    giving in, 54, 55–56, 200
    inventory, 55–56
    stopping, 57
Antagonists, cooperation, 184
Anxiety
    impact, 63–64, 100
    reduction, 91
    results, 49
    struggle, without courage,
        44–45
Apologies, usage, 150
Arbinger Institute, collusion, 147
Ariely, Daniel, on cheating, 110
Aristotle, 7, 39, 74, 196
    courage, the first virtue, 43

courage, the single virtue that makes the others possible, 12

proairesis, intentionality, required to sustain excellence, 196

Artificial core values, 190

Ask Challenges, (third basic CourCom Play), 124, 137–146, 170, 188

    behavioral practice, 146f

    examples, 143–146

    final help question, 143

    leader usage, 143–146

    peer-to-peer Ask Challenges, 143

    steps, 139

    tips, 140

Aspirational core values, 190

Assertive communication, Courageous Communication (contrast), 148

Avoidance, nullifies leadership, 4

Avoids conflict (a Third NO Hideout), 60

Bad habits, facing, 98

Barrie, J.M., all goes if courage goes, 8

Baseline insights/takeaways, 198–199

Battle, the, against our weaknesses, 10

Battle Buddies, personal account-ability to become best self, 41, 52–53, 57, 97, 101

    accountability, 188

    in CBS, 185

    need/assistance, 62, 100

    responsibility, 205

    study, 117

    types, 53

    Life, Personal, Work, 205

    Life Battle Buddy, 71

    Work Battle Buddy, 52–53

Behavioral objectives, identification, 100

Behaviors

    basis of effective courageous leadership training, 5

    changes, 24

    courage is set of practiced, 3

    integrity, 87

    practice of, instead of listen about, 5

Bellevue, Dr. Aiden, scientist, 13–15, 22, 28–29, 32, 156–157, 178–188

Benoit, Principal Anita, on blaming, 69, 70

Bias, 8, 45f, 51, toleration of, 48

BICBOF, Breathe In Courage, Blow Out Fear (part of AeR, first CourCom Conflict Play), 154, 162, 170

Big Lie, The, *you can't handle disapproval*, 43

Biography Form. *See* Leaders of Character Biography Form 5

Blames, 67–70

    NO inventory, 68–69

Bloom, Yale Professor Paul, and Karen Wynn, discover humans are moral beings, 109–110

Blues, Jake, excuses, 43–44

Bodenheimer, UCD Law Professor Edgar, author's mentor, UPR for historic criminals, 90, 103–105, 149

Boisjoly, Roger, NASA
        aerodynamicist,
    celebrated for doing the
        right thing, 63
    courageous stand to save lives, 63
Boomerang Effect of 3 NOs, 48f, 52
Boss Asks for Feedback (BAFF), an
        act of courage, 138
Brand, Paul, M.D., medical mission-
        ary, on lack of American
        hardiness, 5. 114
Breathe In Courage, Blow Out Fear
        (BICBOF, part of AeR, first
        CourCom Conflict Play),
        153, 154, 163, 170
Brian, Michael, upbeat fire-
        fighter, 59
Brown, Professor Brené, author,
        strength in vulnerabilities, 7
Brown, Leon, NBA player, doing
        the right thing, 112
Brown, Stephen, No-
        Thank-You, 176
Buddy Check, behavioral account-
        ability, 57, 58, 112, 117
Buffett, Warren, on saying no, 175

Capstone event (Crossing the River
        of Fear), 119, 213, 215
Carton, Wharton Professor Andrew,
        fear motivates then
        disables, 30
CBS: Cease, Begin, Sustain (third
        CourCom Conflict Play),
        148, 178–188
    Battle Buddy
        Accountability, 185, 188
    behaviors, agreement, 187–188
    example, 179–187
    ground rules, 185

overview of steps, 183
pre-work assignment
        form, 181–182
preparation, 179–183
reconciliation process, 183
share behaviors, 186–187
three stages (Share Behaviors,
        Agree to Behaviors, Battle
        Buddy Accountability), 185
Change, 218
    how to, 53
    inspired others to change, 5
    life-changing, 6
    prediction, 200f
    the self, 51
Character
    no current training in, 4, 44
    improve by changing
        behaviors, 50
    measure of the quality of
        the self, 25
    Moral Character (Rest), 108
    Training in, 7, 117
Character Mirror, seeing the true
        self, 25, 41, 201
    usage, 217
Cheerleading, avoidance, 134
Cheley, Frank, camping leader, 116
CLEAR, the first and central basic
        CourCom Play (Collegiality,
        Listen, Empathy, Ask,
        Relationship) 125–131
    5 parts of CLEAR, 126–128
    behavioral practice, 131f
    Communication Model,
        124–131
    memory cut-out cards, 221
    practice, 129, 131f
    tips, 128
    usage, 166, 176, 178, 180

Coaching, 5–7
  Courage Coaching more effective
    than lectures, 5
  Executive Courage Coach, 11
  few can afford, 4
  mastery by practice, 6–7
  personal, relational, impactful, 5
Collins, Grace C., CNO, nursing
    leader, UPR, 78–82,
    84, 85, 87
Collins, Jim, Stanford Business
    School findings on profit-
    ability and results, 90
Collusion, 147
Communication
  80% of our waking hours, 123
  assertive vs courageous, 148
  basic Courageous
    Communication Plays,
    124
  basis of success or failure, 123
  importance, 123–124
  improvement, 121–122
  requires intentionality to be
    courageous and
    effective, 121
Companies, short-term results
    (selection), 4
Comprehensively Self-govern/Act
    with Humility, 76, 88–103
Comprehensive Self-governance
    Inventory behaviors,
    102–103
Conflict
  avoidance, 60–62
  fear, 39
  NO inventory, 61
  rationales to avoid, 160–161
  resolution, 62
Conflict avoidant, term used to
    replace "cowardice," 59

Conflict Plays, part of Courageous
    Communication,147,
    178–188, 201f
  3 basic Plays (AeR, Fix the
    Fire, CBS), 148
Conscience
  consultation, 109–110
  consulting, "the ignored
    voice," 109
  impact, 28, 40
  research, says to heed, 28
Consciousness, recovery, 91–92
Consult, imitate wise friends, part
    of the Third GO and
    discernment, 111
Corbett, Brian, global poverty
    expert, reports little courage
    left in world, 8
Core Primary Identity, 23f
Core, selection, 189
Core values, 189–191,
  actual, 190–191
  artificial, 190
  personal core values, 195–196
  true core values, 191
Courage
  absence, 160, 44–45
  approved solution,
  as the first and central virtue, 74
  axiom, get courage by practicing
    courage, 3
  core value, 191
  defines your identity, 43
  definition, 6, 49, 73, 195
  denial, opposition, 16
  equips us, 75
  essential in effective
    leadership, 14
  gap, 5, 10
  heroic narrative and life
    pathway, 72

Courage (*Continued*)
  heroic verb, 8
  humility, relationship, 92
  identity in, 48
  impacts everything, 43, 84, 162
  importance, 2, 4–5, 7, 73
  is doing the highest and grandest
    right thing, 2
  journey, initiation, 212
  meaning, 68, 195
  modeling, 49, 133
  moral prowess, comparison, 73
  muscles, flexing, 3
  needed for love, 74
  not a feeling or intuitive, 77
  origin, 195
  pre-wired for, 13
  pursuit, 40
  race and gender neutral, 9, 15
  set of practiced behaviors, 3
  steps, 209
  trainee, 42–43
  training, 218
    absence of, 4
unfriending, mistake, 8
  Courage Quotient, ratio of
    personal fears to personal
    courage, 10
  improve, 10
Courage Training
  for a hospital, 79
  for a university, 112
  helped author overcome his
    fears, 218
  intensives, 112
  origin in radical training
    program, 3
  train others in, 117
Courageous Communication
    (CourCom), 122, 147, 159

assertive communication,
    contrast, 148
basic plays, 124,
  1st play, CLEAR, 125–131,
    (see also, CLEAR)
  2nd play, Encourage Others,
    131–136, (see also,
    Encourage Others)
  3rd play, Ask Challenges, 124,
    137–146, 170, 188 (see also,
    Ask Challenges)
  memory cut-out cards, 220
Conflict Plays, 147,
    178–188, 201f
  memory cut-out cards, 221
Plays, 200f
  goal, 185
  practice, 198
playsets, 123
practice, 200
Sit-Check, 169
types, 124
Courageous destinations, 199f
Courageous Leadership, 14,
    see Courage
Courageousness, 198, 200
Courageous Self, 13
Cowardice
  author slid into, 2; later
    condemns, 40
  banned in usage, replaced by
    "conflict avoidance," 59
  impact, 9; leaving, by quitting
    the NOs, 70
  in human relationships, 116
  life without love, 45
  reactions to fear, 45
  recovery, 50
  seeks to suppress fear and is
    mastered by it, 9

Crooks, Seth, scientist, affirms doing
  the HMA, 112–113
Crossing the River, capstone
  exercise in courage,
  209–215
Cruz, Bella, director, addiction
  treatment services, 29–30,
  32, 34–37, 86, 140–143,
  147–148, 157
Culture
  conflicted, shape-shifting, 9
  divided by fear, 4
  globally shared leadership
    values, 106–107
  multiculturalism, 91
  of fear, 168; and of feelings, 44
  of humility, 91
  of racism, in ancient cultures, 93
  organizational, elevated by doing
    the HMA, 115
Cultural humility, 92
Curiosity mindset, 137
Cussing, doesn't show toughness, 58

Dad and son Jeru, conflicts,
  Reflect-back, 161–162
Dalai Lama, handling life, 88, 92
de Becker, Gavin, fear expert, on
  fear of physical harm, 31
Deeper Country, the, 11, 43, 53,
  195, 211, 213–215
  barrier, crossing, 218
Deke, teen bully, physical Sit-check,
  170–172
Demoralization, 30
Denial (a Third NO Hideout),
  NO inventory, 64
  opposite of courage, 16
Desire, definition, 94

Destructive paralysis, 30
Devil's Disciple, The (Shaw), 176
*The Diagnostic and Statistical
  Manual of Mental Disorders,
  Fifth Edition, DSM-V*, 89
Discern, Act, and Then Train
  Others in the Highest Moral
  Action (DAT), (The Third
  GO) overview, 103–109, 76,
  103–117, 119f, 134
discern the HMA despite feelings,
  anxiety, biases, 108
  consult the conscience, 109–110;
    question prejudices, 110
  consult and imitate wise friends,
    111; morally reason, 111
  differs from standard academic
    reasoning, 112
  do the HMA regardless of risk to
    self-interest or outcome,
    112–116
  train others to do the HMA,
    113, 116–117
  inventory, 118 looking at the self,
    16, 9–10, 49
  practice, 119f
  three parts of, 108
Discomfort
  accepting discomfort a price
    of life, 49
  Americans least able to
    handle, 5, 44
  can't cope with, 45
  feared more than failure, 49
Discretion, Falstaff's fiction of it
  being "the better part of
  valor," 61
Discrimination, 7, 31, 51, 61
  countered by UPR, 92

Disrespects Others (the first NO),
    46, 50–53, 151
  AeR, usage, 156
  infectiousness, 53
  inventory, 50–51
  UPR, comparison, 81
Dobol, CSM Theodore L., role
    model, xi, 111
Doing, knowledge of easier than, 114
Doing the right thing,
  agreement across U.S. subcultures
    regarding, 107
  celebrated for, Boisjoly and
    McDonald, 63
  despite risks to self-interest,
    114–115, or unpopularity,
    job loss, 130
  doing the hardest right, not the
    easier wrongs, 43
  dominating thought to, 10
  global cultural alignment
    regarding,106
  impact, 34f, 35, 114
  personal responsibility to, 118
  pleasure in doing, 130
  produces record-breaking
    results, 90, 114
  strive to, in Tier 4 Deeper
    Country, 211
Duckworth, Angela, author,
    researcher, leverage low
    points to high ones, 7
Dunning, David, 89
Durant, Will and Ariel, his-
    torians, 147

Education (overcoming), denial
    (usage), 63–64
Educational Opportunity
    Program, EOP, 22

Ego, protection, 193
Emotional assessment, 19f–20f
Emotional Intelligence, 148
Emotional reaction, 154,
    156–158
Empathy, part of CLEAR
    communication model,
    81, 126–129, 142
Encourage Others (encourage-
    ment, second basic
    CourCom Play),124,
    131–136, 188
  behavioral practice, 136f
  examples, a teen and an
    employee, 134–136
  performance improves with, 132
  tip sheet, 134
  to change better than
    compensation, 133
Epithumia, desire, urges and
    hungers, 94
ExecuProv, Cherie Kerr behavioral
    training, 117
Excuses
  making, 65–67
  NO inventory, 66–67
Executive Courage Coach,
    guidance, 11

Family, protection,
    54–55
Favoritism, the team killer, 79
Fear, 25, 42–43, 58, 81. See also
    River of Fear
  as a terrible motivator,
    33–34
  culture, creation, 168
  drives negative reactions, 47
  failure to practice facing,
    overcoming, 4

impact, 29–30
overcoming, progress, 198, 200
produces paralysis, demoraliza-
    tion, health problems,
    and failure, 30
reactions, 45f, 48f, 194
replacement, 217
the human knockout punch, 43
triggers, 75
Feedback, 93, 118, 128, 133, 134
Boss Asks for Feedback
    (BAFF), 138
Feelings, culture, 44
Fikkert, Steve, global
    poverty expert, 8
First GO, *see* Unconditional
    Positive Respect
First NO, *see* Disrespects Others
Fix the Fire (second CourCom
    Conflict Play: Reflect-back,
    Situation-Check, No-
    Thank-You Declaration),
    158–161,148
No-Thank-You Declaration,
    175–178
options, 1609
overview, 160
Reflect-Back, when someone
    criticizes you, 161,
    usage, 158–167
Situation-Check, 167–174
Five Steps, The, 118, 195, 217
Flashover event, 66
Foreman, George, world heavy-
    weight champion, 141
Forgiveness, knowing it's right, 44
Frankl, Viktor, author, Holocaust
    survivor, 100

Garbarino, J., childhood
    trauma continues
    to haunt, 17
Getting your own way
    communication skills for, 175
    shows a lack of courage, 168
Gilbreath, Robert, 29, 31
Gillihan, Dr. Seth, fear elevates
    discomfort to existential
    threat, 37
Gives Into Anger, the Second No,
    54–59
    fight or flight mode, 55
    inventory, 55–56
    role play, 58–59
GLOBE, Project, study of world
    leadership cultures,
    106–107
    commonalities in global
        values, 106
    leadership characteristics, 107f
Golden Rule, 86
Gold, Lauren, 60
Good to Great (Collins), 90
Gordon, Thomas, 152
Grit, *see* Self-govern and Humility
Guerrero, Alicia, hi-tech COO,
    avoiding conflict,
    60–62, 147–148

Hardest right vs easiest wrong idea,
    from West Point, 43
Help Query, asking, 141
Heroic moral ideal, 34
    core identity, relationship, 218
    freedom of, 10
    goal of, 10
    identity/Tier 4, 34

Hideouts (third NO), 46, 59, 200
  Avoids conflict, 60–62,
      inventory, 61
  Denies truth, 62–65,
      inventory, 64
  Makes excuses, 65–67, inventory,
      66–67
  Blames, 67–69, inventory, 67–70,
      inventory, 68–69
  inventories, 61, 64, 66–67, 68–69
Hillary, Sir Edmund, conquering
      the self, 15
Highest Moral Action (HMA), 109,
      113, 139, 201
  discernment, 118–119, 217
  doing the, 112–116
  encouragement, 132
  HMA-based listening/speech,
      focus, 148
  identification, 111–112
  internal conflict, 164
  the most right thing,109
  training, 116–119
  UPR to consistently do the, 10
  usage, 163
Hofstede, Geert, social psycholo-
      gist, 89, 106
Home life living conditions, 18f
Hostility, 84
House, Wharton Professor Robert J.,
      GLOBE researcher, 106
Howard, COL Robert L.,
      role model, 58
Hume, David, 94
Humility, 74, 89–90, 97–98,
      139, 162, 200
  accelerates performance, 91
  action/practice, 76, 133, 176
  allows self-transcendence, 91
  born of courage, relationship,
      89, 92

  cultural humility, 92
  impact, 91
  key in Level 5 leaders, 90
  self-governance, link, 89

I Feel Guilty When I Say No, by
      Manuel J. Smith, 175
ICAP, see Individual Courage
      Action Plan
Identity, naming/claiming/
      aiming, 193
  courage defines, 195
  dictated by one's courage, 43
  heroic, 10
  in courage, fundamental to, 3, 48
  inner identity, improved by
      Admit, Quit, Repair, 41
  lifelong process, 189
  narrative informed by courage, 73
  new internal identity, 212
  non-negotiable, in courage, 40
  Oppenheimer killed his previous
      negative, self, 78
I-Message, advancement, 152
Individual Courage Action Plan
      (ICAP), 196, 197
  Accountability and Battle
      Buddies, 205
  basic plays, 200f
  conflict plays, 201f
  courageous destinations, 199
  drafting, 72
  goals, 198, 201–207, into
      objectives,
      202–203
  obstacles/countermeasures, 204f
  overview, 198
  seven questions, 197–198
  strategic plan to overcome fear,
      gain courage, become
      best self, 197

two categories, other and self, 201
what will I change, 200f
Integrity, doing the right thing
    within the self, 44
Intentionality, *proairesis*, required to
    sustain excellence, 196
Intellectual theory, teaching, 4
Intolerance, becomes racism, 51
    complaint, 43
Intuition, seductive power, 77
*Invention of Racism in Classical
    Antiquity, The* (Isaac), 93
"Iron sharpening iron," 93
Isaac, Benjamin, (*The Invention of
    Racism in Antiquity*,) 93
Issues requiring training, 6

Jacobs, COL Jack, MOH recipient,
    if not now, when? 57
Jobs, Steve, 175
Jorgenson, Christine, scientist, did
    the HMA, 112–115
Joshua, bin Nun, needed courage to
    cross the river, 212

Kai, David, father and student Josh,
    Reflect-back, 134–135
Keller, Tim, cowards get
    abandoned, 47
    stop negative self-talk, tell self to
    be courageous, 99
Kennedy, Cal, 60
Kihara, CSM George, on indecisive-
    ness and flat squirrels, 101
King, Jr., Martin Luther, on courage
    and cowardice, 9, 85, 103
Kohlberg, Lawrence, social scientist
    on moral development, 108
Kotter, John, Harvard Business
    School, the leadership
    deficit, 5

Leaders
    courage, modeling, 49
    development, 5
Leadership
    400% deficit, 5
    courage, importance, 4–5
    embracing, 91
    nullified by avoidance, 4
Leaders of Character (LOC)
    Biography Form 5, 15–16,
    82, 195, 197
    Courage, 26–27
    Personal Information, ques-
    tions, 17–22
    Reflections, 22–26
    sections/parts, 16, 198
Leadership
    cannot be done if fearful or
    avoidant, 4
    cannot lead while fearful, 4
    courage essential in, 5
    missing behavioral practice, 5
    practice creates, 9
    requires practice of courageous
    behaviors, 5
Lewis, C.S., courage the form of all
    virtues at the testing point, 74
Life Battle Buddy, 53
Life, gift, 96
Limbic brain instructions, 53
Likert scale, usage, 21, 26, 83
Listening, 124–131, 139
    active listening, 126, 128, 129
    as part of CLEAR, 126–127
    importance, 128
    preparation, 155
Love
    artificiality of self-love, 95
    fails without courage
    requires courage, 74–75
    work out issues with those we, 160

Low Games of the Self, 90
Luce, Clare Boothe, courage the
        ladder for other virtues, 74

Madison, Sean, 75–77, 92
Magical thinking, 57, 93
Male,
    anxious, avoids, boasts, flees,
        guilty, selfish, uses people,
        unstable identity, 130
Man, brave, coherent identity,
        courageous, discerns, does
        the HMA, protects people
        and principles, self-governs,
        trusted, 130
Mandela, Nelson, transformed from
        revenge to forgiveness, 178
McDonald, Allan, 63, 70, 71
    celebrated for doing the
        right thing, 63
McKittrick, Bobb, 49ers offensive
        line coach made Pro
        Bowlers, 7
Memory Cut-out Cards, 201–202
    CLEAR tip sheet, 221
    CourCom basic plays, 220
    CourCom conflict plays, 221
    self-governance, 222
    Three GOs, 220
    Three NOs, 219
Memory tool, usage, 128
Mentors, impact, 40
Merton, Thomas, humility makes
        us real, 92
Mindfulness Pivot, 37
Mindset, 96, see also Tier 4 Mindset
Mistakes, blame, 80
Mom, rescues boy, physi-
        cal Sit-Check
Money, a poor motivator, 133
Moral action, 171

Moral behavior, components,
        108
Moral beings, we are actually,
        109–110
Moral character, courage and
        strength to carry out moral
        intention, 108
Moral critical thinking, 112
Moral imperative, 164
Moral judgment, 108
Moral, meaning, 31
Moral motivation, 108
Moral purpose, 44
Moral reasoning, 109, 111–112
Moral relativism, 105–107; evidence
        against, 106–107
Moral sensitivity, 108
Motivation, autonomy, mastery,
        purpose, better than
        money, 133
Multiculturalism, 92
Murray, COL Charles A., role
        model, xi, 111
Musk, Elon, 1

Narcissism, most Americans suffer
        per study, 89
Narrative, story, set by courage, 73
Negative behaviors, freedom, 184
Negative feeling states, list, 157
Neniis-otoyou'u, the mountain
        guides, 196
Nestor, James, 37
Nishio, Dan, Sit-check, 159
Nin, Anais, life shrinks with lack of
        courage, 2
NOs. See 3 NOs
No-Thank-You Declaration (NTD),
        third CourCom Fix the Fire
        Conflict Play, 158–161,
        175–178

behavioral practice, 178
examples, 174–176
tips, 176
Novak, Caleb, self-governance,
95–103, 123–132, 147–148,
156, 157–158
Nowhere Man, 41

Obesity, 95
OEQ, Open Ended Questions,
asking, 117, 126–129,
137–145, 164, 179
BAFF, Boss Asks for
Feedback, 138
versus closed questions, 138
Oppenheimer, J. Robert, transforma-
tion, 77–78
Outcome, risk, 112–116
Owens, Bradley, humble leaders are
self-transcendent, 91

Pathological narcissism, 89
Patience, 162
Pattee, Emma, 55
Peer-to-peer Ask Challenges, 143
Performance
acceleration, humility
(impact), 91
Ask Challenges, leader
usage, 143–146
Personal behaviors, ranking, 22
Personal core behaviors, evolu-
tion, 190–191
Personal core principles, 195–196
Personal health problems, 30
Personal needs, question-
ing, 109, 110
Persons, Dr. Gary, 13–15, 21–22,
28–29, 32, 86, 156–157,
178–188
Physical situation-check, 170–174

Piaget, Jean, 108
"Pick our battles," excuse, 115
Pink, Daniel, money a poor motivator, 30, 133
Plays. *See* Courageous
Communication
Plays, how many do you know, 7
Power, malignant drive, 32
Practice
achieve mastery, 12
error of thinking it unnecessary,
8
get courage by, 116
practice partners, 86–87
practice, practice, practice, 6–7
principled conduct under
pressure, 44
specific skills under realistic
conditions, 7
Prejudice, 92
questioning, 109, 110
Pride, protection, 193
Principled conduct, practice, 44
Proairesis, Aristotelian intentionality
for excellence, 196
Problems, multiplication, 115
Professional, meaning in
behaviors, 184
Project GLOBE, 106
leadership characteristics, 107
Promotions/bonuses, 133

Questions, asking, 117, 125
Ask Challenges Play, see Ask
Challenges
Asking, 117, 125
Big Question, UPR
dynamite question, changing
ourselves first, 145
burning question, will we cross
the river, 211

Questions, asking (*Continued*)
final help question, in Ask
Challenges,143
Open-Ended, see Open-
Ended Questions
Seven questions, identity,
197–198
we avoid, 21
Quitting, 70–72

Racism, 51
courage counters, 9
destructiveness of, 93
feature of Tier 1 character, 32
fueled by the First NO,
Disrespects Others, 46
results from disrespect,
intolerance, 50
Reaction, forced into,
excuse, 115–116
Reason morally, 112
Reconciliation, instead of firing, 178
Redo question, usage, 138
Reflect-Back, the first Fix the Fire
Courcom Conflict Play, 187
behavioral practice, 167f
echo-back, contrast, 166
pushback against, 164
tips, 165–166
usage, 158, 160, 161–166
Relationship
as part of CBS, (professional
principled, admirable, free
of negative behaviors), 184
challenges, solving, 34
closing element of the CLEAR
communication model,
128, 156, 180
dialogue, 126, 128, 129
valuation, 179

Repairing, 70–72
Research
80% of our time spent in
communication
Americans, see, Americans
collectivism vs. individualism, 88
discrimination, 93
profitability and results,
34f, 35, 90
self-esteem, 88
Respect, 162
difference, 84
Respect Challenge, 84
Rest, James, social scientist, Four
Components of Moral
Development, 108
Results, impacted by courage,
34f, 35, 114
Reynolds, Jack, NFL linebacker, his
character changed team, 6
Risk to self-interest, 114–115
River of Fear, 209
barrier to our best selves, 4
crossing, 209–211
exercise, 211–216
Role plays, Courageous
Communication, 141–142

Samwise Gamgee, exceeding
limits despite despair,
9, 39–40
Saying no, Warren Buffett, Steve
Jobs, Manuel J. Smith,
Stephen Brown, General
John Burgoyne, 174–176
Schaffner, Anna Katherina, PhD,
researcher, on impact of
humility, 91
Schultz, Howard, CEO,
Starbucks, 116

Schwarzkopf, General H. Norman,
    author's mentor,
    consult wise friends, 111
    lead by example, 149
Scientific Method, 15
Second GO, see *Self-govern
    and Humility*
Self-absorption, impact, 39
Self-assessment, 15
Self-care, grit/gratitude/courage, 98
Self-centeredness, costs, 73
Self-concern, feeling, 40
Self-destructive habits/impulsivity,
    29, 159
Self-esteem 88, initiatives, 133
Self-govern and Humility (Second
    GO), 76, 88–103, 100, 162
    behavioral practice, 103f
    challenges, 101
    courage in self-care, 98
    evidence for, 95
    facing addiction and bad
        habits, 98
    grit and gratitude in self-care, 98
    humility, link, 89
    impact, 99
    inventory, 97–98
    memory cut-out cards, 222
    no happiness or joy without inner
        discipline, Dalai Lama, 88
    overview, 88–89
    usage, 154
Self-improvement, 49–50
Self-indulgence, 102
Self-interest, 32–33, 133, 150
    benign interest, 33–34
    risk, 112–116
Selfless curiosity, usage, 140
Self-pity, 101
Self-regulation, 108

Self-talk, 98, 99, 204f
Sexual harassment, 51
Shanahan, offensive coordinator
    Mike, 49ers, wrote complex
    playbook, 206
Shaw, George Bernard, 176
Singleton event, 155
Situation-Check (Sit-Check), the
    second Fix the Fire Play,
    CourCom Conflicts,
    158–161, 167–174
    collegial greeting (CG), 169
    behavioral practice, 174f
    examples, 169
    physical situation-
        checks, 170–174
    tips, 170
    United Airlines Flight
        173, 168–173
    Verbal Sit-Check, 173
Skydiving, not like military
    parachuting, 94
Smith, Manuel J. (*When I
    Say No*), 175
Smith, Fitz, fire battalion chief,
    46–47, 56–59, 70, 138–139
Stanford Business School,
    research, 35
Steps, Step One, 15; Step Two, 39;
    Step Three, 73; Step
    Four, 123;
Step Five, 147
Storytelling, usage, 117
Streat, Dr. Toussaint, MD, role
    model, 111
Stress, 133
    impact, 29, 63–64
    principled conduct,
        modeling, 163
    reduction, 91

Stretch Master, impact, 47
Subject Matter Expert, ability, 142
Success, results (impact), 33–34
Sullivan, Dr. James P., practice
    behaviors of courage
    instead of listen to
    talks about, 3
Sutcliffe, Clifton, board member,
    Reflect-back, 149–152,
    154, 156, 193

Team members, struggles, 144–146
Teenager, encouragement, 134–135
Temptations, preparation, 100
The most important person in the
    world (TMIPITW),
    treatment, 127
Theoretical core values, 190
Therapy, 17, 97, helpful for those
    with Narcissistic Personality
    Disorder, fn 53, 234
Third GO, see Discern, Act, Train
Thought-based education,
    impact, 6
Tier 1 (dishonor), 31, 86
Tier 2 (disrespect), 31–32, 86
Tier 2 supervisor, work, 76
Tier 3 (uncertainty), 33–34, 86
Tier 3 behaviors, trap, 76
Tier 4 (UPR), 34, 86
Tier 4 Deeper Country, 214–215
Tier 4 Earnings & Results Power, 35f
Tier 4 Global Positioning System
    (GPS) Tool, 29–37, 30f,
    85, 194
  First GO (relating to people), 86
  overview, 30f
  usage, 93, 194
Tier 4/Heroic Moral Ideal, 34
Tier 4/Highest Moral Action, 139

Tier 4 Mindfulness Pivot, looking at
    the self first, 37
Tier 4 Mindset, 96
Tier 4 Pivot, *fix me first*, 178
Tier 4 Table, examples, 36f
Tier 4, overview, 29–31, an inner
    country, 211
  earnings and results, 34f
  set direction, 194
Tiers, team leader response, 31
Tolkien, J.R.R., 9
Train others to do the HMA,
    113, 116–117
Training, initiation, 86
Transformation
    mindset, 97
    possibility, 218
Trigger Bill, iconic wrangler's saying,
    all fires start the
    same size, 116
Triggers, to disrespect others, such as
    interruption, 87
True core values, 191
Trust
    earning, 84
    killing (3 NOs boomerang
    effect), 48f
    not the same as respect, 84
Truth
    denial, 62–65
    statement, 152
Turner, Ted, CNN, 92
Twain, Mark, on courage, 44

Unconditional Positive Respect
    (UPR) (First GO), founda-
    tion of courage, 87, 75, 76,
    77–88, 105
  10-week Dynamic Practice
    Routine, 88f

basis/power, 137, 164
behavioral practice, 88f
behavior, improvement
    (practice), 86–87
Big Question, 83–84
commitment, 214
disrespect, comparison, 81
dynamic practice routine, 87
examples, 80–81
inventory, 83
listening, impact, 165
not mean approval or
    endorsement, 84
practice, 103, 180, 201
reason for being the First GO, 85
relating to people, 86f
sustaining, 179
universal stance of courage, 84
usage, 126–129, 139, 141,
    152, 170, 176
warmth element, prob-
    lem, 154–155
Wheel, 82f
United Airlines Flight 173, 168–173
    Culture of fear in the ranks, 168
    Verbal Sit-check, 173

Values
    human commonalities, 106
    naming, 194
Verbal Sit-Check, 173
Virtue ethics, 104
Virtues,
    controlling emotions, 88
    we disregard, 88–89

Walsh, Coach Bill, 49ers; on charac-
    ter first in leadership, 6;
    practice, practice,
    practice, 6–7
Warm, open, and welcoming
    (WOW), a part of CLEAR
    and UPR, 126, 128–130,
    131f, 141–142
Washington, General George,
    crossing the river, 212
West Point, the principle of
    self-sacrifice, 149
    character development, xviii
    do the hardest right, not the
        easiest wrong, 43
    do something vs. nothing, 100
    train trainers, 117
Willpower and Wishpower, 94
Wisdom, 110
Wise Friends, consultation,
    109, 111
Work
    disengagement, 132
    Encouraging Others,
        135–136
Work Battle Buddy, 53
    committing/selection, 71
WOW, Warm, Open, Welcoming,
    part of Collegiality in
    CLEAR, 126, 142
Wynn, Karen, 109–110

Young, Steve, 49ers quarterback,
    memorized complex
    playbook, 206